P9-CAS-881

FRAME RELAY

FRAME RELAY

TECHNOLOGY AND PRACTICE

Jeff T. Buckwalter, Ph.D.

ADDISON-WESLEY

An imprint of Addison Wesley Longman, Inc.

Reading, Massachusetts • Harlow, England • Menlow Park, California
Berkeley, California • Don Mills, Ontario • Sydney
Bonn • Amsterdam • Tokyo • Mexico City

Many of the designations used by manufacturers and sellers to distinguish their products are claimed as trademarks. Where those designations appear in this book and Addison Wesley Longman, Inc., was aware of a trademark claim, the designations have been printed with initial capital letters.

The author and publisher have taken care in preparation of this book, but make no expressed or implied warranty of any kind and assume no responsibility for errors or omissions. No liability is assumed for incidental or consequential damages in connection with or arising out of the use of the information or programs contained herein.

The publisher offers discounts on this book when ordered in quantity for special sales. For more information, please contact:

Corporate and Professional Publishing Group
Addison Wesley Longman, Inc.
One Jacob Way
Reading, Massachusetts 01867

Library of Congress Cataloging-in-Publication Data
Buckwalter, Jeff T.
   Frame relay : technology and practice / Jeff T. Buckwalter.
      p.   cm.
   Includes bibliographical references and index.
   ISBN 0-201-48524-9
   1. Frame relay (Data transmission)   2. Computer networks.   I. Title.
TK5105.38 B83 1999
004.6′6—dc21   99-051438
                                                                         CIP

Copyright © 2000 by Addison Wesley Longman, Inc.

All rights reserved. No part of this publication may be reproduced, stored in a retrieval system, or transmitted, in any form or by any means, electronic, mechanical, photocopying, recording, or otherwise, without the prior written permission of the publisher. Printed in the United States of America. Published simultaneously in Canada.

Text printed on recycled paper.

ISBN 0-201-48524-9

1 2 3 4 5 6 7 8 9 – MA – 03 02 01 00 99
First printing December 1999

To Regina and Derek

Contents

Preface

Networking professionals who are trying to learn about or use frame relay technology have many questions. Why has frame relay been so successful in the marketplace? How does frame relay work? What are the potential problems when migrating to frame relay? How does frame relay compare to other technologies? The answers to these general questions and many more are here.

This book takes a current, practical, wide-ranging look at the issues a network manager must face when migrating to a frame relay network. It collects what is known about, and what is important about, frame relay networks in one place.

My intent was primarily to write a book that is *useful*. Thus, this book explains frame relay technology, gives relevant facts, interprets frame relay standards, discusses issues, spotlights "gotchas," and compares alternatives. It pulls together information from many sources, such as vendor white papers, Web sites, standards documents, trade journal articles, email newsletters, seminar discussions, private conversations, Usenet newsgroups, and conference proceedings.

Intended Audience

This book is aimed at readers who are new to frame relay or who want to extend their understanding of its technology and practice. The primary audience is network managers who are considering migrating to or expanding their use of public frame relay services. Until the foundations are understood, it can be easy to make the mistake of believing that data networking is now a commodity marketplace. However, in my opinion there are real technical differentiators among data services and products that many managers are unaware of. This book can help lay the foundations for becoming an intelligent consumer.

In addition to networking managers, several other related groups will find this book helpful:

- Network engineers, designers, architects, and administrators who need to ramp up on their frame relay knowledge.
- Staff members who are responsible for implementing a frame relay network.
- Network managers who are building private frame relay networks for their enterprises instead of purchasing services from public carriers.
- Sales and marketing professionals and sales engineers who need to be able to talk more knowledgeably with their customers about frame relay services and products.
- Computer science, engineering, and technical students who need more education about a technology they will likely be using during their careers.
- Consultants who want to better understand frame relay technology so that they can make useful recommendations to their clients.
- Vendors' research and development engineers who want a foundation for reading the frame relay standards documents and trade literature.
- Technicians and operations personnel who need a basic background for understanding their product manuals and procedures.

In short, the audience includes anyone involved in the commissioning, design, pricing or costing, selection, installation, and day-to-day operation of a frame relay network.

I have attempted to provide an international perspective so that the book will be useful worldwide.

Recommended Background

This book assumes no particular knowledge of frame relay. However, some background about the larger field of networking and data communications is helpful. Professionals already working in the networking field will likely have sufficient background. To help with unfamiliar terms encountered, an extensive glossary is included.

Plan of the Book

The general approach here is to introduce the basic terms, concepts, and organizations involved with frame relay in the first two chapters, then to expand on all of these topics in later chapters.

Thus, Chapter 1 explains why frame relay has been so successful, introduces the basic components of a frame relay network, describes benefits and limitations of the technology, and compares frame relay to other networking technologies in use today. Chapter 2 sketches the standards organizations, service providers, and vendors involved in frame relay.

Chapters 3 through 6 provide a solid description of frame relay technology, including architecture, interfaces, virtual circuits, and traffic management. These are important chapters for grasping how frame relay technology works, and they are frequently referenced in the remaining chapters.

Chapters 7 through 11 deal with additional topics of interest to a network manager, such as differences between carrier implementations of frame relay, network management, pricing, procurement, and design of frame relay networks.

Finally, Chapters 12 through 14 describe how frame relay networks interact with other traffic, such as voice, TCP/IP and other router-based protocols, IBM's System Network Architecture (SNA), and asynchronous transfer mode (ATM).

Scope

Frame Relay: Technology and Practice covers all the important topics related to frame relay networks, although not in exhaustive detail. For instance, I include current "hot" topics—voice over frame relay, data-oriented virtual private networks (IP VPNs), integration of frame relay and ATM, new options for accessing frame relay networks, service level agreements (SLAs), quality of service (QoS) offerings from carriers and vendors, and switched virtual circuits (SVCs). The focus is on fundamentals and content valuable to practitioners, such as network managers, rather than on esoteric topics. Only topics that are related to frame relay are included. In short, this book is *not* a primer on computer networks in general. The intent was to be vendor neutral and unbiased in the discussion of service providers.

Features

This book evolved from the third edition of a 250-page manual that I wrote to accompany the two-day seminar, Frame Relay Technology and Applications, offered by *Business Communications Review*. Thus, the core material has been field-tested by hundreds of networking professionals in dozens of seminars over three years. This has benefits for the reader: crisper explanations, sharper focus, streamlined flow, added experience "from the trenches," and field checking of facts and conclusions.

The following are some more specific features of the book:

- Over 85 diagrams and charts, which are especially beneficial for those of us who learn visually
- Wide-ranging sources for preparing the book, which provide the reader with a current, balanced, and broad perspective on frame relay
- Several exercises, with answers supplied, which allow the reader to reinforce certain key concepts
- An unusually extensive glossary, which can help fill in any holes in the reader's networking background
- An extensive index so that the book can be used as a quick reference
- An appendix on general sources of information about frame relay topics, which will be helpful for readers who want to keep up with the field
- Footnotes to books, articles, and Web sites so that the reader can further explore topics mentioned in the book

The overall benefit of this book is that it helps readers understand what they should be looking for when investigating frame relay services and products. It is estimated the the global revenue from frame relay products and services in the year 2000 will be $15 billion. Many people will be investigating this technology.

Acknowledgments

Many people have contributed to this book in many ways. I would like to express my deep thanks to:

Alan Schaevitz of AYS Associates, who inspired me to write the manual on which this book is based and who carefully discussed many aspects of this material and its presentation with me.

The hundreds of networking professionals who have attended my frame relay seminars and the hundreds of university students who have attended my graduate and undergraduate networking classes. I have learned much from all of you.

My family, Regina and Derek, who were so cooperative and supportive of my writing this book.

The Computer Science Department and administrators at the University of San Francisco, who provided an extended leave so that I could write this book.

The book's reviewers who contributed so marvelously with suggestions and critiques—Lou Breit, First Data Corporation; Guptila de Silva, Australian Federal Police; Michael Easley; Michelle Famiglietti; Larry Greenstein, Nuera Communications and the Frame Relay Forum; Richard P. Jussaume, Breakaway Solutions, Inc.; Mark Kaplan, Newbridge Networks, Inc.; Dana Love, Radnet, Inc.; Ravi Prakash, Cisco Systems, Inc.; Dr. Robert C. Raciti; Richard Rogers, Intel Network Systems; Lawrence A. Van Buren; Linas Vepstas; Joanie Wexler, independent technology analyst and editor; and the anonymous reviewers.

The people who helped by sharing information, giving advice, telling stories, or offering encouragement—Gary Audin, Delphi, Inc.; Bill Branson, Frank Russell Co.; Zak Cohen, Briarwood Associates; Liz Duncan, Electronic Payment Systems; Keith Falter, AT&T; Michael Finneran, dBrn Associates, Inc.; Russ Hansen and Chuck Jarzbek, Williams Communications Solutions; Chris Johnson, Bell Atlantic; Michael Kudlick, University of San Francisco; Gerry Litton, User-Friendly Consulting; Loren Meissner, University of San Francisco; Mark O'Leary, AT&T; Dave Pace, BCR Enterprises, Inc.; David Peterson, Transition Data Group; Rick Sant'Angelo, LAN Tech Systems; Buddy Shipley, Shipley Consulting Intl.; and Mehdi Sif, Nortel Networks.

The publishing professionals at Addison Wesley Longman, who turned ideas and diskettes into a real book. Thanks go especially to Mary Hart, project editor, for her continual support; Marilyn Rash, production coordinator; and Dianne Cannon Wood, copy editor.

FRAME RELAY

Introduction

This chapter introduces changes in the business and technical communities that are driving demand for new communications services—in particular, frame relay services. An understanding of these trends provides a context for evaluating frame relay and other emerging technologies.

We introduce a simple block diagram for a frame relay network and briefly discuss the basic components. Frame relay networks will be discussed in much more depth in later chapters.

Next, we describe the major benefits of frame relay technology. These benefits are why frame relay has become so popular within the last few years. For balance, we also describe the major disadvantages of the technology.

Lastly, we briefly discuss the relation of frame relay to other technologies. We point out its major advantages and disadvantages as compared to leased lines, ATM, X.25, switched digital facilities, virtual private networks (VPNs), and other emerging technologies. These comparisons will be discussed further in later chapters.

Driving Forces for Frame Relay

Frame relay has been one of the major success stories in the data communications arena. From its introduction in the early 1990s, the combination of frame relay products and services has grown rapidly to an estimated $15 billion in annual global revenues in the year 2000 [VerticalSG99]. Growth rates have often been over 100% per year. *Why?*

The Need for Frame Relay

For a number of years, managers of **wide area networks** (WANs) have had several needs on their wish lists. Frame relay technology was developed to specifically address these needs, which are

- A higher performance packet technology
- Integration of traffic from both legacy and LAN applications over the same physical network
- Simpler network management
- More reliable networks
- Lower network costs

We now explore each one.

A Higher Performance Packet Technology

"High performance" means high throughput, low delay, and high efficiency. Good throughput and delay are requirements for a wide area network. High efficiency is desirable in order to obtain good return on investment.

Network managers have seen a dramatic increase in the volume of data traffic over the years. Some of the reasons for this, such as LAN internetworking and the shift from text to graphics, we will discuss in the next subsection. The result has been a need to handle much higher throughput, in bits per second, than previously.

In addition to the need for higher raw throughput, network managers also need low network delay, especially across the wide area network. Low delay (also known as latency) is necessary in part because of the expectations that LAN users have for very fast response time. Typically, users do not care and do not want to know whether the resources they are using are on their own LAN or on a distant one. In either case, they want fast response time, even though it is technically much harder to provide it across the wide area.

Lastly, network managers need a technology that efficiently handles bursty traffic. Most *data* traffic is bursty, meaning that an end user may want to transfer a 10-Mbyte file across the network and then do no more transfers for 20 minutes. This tends to produce very high circuit utilizations for *short* periods of time, then no utilization at all for *long* periods of time, resulting in a low *average* circuit utilization. (For our purposes, circuit utilization is the percentage of time the circuit is busy.) Network managers find it hard to cost-justify an expensive long-distance circuit that may be busy for only 5% of the time on the average. For that reason, they need a technology that will handle bursty traffic as efficiently as possible, by maintaining a high average circuit utilization when possible. We will explore this performance issue more thoroughly in Chapter 11, Design of Frame Relay Networks.

Circuit-switched technologies, such as T1/E1 lines or ISDN lines, all of which use time division multiplexing, are notoriously inefficient for transporting bursty data traffic. (See the Glossary for brief explanations of T1, E1, and ISDN.) They are much better for transporting low-volume, continuous data streams, such as voice or video. Hence, network managers have a need for a *packet*-switching technology as an alternative to the less efficient circuit-switching technologies.

In general, frame relay is a high-performance technology with good throughput and acceptable delay. It is also relatively efficient, for two technical reasons: its ability to statistically multiplex many logical connections over the same physical circuit and its ability to "burst" extra data into the network. More on these two issues in Chapter 3, Frame Relay Architecture, and Chapter 5, Frame Relay Virtual Circuits.

Traffic Integration

Historically, in many companies one department, often called Management Information Systems (MIS), built and supported the centralized MIS applications. These applications, which were and still are mission critical, were often based on IBM's **Systems Network Architecture** (SNA) and are now often called legacy applications, although the term "legacy" also more generally refers to any older application. In contrast to the wide area networks that support SNA, LANs were often built, supported, and interconnected by whatever departments needed the connectivity. This resulted in many companies developing parallel networks, one for the LAN file transfers and one for the MIS applications. With the current competitive business environment and the emphasis on cost justification, there is increasing pressure to consolidate these LAN and legacy networks.

Frame relay technology is able to consolidate both types of data traffic over the same physical network. In addition, under certain conditions voice and video traffic can also be carried over a frame relay network (see Chapter 12, Voice over Frame Relay). This consolidation is often called network convergence.

Simpler Network Management

Network management has become increasingly complex. This is due to such factors as

- Mergers and acquisitions among companies, which result in the merging of disparate networks
- More types of traffic that must be carried, such as digitized voice and images
- The proliferation of "new" protocols, such as ATM, while "old" protocols, such as IBM's Bisynch, continue to live on despite attempts to eradicate them
- Deregulation of the communications industry, which has led to increased product and services choices for network managers

These factors, combined with pressure to control costs and a shortage of trained network staff, have created a need for simpler network management. Some network managers have responded by outsourcing pieces of their management or at least making increasing use of carriers' services.

When frame relay is used in a network, overall network management usually becomes simpler. This issue is discussed more fully in Chapter 8, Network Management.

More Reliable Networks

As companies have become more dependent on their networks, the need for overall reliability has increased. Companies want high availability and long **mean time between failure** (MTBF), both for individual components and for the network as a whole. Having any potential single point of failure becomes a great concern.

Lower Network Costs

As the traffic volume on networks has increased, and the need for higher performance networks has grown, so has the cost of paying for the network. Network managers are under pressure to keep costs from escalating. In keeping with the corporate trend toward downsizing, they need to do more with less.

As we will see in the later section on the benefits of frame relay, the use of frame relay technology often leads to lower costs.[1]

---

[1]The term "frame relay" is used in at least three related ways. It refers to a particular type of packet-switching technology. It also refers to a set of standards (protocols) that describe how a company interfaces its equipment to a frame relay network. And it refers to a set of services offered by public frame relay service providers. The context usually makes it clear which is the appropriate meaning.

Accelerators for the Growth of Frame Relay

Equipment vendors and service providers saw that a "fast packet" technology, such as frame relay, could help satisfy the needs of network managers discussed above. Frame relay technology could improve performance, integrate traffic types, and simplify network management, all for a reasonable price.

However, several trends also have accelerated the growth and acceptance of frame relay far beyond its being just another technology. In the communications arena these trends are

- A shift to "cleaner" digital networks
- Increasingly intelligent network devices
- Experience with packet networks
- Availability of ISDN standards as a basis for frame relay
- A shift from the centrality of voice to the centrality of data communications
- Increasing use of LANs and client/server computing
- Increasing use of digitized voice and video, multimedia, and digital imaging
- Increasing importance of computer networks for businesses

Shift to Cleaner Digital Networks

During the 1980s, sophisticated fiber optic networks were installed throughout the United States. Fiber optic lines significantly increase the quality of transmissions, resulting in far lower error rates for packets sent across the network.

Cleaner digital circuits allow frame relay to dramatically simplify the processing of errors, as Chapter 3, Frame Relay Architecture, will show.

Increasingly Intelligent Network Devices

The often quoted Moore's Law states that computer chip complexity doubles roughly every 18 months [Newton98]. Compounded over many years, this evolution has led to vast increases in the processing power of both end-user devices (customer premises equipment) and network devices, such as switches. Intelligent end-user devices, such as routers and access concentrators, have taken over much of the error processing that used to be performed within the network itself. Thus, the frame relay network protocol, which does only simple error processing, can function well in this environment by handing off the heavyweight error detection and correction to the end-user devices.

In addition, the increase in processing power has produced inexpensive network switches, such as frame relay switches, that can handle large amounts of traffic.

Experience with Packet Networks

In many ways, frame relay is the next evolutionary step beyond X.25 packet switching. As we will see in Chapter 3, Frame Relay Architecture, there are many similarities, and some vital differences, between the two. Thus, years of experience with X.25, and with its relative, the Internet Protocol (IP), have made it easier for networkers to learn about and feel comfortable with frame relay.

Availability of ISDN Standards as a Basis for Frame Relay

ISDN standards were the basis for the frame relay standards. In 1988 the ITU-T Recommendation I.122, now called *Framework for Frame Mode Bearer Services*, introduced the frame relay protocol as a part of the ISDN standards. In particular, the ISDN D channel protocol, ITU-T Q.921, which is used by ISDN equipment to set up calls, was the basis for much of the frame relay work. Since then, ANSI, ITU-T, and other organizations have picked up and extended the frame relay standards. (More about these organizations in Chapter 2, Who's Who in Frame Relay.)

Around 1990, when equipment vendors were looking for a newer, higher performance packet-switching technology, they were attracted to the careful and substantial ISDN work that had already been done.

Shift from the Centrality of Voice to the Centrality of Data Communications

Historically, wide area data communications were an add on to the existing well-established analog voice communications network. During the 1990s the trend has reversed. The handling of voice traffic is rapidly becoming less of a standard for justifying corporate communications networks, while data communications demands are soaring. The data communications market is increasing at a rate of about 25% per year, while the voice market is increasing at less than 5% per year.

This shift from analog to digital traffic has helped the growth of frame relay, which is a digital protocol, by increasing the amount of digital traffic that must be carried.

Increasing Use of LANs and Client/Server Computing

LANs have grown up from a local resource-sharing method to an inter-connected infrastructure that supports a client/server environment. Applications that run on LANs typically have expectations of quick response time and the ability to handle large quantities of data. The advent of multimedia makes the demand for communications capacity all the greater. The interconnection of high-speed LANs over a low-speed WAN poses problems for LAN-based applications.

Frame relay has enjoyed growth because of its ability to cost-effectively interconnect LANs at a reasonable performance level.

Increasing Use of Digitized Voice and Video, Multimedia, and Digital Imaging

From the Web to corporate intranets to new Windows operating systems, we see increasing emphasis on digitized voice, video, and images. This trend is fueled in part by more powerful compression algorithms, such as MPEG-2, which make the handling of large data files more feasible. The vastly increased processing power of microprocessors, as discussed above, also allows larger files.

Digitized multimedia files are large. Frame relay technology helps handle the huge traffic volumes.

Increasing Importance of Computer Networks for Businesses

Computer communication is becoming ever more critical throughout the entire organization. Failure of the network can have disastrous consequences for the business. For many companies, frame relay technology is a piece of the answer for building reliable networks.

Frame Relay Network Basics

Here we briefly discuss a diagram (Figure 1.1) that illustrates the simplest case of a frame relay network. We will discuss more complex frame relay scenarios in later chapters; however, this diagram is the one to keep in mind as the "basic" design layout.

Descriptions of the six components of a typical frame relay network follow.

Frame relay customer premises equipment (CPE), which converts the user's data into frames that are compatible with the frame relay

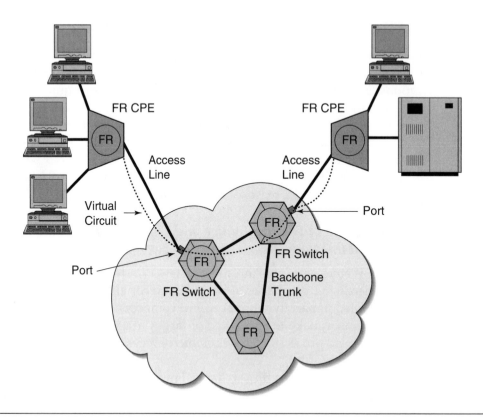

FIGURE 1.1 Basics of a Frame Relay Network.   *A frame relay network has five major physical components and one "virtual" component.*

interface standards. The access equipment may be a router, a **frame relay access device** (FRAD), a front end processor, or any other frame relay DTE. Usually, the same frame relay access equipment may be used with either private frame relay networks or public frame relay services.

Access line, which connects the customer's equipment to a port on the frame relay switch. The access facility[2] must be appropriate for the port speed and is usually a 56/64-Kbps or a T1/E1 link. When a fractional T1/E1 is desired, a full T1/E1 is still generally used for access, although the unused portion may transport other traffic. At the customer's site, a standard **data service unit/channel service unit** (DSU/CSU) is used to

---

[2]The terms "line," "circuit," "link," and "facility" are used interchangeably when describing the access line.

terminate the access circuit. (See Chapter 4, Connecting to the Network, for more about access options and DSU/CSUs.)

Port connection on the frame relay switch, which is the point of entry into the frame relay backbone network and is usually associated with an individual site. A single port connection will support multiple logical connections to many different remote locations (as discussed in Chapter 5, Frame Relay Virtual Circuits). The purpose of the port connection is to dynamically allocate network capacity to meet the changing needs of users. The connection is defined in terms of speed. The most common speeds available range from 56/64 Kbps to 1.544 Mbps (2.048 Mbps in Europe), although higher speeds are available.[3]

Frame relay switch, which does the actual processing and routing of the frames once they enter the network. The frame may transit one or more intermediate switches before it reaches the destination switch. The switching equipment may be a specialized frame relay switch, an I/O card on a T1/E1 multiplexer, or a packet switch that also supports frame relay as long as it implements the frame relay interface standards. A frame relay switch may be part of a private network or part of a public frame relay service.

Backbone trunks, which connect the frame relay switches within a frame relay network. The backbone circuits are often T1 or T3 lines. (See the Glossary for T3.) They are meshed to provide alternate routes though the network. For public frame relay services, the backbone is handled completely by the carrier and is not seen by the user. In fact, for the major carriers the backbone is actually an ATM network rather than meshed trunks.[4] For public frame relay networks, the combination of frame relay switches and backbone facilities is often called the frame relay **cloud**, perhaps because the user's frames seem to disappear into the fog and then magically reappear on the other side.

---

[3]Lower port speeds are typically quoted as multiples of 56 Kbps or 64 Kbps. The port speed will be a multiple of 56 Kbps if the speed of the access line is a multiple of 56 Kbps; and similarly for the 64-Kbps case. However, for a T1 access line some service providers quote the port speed as 1.544 Mbps, which is the raw speed of the circuit, with framing bits included (see the Glossary for more about T1). Other service providers quote the port speed as 1.536 Mbps, which is the usable speed of the T1 circuit after framing bits have been excluded. The relevant calculation is 24 channels × 64 Kbps per channel = 1.536 Mbps. Similarly, for E1 access circuits the port speed is sometimes quoted as 2.048 Mbps (raw rate) or as 1.920 Mbps (usable capacity; 30 channels × 64 Kbps per channel = 1.920 Mbps). Some service providers duck the issue of exact T1 port speed by quoting "T1 speed" or just "1.5 Mbps."

[4]Some carriers are also beginning to send frame relay traffic over IP VPNs based on Multiprotocol Label Switching (MPLS). See [Wex99] for a survey.

Virtual circuits, which are the "nonphysical" component of a frame relay network. Sometimes also called **virtual connections** or **logical connections**, they are the frame relay equivalent of dedicated physical lines. A virtual circuit appears to the user as a physical link, but no actual bandwidth is allocated to it—hence, it is "virtual." Two types of virtual circuits exist, **permanent virtual circuits** (PVCs), which are the most common, and **switched virtual circuits** (SVCs). When PVCs are used, the network operator assigns the end points of the circuits at the time of circuit provisioning. With SVCs the virtual circuit is set up dynamically, in real time, much as a phone call is set up. More on this in Chapter 5, Frame Relay Virtual Circuits.

Benefits and Limitations of Frame Relay

Frame relay technology is one solution to some of the problems that corporate network managers are facing.

Benefits

In this subsection we outline its typical benefits. These benefits are of course related to the needs of network managers discussed earlier. In later chapters we elaborate on how users can design their networks to achieve them. In other chapters, after we have discussed more details of frame relay technology, we will outline its technical advantages (Table 1.1).

Cost Reductions

Tariff Savings.   For public frame relay services, the cost of frame relay connections is usually lower than that of equivalent dedicated leased lines,

TABLE 1.1 The Benefits and Disadvantages of Frame Relay

Costs	⇓
Complexity	⇓
Flexibility	⇑
Performance	⇑
Upgrade capability	⇑
Traffic reporting	⇑

typically by 20% to 50%. This is due, in part, to the ability of frame relay networks to statistically multiplex many PVCs over a single physical line. (Statistical multiplexing is discussed more fully in Chapter 5, Frame Relay Virtual Circuits.) Thus, more logical connections can be supported by a given physical line, which is more cost effective for the carrier. The same economics work for private frame relay networks also.

However, we shouldn't overgeneralize about pricing. In the United States, frame relay pricing is usually not distance sensitive. Hence, the price advantage of frame relay is more apparent only for longer distances. In other countries, because of regulatory policies, frame relay may actually be priced higher than equivalent leased lines.

Wide Area Circuit Savings.　Since frame relay allows many logical connections to be shared over the same physical circuit, the number of physical circuits can often be reduced, particularly for highly meshed networks.

Equipment Savings.　For the same reason that the number of physical circuits can be reduced, the number of wide area network ports to remote locations can be reduced, often significantly. Thus, smaller and less expensive routers may be feasible. Fewer physical circuits also translate into a reduction in the number of DSU/CSUs needed.

Local Access Savings.　Again, for the same reason that the number of physical circuits and the number of ports can be reduced, the number of local access circuits can be reduced. Here, the local access circuits include the local connections to long-distance leased lines. In addition, separate applications, such as LANs and IBM's SNA and possibly voice, can often be consolidated into a single network, further reducing the number of local access circuits.

Savings Example.　As an illustration of the potential savings described above, consider Figure 1.2(a). We have 5 routers that are fully meshed, requiring a total of 10 long-distance leased lines, 20 router WAN ports, 20 DSU/CSUs, and 20 different local access circuits. Assume that the local access circuits connect to long-distance leased lines at a long-distance carrier's **point of presence** (POP). In Figure 1.2(b), we have the same 5 routers, but only 5 total router WAN ports, 5 DSU/CSUs, and 5 local access circuits. The 10 long distance leased lines have been replaced by 10 PVCs, which are "logical," not "physical." The equipment within the provider's frame relay network, such as DSU/CSUs, frame relay switches, and trunks, is the responsibility of the service provider. Although the reduction

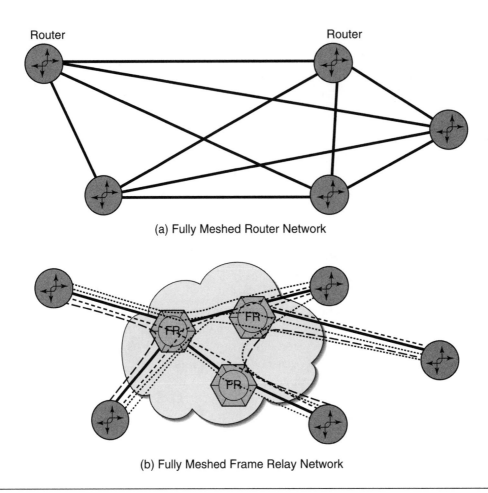

(a) Fully Meshed Router Network

(b) Fully Meshed Frame Relay Network

FIGURE 1.2 Example of Savings When Using Frame Relay.   *Fully meshed leased line networks need more CPE than fully meshed frame relay networks.*

in the amount of equipment is more noticeable than the tariff savings in our example, the reduction in monthly recurring charges typically produces a greater savings in the long run.

With more routers in a fully meshed configuration, the savings only become more dramatic.[5]

---

[5]However, no one builds *large* fully meshed router networks based on leased lines because the costs increase as the square of the number of routers. Large router networks are partially meshed, often with a hierarchical structure.

Decreased Complexity

Frame relay can simplify network architectures and reduce the number of leased lines, parallel networks, ports, and equipment. This translates into decreased complexity and lower operating costs. Also, frame relay providers typically offer the option of bundling everything together, including the equipment. Even if this option is not taken, a public carrier will assume a larger burden for network operations and availability. Network administration and provisioning is often easier and faster than with traditional dedicated networks. Hence, it is often easier to manage growth of a frame relay network.

Improved Performance

By eliminating the packet layer processing of packet-switched and X.25 networks (as discussed in Chapter 3, Frame Relay Architecture), frame relay gives higher throughputs. This is why it is often called a "fast packet" technology. Also, frame relay solutions often allow a higher level of direct connectivity (more meshing) between remote locations. Bypassing intermediate network hubs can reduce congestion and decrease response times.

In fairness, however, frame relay solutions will usually incur longer and more variable delays than equivalent leased line scenarios, although such delays are usually within acceptable limits. The delays may also be mitigated by more meshing, which reduces intermediate router hops. More on this in Chapter 11, Design of Frame Relay Networks.

Increased Upgrade Capability

Existing equipment can typically be upgraded to support frame relay standards rather easily. For instance, access devices often require only software changes or simple hardware upgrades. This benefit is of more direct value to vendors, but can also spin off to customers. Upgrade capability is improved because the frame relay standards are well defined, coherent, and widely supported by equipment vendors and service providers.

Improved Traffic Reporting

Frame relay can measure and report on traffic patterns, traffic amounts, peak traffic times, and so forth. For some networks, this information can give network managers their first view of what is really happening in the network.

Limitations

Like every other networking technology, frame relay has limitations, as follows.

- It is a shared-medium technology, which means there is inherent potential for a heavy user of the medium to create congestion for other users. This is true for any type of shared medium, such as Ethernet or ATM, although good engineering can minimize the impact of congestion in the network. Congestion results in long, and variable, delays for the user.
- Like all packet networks, it introduces finite, though small, delays at the switching nodes, even when there is no congestion. Thus, although the signal propagation delay across a frame relay network will be about the same as across a leased line network, the total delay will be somewhat longer. More about this in Chapter 11, Design of Frame Relay Networks.
- It was originally intended for data-only applications because it was designed for bursty, delay-tolerant, variable-block-size data. This environment is the opposite of what is needed for good-quality voice. Voice can be carried, but not at *consistent* "toll quality." High-quality video is quite difficult, although lower-quality video is possible.
- Typically, frame relay service providers offer only one class of service to the customer. Thus, the frame relay network does not distinguish between voice and video traffic on the one hand and ordinary data traffic on the other. Nor does it distinguish between different types of data traffic, such as interactive versus file transfer. This one-size-fits-all service may not be particularly appropriate for certain types of traffic, such as voice, which has tight delay requirements. Some carriers are offering different classes of frame relay service, but such differentiated service is not yet widespread.
- In order to lay out a frame relay network, the designer must have some grasp of traffic in the network. Although it is possible to wing it, then collect traffic statistics from the frame relay devices after the network is built, and then redesign the network, the most efficient method is to know initially where traffic is going, how much, and what kinds.
- For public frame relay networks only certain speeds are available, and this will depend on the carrier. Standard offerings are usually limited to a few sub-64-Kbps choices plus any increment of 64 Kbps up to 1.5 Mbps, or sometimes higher. These limitations are primarily

for marketing reasons, not technical constraints. However, in practice these limitations are not extremely troublesome.

Frame Relay and Other Networking Technologies

Frame relay is one of the technologies for solving the needs of wide area network managers discussed earlier. However, several other technologies also have a role. Three are emerging technologies: **asynchronous transfer mode** (ATM), data-oriented virtual private networks, and **Switched Multimegabit Data Service** (SMDS). Four are technologies from the 1980s that have been brought forward: dial-up analog phone lines with modems, ISDN, leased lines, and X.25 packet switching.

Each of these networking solutions has advantages and disadvantages. No single solution is optimal for every site in a network. In Figure 1.3 we attempt to show where each of the technologies has its zone of advantage [Heckart94]. However, there is *considerable* overlap among them, and in the figure the boundaries are by no means firm (see also Table 1.2). New developments, such as switched virtual circuits and higher speeds, will increase the amount of overlap.

Now, we make some comments about the role of each technology in relation to frame relay.

Dial-Up Modem Lines

Dial-up lines have the advantage of any-to-any connectivity (ubiquity). However, call setup times are long (4 to 10 seconds) and data rates are low (up to 56 Kbps).

For frame relay, PVCs have no call setup time at all and SVCs have only a small one. Frame relay data rates vary, but often go as high as 1.5 Mbps, or higher. Frame relay is not ubiquitous, but can be accessed remotely via leased lines or dial-up modems or ISDN. However, it is more complex and requires more equipment than analog phone lines with modems.

ISDN and Other Switched Digital Facilities

Switched digital lines have the advantages of bandwidth-on-demand and that connections to different destinations can be made on a per-call basis. However, once a call has been established, the line behaves like a leased line and does not provide any efficiency advantage for bursty traffic. Also, ISDN facilities are only now becoming widely available. For other switched

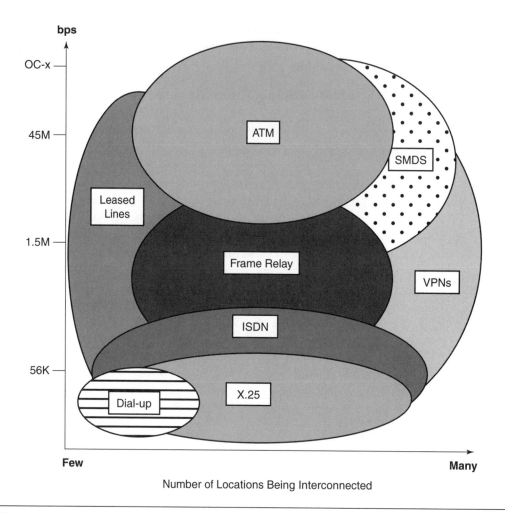

FIGURE 1.3 Zones of Advantage in WAN Technologies.   *Frame relay has a zone of advantage compared to other networking technologies.*

Source: Adapted from C. Heckart, *The Guide to Frame Relay Networking (1994).*

digital facilities, such as switched-56, service offerings are scattered and often incompatible across carriers.

As mentioned earlier, frame relay handles burst traffic well and can accommodate intermediate data rates. And frame relay services are flexible because they can be accessed through either local leased or local switched lines. However, until frame relay SVCs become more commonplace, the PVCs will not have the advantage of being able to make connections to different locations on a call-by-call basis.

TABLE 1.2 Comparison of WAN Technologies

Technology	Connection Type	Data, Voice, or Video	Data Transmission Unit	Bandwidth Supported (bps)	Maturity Level
Dial-Up Modem Lines	Physical	Data, voice	Transparent bit streams	Up to 56K	Mature
ISDN and Switched Digital	Physical	All	Transparent bit streams	Up to 1.5M	Mature
Leased lines and MUX Nets	Physical	All	Transparent bit streams	Up to 1.5M, 45M, and OC-x	Mature
X.25 Packet Switching	Virtual	Data	X.25 packets	Up to 64K and higher	Mature
Frame Relay	Virtual	Data, some voice, video	Frames	Up to 1.5M and higher	Newly mature
ATM	Virtual	All	Cells	1.5M to gigabit	Maturing
Data VPNs	Virtual	Data, some voice, video	IP packets	Up to 1.5M and higher	Emerging
SMDS	Connectionless	Data	Frames and cells	1.5M to 34M+	Withering

Leased Lines

Leased lines and multiplexer-based networks can be obtained in varying data rates to meet customers' needs and are also quite common in customer networks.[6] However, they are not usage-based—the customer pays for them whether they are used or not. They have no inherent efficiencies

---

[6]Vertical Systems Group estimates that for the year 2000, there will be 1.4 billion leased line end points in the United States, but only 1 billion frame relay service end points [Vertical SG98]. As another perspective, the estimated global revenue in 1998 from leased line services was $15.6 billion, but the estimated revenue for frame relay services was $6.2 billion [DC97Dec]. Leased lines are by no means dead.

for bursty traffic (they may run at only 5% to 20% of capacity even during peak periods). Moreover, fully redundant interconnectivity requires expensive mesh topologies.

Frame relay can be provisioned according to usage. It is naturally suited to bursty traffic, and fully redundant interconnectivity can be provisioned for a relatively low marginal cost. However, frame relay is likely to be more expensive than heavily utilized leased lines, and its delay is both somewhat longer and considerably less predictable.

X.25 Packet-Switching Services

X.25 has the advantage of more network services available to the end user (such as error detection and correction and network routing and management). It also allows statistical multiplexing access to the available bandwidth and provides virtual circuits for any-to-any connectivity within the network. However, because of the extra overhead of processing the packets, and by tradition, X.25 is typically limited to lower access speeds—2.4 to 256 Kbps.

Since frame relay is a follow-on technology to X.25, it shares many of the same advantages. But it has the extra advantages of higher access speeds (up to 1.5 Mbps and higher) and typically lower prices because of its greater efficiency. We will discuss frame relay and X.25 more in Chapter 3, Frame Relay Architecture.

Asynchronous Transfer Mode

Asynchronous transfer mode (ATM) can be considered a direct outgrowth of circuit switching, packet switching, and frame relay. Like frame relay, it provides statistical multiplexing access to available bandwidth, makes use of virtual circuits, is suitable for WANs, and carries data traffic well. Unlike frame relay, ATM is scalable to much higher speeds, is also suitable for LANs, and carries voice and video traffic well.

ATM transmits only fixed-size frames, called cells, not variable-size frames, as frame relay and packet switching do. Hence, ATM is a type of cell relay. The standard for ATM cell relay is 53-byte cells (48 bytes of user data, 5 bytes of header). With only fixed-size cells to process, cell relay can use hardware switching and thus perform significantly faster than either frame relay or packet switching. More important, fixed-size cells allow ATM to handle "isochronous" traffic (see the Glossary), like voice and videoconferencing, which is difficult for frame relay to handle.

ATM is already common as the cell-switching backbone for frame relay and other technologies. We may see ATM become more common for end-to-end services, although its use within customer premises is less certain.

ATM has become mature as a technology only recently. Some standards still need to be refined. The technology needs to be further implemented in silicon, costs need to come down, and users need to gain experience with it.

One often hears that frame relay is only a transitional technology along the path to ATM. However, frame relay has the advantages of being currently available, widely supported, relatively well understood, and cost effective for a large niche of data networks. In particular, frame relay is better suited than ATM for data-only, medium-speed (56/64 Kbps, T1) requirements. Its ratio of header size to frame size is typically much smaller (often less than 1%) than the overhead ratio for ATM (9.4%). Thus, it is considerably more efficient in terms of overhead. In addition, frame relay will likely be used for quite some time as an access network for higher speed backbone ATM networks.

We discuss the relationships between these two technologies more fully in Chapter 14, Frame Relay and ATM.

Data-Oriented Virtual Private Networks

Data virtual private networks, also know as Internet VPNs or IP VPNs, are an intriguing new arrival on the networking scene. By data VPNs we mean that customers use special VPN products or special VPN services from an ISP to create secure "tunnels" through the Internet. They have two major advantages: the widespread use of the Internet and low cost. Compared to frame relay, VPNs have the potential of noticeably lower cost.

However, at present VPNs also have serious drawbacks. Reliable security is still a great concern for the Internet, complicated by the lack of interoperability among many VPN products and by the hassles of security administration. Congestion on the public Internet can wreak havoc on time-sensitive traffic, unless the ISP offers less-congested facilities and quality of service guarantees specifically for VPN users. Moreover, the Internet is far less robust than frame relay, which raises the possibility of a company needing a frame relay backup for a VPN application. Nonetheless, data VPNs bear watching, especially for remote access and extranet applications.

Note that VPNs and frame relay are not head-to-head competitors. VPNs operate at the IP layer, layer 3, whereas frame relay operates at layer

2. Hence, a frame relay network can carry secure VPN tunnel traffic. For instance, a company could connect to the Internet via frame relay and then establish secure tunnels over the frame relay connection.

In addition, some analysts have noted that frame relay can be considered as a layer 2 VPN because frame relay virtual circuits act like secure tunnels [Sif99]. However, not everyone agrees that frame relay should be considered as a VPN type.

Switched Multimegabit Data Service

Switched Multimegabit Data Service (SMDS) is a high-speed, connectionless form of packet switching, and so it is like the postal service of data communications. Data is given a complete address and dropped into the network, and the network then makes a best-effort attempt to deliver it. SMDS is advantageous when the user group is open and less well defined, for instance, for traffic between companies. However, SMDS is expensive, is offered only by public carriers, and is available only as a metropolitan area network.[7] As such, it appears to be withering on the vine, and we will not discuss it further.

---

[7]As one wag at Pacific Bell put it, "Frame relay is a Chevy; SMDS is a Cadillac. Who needs a Cadillac if you're just carrying orange crates?"

Who's Who in Frame Relay

Several organizations are involved in the development of frame relay standards, the documentation of implementation agreements, or the encouragement of frame relay products and services. This chapter discusses these organizations and their roles in frame relay. Also included is a brief survey of service providers and vendors.

Standards Organizations

International Telecommunications Union–Telecommunication

The organization that has done much of the work on developing frame relay standards is the **International Telecommunications Union–Telecommunications Standardization Sector** (ITU-T). Formerly known as CCITT until 1993, the ITU-T is one of four permanent parts of the ITU, which is a United Nations agency based in Geneva, Switzerland. All UN members may belong to the ITU, representing their governments. In the United States the State Department additionally authorizes Recognized Operating Agencies (ROAs) and some vendors and scientific organizations to participate in the work of the ITU-T.

The ITU-T is subdivided into over a dozen Study Groups (SGs) that investigate and develop standards for specific areas of communications technology. Each SG in turn has Working Parties to do the actual investigation and standards development. Because of the number of groups involved, the process of setting standards is slow but relatively democratic.

The resulting standards are called recommendations. They are nonbinding, but in practice most vendors adopt them because of self-interest and market pressure.

The ITU-T standards can be recognized by their format: a letter followed by a period, followed by a number (for example X.25 or V.35). The letter generally indicates the area of communications technology to which the standard applies. "X" represents digital packet networking standards, such as X.25 and X.75; "V" represents standards for digital transmission over analog facilities, such as V.24 and V.90; "I" represents ISDN standards, which includes some frame relay standards, such as I.122; and "Q" represents other frame relay standards, such as Q.922. (See Figure 2.1.)

The American National Standards Institute

The American National Standards Institute (ANSI) has contributed significantly to the development of frame relay, among many other technologies. Despite its name, ANSI is a private, nongovernmental, nonprofit federation of standards-making and standards-using organizations. Its members are manufacturers, common carriers, professional societies, trade associations, consumer groups, and other interested parties. ANSI is the national clearinghouse for voluntary standards of many kinds in the United States.

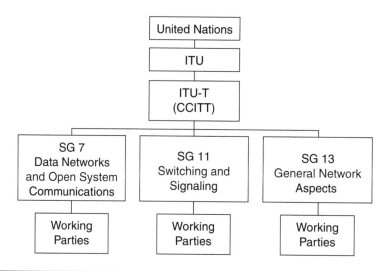

FIGURE 2.1 ITU-T Structure. *The International Telecommunications Union–Telecommunications has developed frame relay standards.*

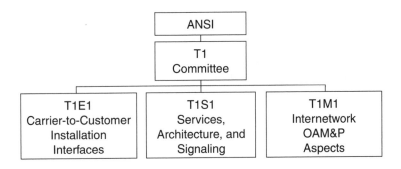

FIGURE 2.2 ANSI Structure. *The American National Standards Institute has also contributed to frame relay standards.*

ANSI works actively with international standards bodies such as ITU-T and ISO as a U.S. representative. Its standards are frequently adopted internationally.

Within ANSI, the T1 committee is charged with communications standards. In turn, this committee is subdivided into working groups for the study and development of standards in specific areas. ANSI standards published by the T1 committee can be recognized by their format: "T1" followed by a period, followed by a number—for example, *ANSI T1.606 Frame Relay Bearer Service–Architectural Framework and Service Description.* (See Figure 2.2.)

The Frame Relay Forum

The Frame Relay Forum is described as "an association of vendors, carriers, users, and consultants committed to the implementation of Frame Relay in accordance with national and international standards." It was formed in 1991 and now maintains chapters in North America, Europe, Australia/New Zealand, and Japan.

> The Forum's technical committees take existing standards, which are necessary but not sufficient for full interoperability, and create Implementation Agreements (IAs). These IAs represent an agreement by all members of the Frame Relay community as to the specific manner in which standards will be applied, thus helping to ensure interoperability. At the same time the Forum's marketing committees are chartered with worldwide market development through education as to the benefits of Frame Relay technology [*www.frforum.com*].

Currently the Frame Relay Forum has over a hundred Full Members, most of whom are manufacturers and carriers. Its marketing materials

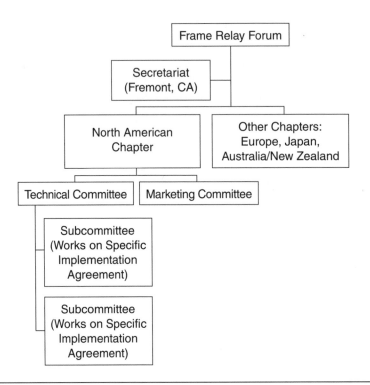

FIGURE 2.3 Frame Relay Forum Structure. *The Frame Relay Forum furthers the implementation of frame relay standards.*

include newsletters, application guides, white papers, slide presentations, fax-on-demand, and a Web page. Marketing activities include seminars, trade show participation, a speaker's bureau, and user roundtables. (See Appendix A for contact information.)

The Frame Relay Forum also works with the ATM Forum on interworking issues. An example, which also shows how to recognize Frame Relay Forum publications, is *FRF.5 Frame Relay/ATM PVC Network Interworking Implementation Agreement.* (See Figure 2.3.)

The Internet Engineering Task Force

The Internet Engineering Task Force (IETF) is one of the major organizations that cooperate to produce the standards and conventions of the Internet. Working groups of the IETF develop documents called Internet drafts (see Table 2.1). After these are circulated and approved by the **Internet Engineering Steering Group** (IESG), they become **Requests for Comments**

TABLE 2.1 The Internet Engineering Task Force Produces the Internet Standards

Functional Area Directorates

- Applications
- Internet
- User Services
- Operational Requirements
- Next-generation IP
- Routing
- Security
- Transport
- Network Management

(RFCs). The acronym "RFC" is of historical importance only, because in practice the comments have already been made on the Internet drafts. RFCs may describe standards or they may be simply informational.

In keeping with the "anarchy" of the Internet, working groups do not have official membership. Their members are defined by participation and are viewed as individual technical contributors rather than representatives of companies. They are primarily developers and users of protocols, not standards people.

For a proposed protocol to advance into standardization, there must be working implementations, as opposed to the paper specifications all too common in formal international standards work. This is one of the reasons that Internet protocols have a reputation for being practical.

From the point of view of frame relay, one particularly important IETF standard, which also shows how IETF standards are named, is *RFC 1490–Multiprotocol Interconnect over Frame Relay.*

Other Standards Organizations

ITU-T, ANSI, the Frame Relay Forum, and the IETF are the most important developers of frame relay standards. However, some other groups also play a role:

ATM Forum, which works with the Frame Relay Forum to resolve migration path and interworking issues

International Standards Organization (ISO) and the **International Electrotechnical Commission** (IEC), which produce many types of standards, including the **Open Systems Interconnection** (OSI) architecture and standards

Institute of Electrical and Electronics Engineers (IEEE)

Electronics Industries Association/Telecommunications Industries Association (EIA/TIA)

National Institute of Standards and Technology (NIST), formerly the National Bureau of Standards

European Computer Manufacturers Association (ECMA)

Commercial Organizations

Frame Relay Service Providers

United States

As with other public networking services, frame relay service providers fall roughly into two categories:

Interexchange carriers (IXCs) offer frame relay services on a wide scale, typically across **Local Access and Transport Areas** (LATA) boundaries (see Glossary). Many operate nationally or internationally; others are only regional. The larger carriers, such as AT&T, Sprint, and MCI WorldCom, offer frame relay over their own physical networks, and so they are also called facilities-based carriers. These networks, which typically are based on ATM running over **Synchronous Optical Networks** (SONETs) fiber optics, also carry many other kinds of network traffic over the ATM backbone. Other carriers, sometimes called resellers, or value-added networks (VANs), lease high-speed lines from the major carriers and then resell frame relay services over the leased lines.

Local carriers offer frame relay services within the same LATA. They include the **regional Bell operating companies** (RBOCs) and **competitive access providers** (CAPs). The local carriers are also known as incumbent local exchange carriers (ILECs) and competitive local exchange carriers (CLECs).

With passage of the Telecommunications Act of 1996, the traditional distinctions between IXCs and local carriers are fading. Many IXCs offer intraLATA frame relay connectivity. Many CAPs provide end-to-end frame relay services that cross LATA boundaries. The regulatory situation is likely to become even more murky in the future as other groups, such as cable companies, increase their presence in the telecommunications field.

International

Compared to the United States, international frame relay services have problems. Reliability is a concern, especially in those countries where leased lines already have a reputation for going down frequently. Some countries are plagued by regulatory obstacles and difficulty in obtaining access circuits. Also, prices are typically higher than in the United States. Frame relay switches may be sparsely located, especially for international providers seeking to extend their reach. And gateways between different providers' backbones are relatively rare, although this can be a problem in the United States as well.

When a service provider wants to extend its backbone into another country, it has two options: Lease lines from the national PTT or link up with the frame relay networks that already exist in the country. Thus, a number of international providers have bilateral agreements with other international or local providers. These agreements are easiest to implement when the two providers use the frame relay switches from the same vendor. Otherwise, linking dissimilar networks can be difficult, especially for provisioning, billing, and troubleshooting.

On the positive side, decreasing regulation in many countries is leading to more service offerings, lower prices, and more providers to choose from. Some areas, such as Western Europe and Brazil, are experiencing strong growth in frame relay.

Frame Relay Vendors

As with other kinds of data communications equipment, vendors may specialize in one category of frame relay equipment or may manufacture in many categories. The major categories are

- Routers, bridges, and LAN switches with frame relay support
- Frame relay access devices (FRADs)
- Frame relay switches
- Add-on devices, such as adapter cards, and frame relay testing and monitoring equipment

See the Frame Relay Forum Web site for vendors of frame relay equipment [*www.frforum.com*].

Chapter $\boxed{3}$

Frame Relay Architecture

In this chapter we discuss the architecture of frame relay networks, focusing on their logical layered structure rather than their physical components. We also discuss related issues such as interfaces, frame format, and identifying virtual circuits.

We see how frame relay is a natural evolution of X.25 packet-switching networks. Frame relay keeps many of the good features of packet switching, but improves on speed and simplicity.

Once we have a good grasp of the architecture of frame relay, we discuss the physical components in the next chapter. Together, these two chapters lay the foundation for understanding frame relay technology.

Frame Relay Layers

Frame relay operates at layers 1 and 2 of the Open Systems Interconnection (OSI) model (Figure 3.1). As usual, layer 1, the physical layer, handles the actual physical transmission of the frame relay bit stream. We will discuss the physical connection in the next chapter. The more novel part of frame relay is the layer 2 interface, at the data link layer.

Note that frame relay is an *interface* standard. It specifies what frame relay customer premises equipment (CPE) must do in order to connect to a frame relay network. The frame relay standards say nothing about how a frame relay network operates internally. In fact, the *internal* operation of the network is vendor proprietary and depends both on how the vendor

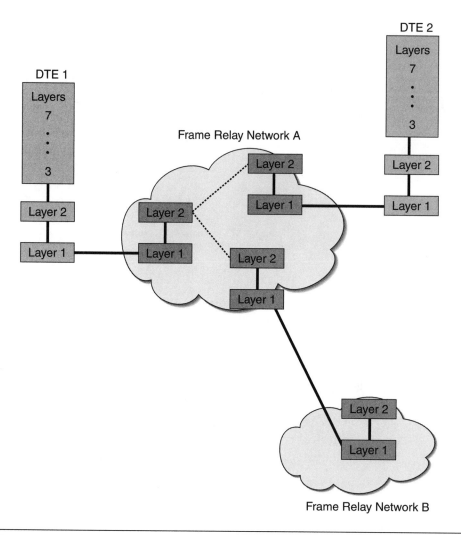

FIGURE 3.1 Frame Relay Layers.   *Frame relay operates at layers 1 and 2 of the OSI model.*

designs the frame relay switch and on how the service provider makes use of the switch features.

The basic frame relay protocol is a subset of the **Link Access Procedure for Frame Mode Bearer Services** (LAPF), as defined in ITU-T Q.922.[1] This

---

[1]The international standard, *ITU-T Q.922 (1992) ISDN Data Link Layer Specification for Frame Mode Bearer Services*, is closely aligned with the U.S. standard, *ANSI T1.606-1990 Architectural Framework*

subset is known as the LAPF Core protocol and sometimes as the data link core functions. The core functions provide the bare service of transferring data link frames from one subscriber to another, with no sophisticated flow control or error control. The core functions are

- Frame delimiting, alignment, and transparency
- Frame multiplexing using the DLCI field in the frame header (discussed later)
- Detection of format or transmission errors

Thus, from the point of view of OSI layering, frame relay sits in a sublayer of layer 2, the core sublayer. The core sublayer is the lowest sublayer of the data link layer, which is why it can carry other link layer protocols, such as **Synchronous Data Link Control** (SDLC).

Note that frame relay, unlike the full LAPF protocol, does *not* provide frame sequencing, acknowledgments, window sizing, or supervisory frames. How are these functions handled? The higher level protocols in the intelligent end equipment handle these important functions. This is a vital point. By moving the flow control and error control functions up to higher layer, where they are typically done anyway, the frame relay layer can concentrate on what it is good at—raw throughput.

As an example from the TCP/IP world, TCP, which operates at layer 4, has its own extensive error checking and flow control built in. So, why should the frame relay sublayer, which is part of layer 2, repeat all of that overhead? If the transmission lines are clean, which fiber optic circuits are, then there is no need for the frame relay protocols to repeat all that work.

What frame relay does provide is a small probability of frame loss, nonduplication of frames, and preservation of the order of frame transfer from one edge of the network to the other.

Since frame relay operates at layer 2, we use the term "frames" instead of "packets" for the blocks of data that are transferred. "Packets" typically refers to blocks of data that are transferred at layer 3, the network layer. However, as is often the case with networking jargon, people sometimes use "frame" and "packet" interchangeably.

---

and Service Description for Frame-Relaying Bearer Service. However, note that any given standards document is often highly dependent on previous documents. For instance, *Q.922* refers back to *Q.921 Digital Subscriber Signaling System No. 1 (DSS 1), Data Link Layer*, for many concepts and definitions. In addition, the Frame Relay Forum's *FRF.1.1 User-to-Network Implementation Agreement (UNI)* defines how the international standards should be interpreted to assure interoperability. Thus, the basic frame relay protocol should perhaps be called FRF.1 rather than LAPF Core.

Frame Relay and X.25 Packet Switching

Frame relay can be thought of as the "son of X.25 packet switching." As the "natural" successor to X.25, it shares many similarities and some notable differences with it. (See Figure 3.2.)

X.25 was developed at a time when the majority of communications facilities were analog, the maximum speed available was 56 Kbps, and circuits were prone to data errors. The X.25 standards were intended to compensate for these limitations. Nowadays, with clean fiber optic digital circuits and much faster microprocessors, many of the specifications in X.25 are unnecessary and limit performance. Frame relay is a "lightweight" version of X.25 that also adds some new features.[2] The simplicity of frame relay compared to X.25 is one of the reasons for its rapid acceptance.

The similarities between X.25 and frame relay are these:

- Both are based on the idea of connection-oriented packet switching as implemented by virtual circuits, rather than on the idea of circuit switching as implemented by **time division multiplexing** (TDM).
- Both allow a single physical access circuit to support many virtual circuits. This is a form of logical multiplexing.
- Both allow statistical multiplexing access to the available bandwidth, also known as dynamic bandwidth allocation, so that the physical circuit can be used more efficiently.
- Both can be deployed in public, private, or hybrid networks.
- Both are designed primarily for data, which means that both are well suited for variable-length frames, and delay-tolerant, bursty traffic.
- Both are *interface* specifications only and do not say anything about the *internal* design of the network.

The differences can be summarized as follows:

- X.25 networks are generally limited to 56-Kbps access speeds. Frame relay networks begin at 56 Kbps and support access circuits up to 1.5 Mbps and beyond.
- X.25 specifies headers at both layer 3 (the X.25 packet header) and layer 2 (the **Link Access Procedure-Balanced**—LAPB—header). Frame relay specifies a header *only* at layer 2 (the frame header).

---

[2]One consultant refers to frame relay as "X.25 on steroids" because frame relay is leaner, meaner, and faster than X.25.

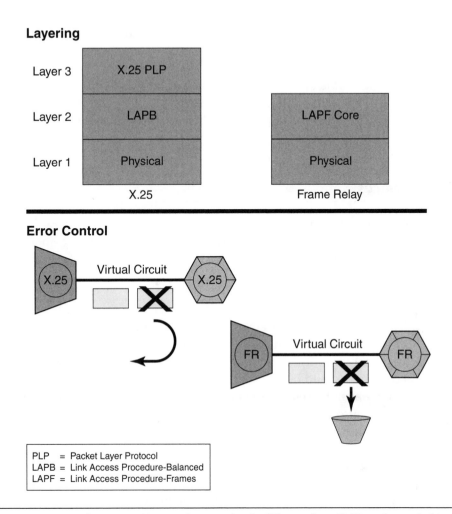

FIGURE 3.2 Frame Relay versus X.25. *Frame relay is different from X.25 packet switching in layering and error control.*

Thus, multiplexing and switching of virtual circuits takes place at layer 2 instead of layer 3, eliminating one layer of processing.

- In X.25, both layer 2 and layer 3 include flow control and error control. X.25 does both error detection and error correction (through its acknowledgment protocol). In frame relay, there is no hop-by-hop flow control or error control at all, only error detection. Damaged frames are simply discarded without comment. End-to-end flow control and error control are the responsibility of a higher layer—hence the need to run a protocol like TCP or Novell's IPX/SPX or HDLC at a higher layer.[3]

- X.25 uses inband signaling—that is, call setup packets are carried on the same virtual circuit as data packets. Frame relay uses out-of-band signaling. Call control packets for SVCs are carried on a separate logical connection from the user data. This simplifies the work of intermediate nodes in a frame relay network.

Network Interfaces

The three frame relay network interfaces are the User-Network Interface, the Network-to-Network Interface, and the Local Management Interface. They are depicted in Figure 3.3.

User-Network Interface

The **User-Network Interface** (UNI) is simply the set of procedures that allows the frame relay access equipment to communicate with the frame relay network. It is the LAPF Core protocol described earlier. The access equipment could be a router, FRAD, multiplexer, concentrator, bridge, or simply a frame relay I/O board in some piece of equipment. This equipment is also known as frame relay **data terminal equipment** (DTE). Every type of frame relay access device has a UNI with the network to which it is connected.

Details of the frame relay UNI are described further in the Frame Relay Forum's *FRF.1.1 User-to-Network Implementation Agreement* [FRF1.1-96]. However, outside of the standards documents, the term "UNI" is not as commonly used as it is in the ATM arena.

Network-to-Network Interface

A **Network-to-Network Interface** (NNI) interconnects two frame relay networks. It is based on the same standards as the UNI, but has added

---

[3]Note that in some cases, such as transmitting voice, it is better *not* to do error correction because the error correction process would introduce too long a delay in the output of the voice at the destination. A better approach is to allow a short gap in the voice output (because of the damaged frame) and then continue with the generation of the voice at the destination as new frames continue to arrive.

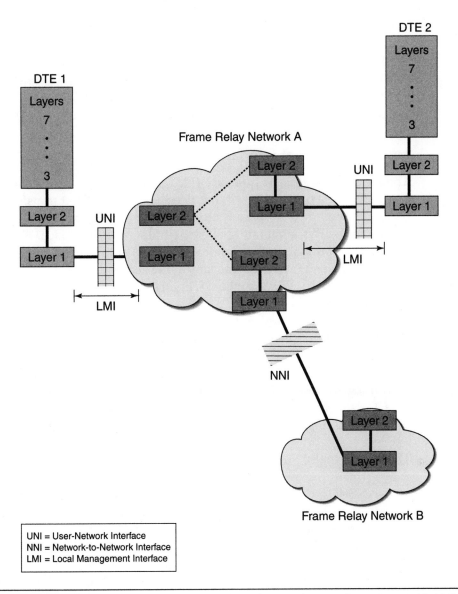

FIGURE 3.3 Frame Relay Interfaces. *There are three frame relay interfaces: UNI, NNI, LMI.*

features for high-speed data transfer, congestion management, and exchange of management information, such as error handling and link integrity. Carriers do not need an NNI to connect two frame relay networks. However, it provides benefits to the carriers and provides better management information to the end user. For instance, an NNI is particularly useful for connecting RBOC frame relay networks across IXC networks that act as transit networks.

Details of the frame relay NNI are given in the Frame Relay Forum's *FRF.2.1 Network-to-Network Implementation Agreement* [FRF2.1-95]. We also discuss the NNI more extensively in Chapter 4, Connecting to the Network.

Local Management Interface

The **Local Management Interface** (LMI) helps to ensure the valid operation of the local frame relay UNI. It does not do any direct transfer of user data, but provides the user with status and configuration information related to the PVCs operating over the frame relay interface. The LMI is considered optional by the standards bodies, but in practice it is always implemented and enabled on a frame relay access device.

With the LMI, the frame relay DTE can query the network "on the other side of the UNI" about

- The status of the virtual circuits that cross the UNI.
- The status of the local loop connection between the DTE and the network's port. The LMI uses a periodic polling procedure (link integrity, keep-alive signal, or heartbeat) across the UNI.
- Groups of downloadable network addresses that help simplify network configuration. This eliminates some manual updating of tables.

There are actually three versions of the LMI:

- ANSI T1.617a Annex D, the most common, which uses virtual circuit 0 for the LMI. This is often called just **LMI Annex D** or the **ANSI LMI**. There is also an older variation, ANSI T1.617 Annex D.
- ITU-T Q.933 Annex A, which is closely aligned with T1.617 Annex D. This is often called simply **LMI Annex A**.
- The Frame Relay Forum's first-generation LMI, which uses virtual circuit 1023 and is now largely outdated.

"LMI" is a de facto, but common, term. In the Frame Relay Forum documents, LMI mechanics are known as control procedures, signaling procedures, or management procedures, especially for PVCs.

We discuss the LMI more extensively, especially the format of LMI messages, in Chapter 8, Network Management.

Frame Relay Layer 2 Formats

Frame Format

The frame format for frame relay (Figure 3.4) is a streamlined version of the formats for HDLC, SDLC, LAPB, and the other "bit-oriented" synchronous data link layer protocols.[4] As described earlier, the frame relay link layer protocol is called the LAPF Core (Link Access Procedure for Frame Mode Bearer Services—Core Functions). It does not include error recovery, flow control, or management frames. Various texts describe High-level Data Link Control (HDLC) and related protocols. For a particularly readable overview of HDLC and many other networking topics, see Tanenbaum's *Computer Networks* [Tanenbaum96].

The full LAPF is described in ITU-T Q.922, which is based on the ISDN standard LAPD of Q.921. (Thus, it is not surprising that the frame relay standards use a lot of terminology adapted from ISDN.) One major advantage of basing the frame relay frame format on earlier bit-oriented protocols is that equipment already supporting HDLC, SDLC, or LAPB can be relatively easily modified by manufacturers to support frame relay.

The actual format of a frame relay frame is fairly simple. First comes the familiar **flag** (01111110 in binary, 7E in hexadecimal) indicating the beginning of the frame. Next comes a **header field**, which is 2 octets long.[5] The header contains addressing and various status information, discussed later in this chapter.

Then comes the **information field**, or "payload" of the frame. The payload can contain any arbitrary bit patterns,[6] but must consist of an integral number of octets. The length of the information field is variable. The minimum is 1 octet; the maximum is negotiated with the service provider at subscription time.[7] However, the frame check sequence (FCS—see

---

[4] The frame relay format (LAPF Core) is the same as the 2-octet address version of HDLC, but with the HDLC control field missing. The 2-octet address field is called simply the header in frame relay parlance and contains a few control bits in addition to address bits.

[5] We use the term "octet," meaning exactly 8 bits, instead of the term "byte" because "octet" is used throughout the standards documents. Also, the term "byte" has an IBM flavor disliked by some of the international standards representatives.

[6] The ability to transmit arbitrary patterns of user data, including even the bit pattern 01111110, is due to a technique called bit stuffing, or zero insertion, which is a standard feature of protocols in the HDLC family.

[7] FRF.1.1 states, "A maximum frame relay information field size of 1600 octets shall be supported by the network and the user. In addition, maximum information field sizes less than or greater than 1600 octets may be agreed to between networks and users at subscription time."

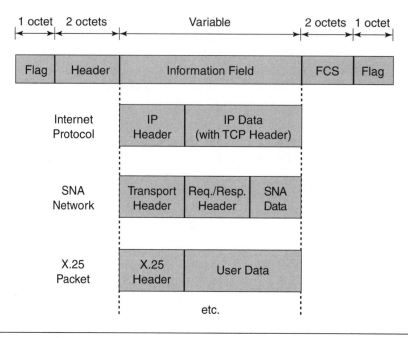

FIGURE 3.4 Frame Relay Layer 2 Frame Format.   *The frame structure for frame relay is simple.*

later) does not provide effective error checking for frames longer than about 4000 octets.

Typically, the payload will contain packets from layer 3 or other kinds of user data that are wrapped in headers. As usual, the information field is passed through the frame relay network transparently, regardless of its contents, via the technique of bit stuffing.

The Frame Relay Forum's *FRF.9 Data Compression over Frame Relay Implementation Agreement* describes how the information field can be compressed prior to transmission over a frame relay link. However, it does not appear to be widely supported at this time.

Next comes the **frame check sequence** field. This is the familiar **cyclic redundancy check** (CRC) error-detecting code calculated from the remaining bits of the frame, exclusive of the flags. Frame relay switches use the FCS to determine if the frame suffered a transmission error. If so, the node simply discards the damaged frame as soon as it detects the error.

The frame ends with another flag (01111110 in binary) to indicate the end of the frame. Note several points about the frame format:

- The total amount of overhead is only 4 octets, plus 2 flags, for a total of 6 octets. When compared to an information field length of, say, 1600 octets, this gives an overhead ratio of only 0.4%. This is one major reason why frame relay is considered so efficient.
- There is only one frame type, used for carrying user data. Unlike HDLC and SDLC, there are no control frames.
- Frames are *variable* length, not fixed length as in ATM cells. Thus, buffering of frame relay frames is somewhat more complex than in the ATM case.

Header Format

The frame relay header contains addressing and various status information. (See Figure 3.5.)

The high-order 6 bits of the first octet, together with the high-order 4 bits of the second octet, make up the **data link connection identifier** (DLCI). As the name suggests, the DLCI is used to identify the logical connection that the frame travels over. In particular, it points to a specific PVC or SVC on the frame relay network. The use of DLCIs allows multiple logical connections to be multiplexed over the same physical channel.

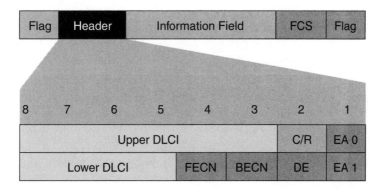

FIGURE 3.5 Frame Relay Header Format.   *The frame relay header field contains addressing and status information.*

The DLCI serves the same function as the virtual circuit number in X.25. Loosely, the DLCI can be thought of as just the frame relay address within the header.

The **command/response bit** (C/R) is application specific and is not used by the LAPF protocol. It is passed transparently by the frame relay network for applications that need command/response logic.

The last bit (EA 0) in the first octet is one of two **extended address bits**. Its value is a binary 0. The extended address bits allow the DLCI addressing structure to be expanded to handle more addresses (as described in ITU-T Q.922) by increasing the number of octets in the header. However, the Frame Relay Forum's *FRF.1.1 UNI Implementation Agreement* does not allow the use of more addresses. It states that a 2-octet header, which provides a 10-bit DLCI address, is sufficient.

The **forward explicit congestion notification bit**, the **backward explicit congestion notification bit**, and the **discard eligibility bit** (FECN, BECN, and DE) are used for congestion control and are discussed in Chapter 6, Traffic Management.

The last bit (EA 1) in the second octet is the final extended address bit. Its value is a binary 1.

Note a few points:

- Unlike HDLC and its cousins, there are no sequence numbers and no acknowledgment fields. Hence, frame relay (in its LAPF Core form) cannot directly support any flow control, sliding windows, error recovery, or **ARQ** (see Glossary) between the end user and the frame relay network.
- Also unlike HDLC, there is only one *type* of frame, used for carrying user data. Hence, it is not possible to use inband signaling to set up a virtual circuit. For SVCs, call setup must be over a separate virtual circuit, namely, DLCI 0. For PVCs, dynamically negotiated call setup is not necessary or possible because the circuit is set up at provisioning time and remains in place "permanently."

Data Link Connection Identifiers

How DLCIs Identify Virtual Circuits

As shown in Figure 3.6, DLCI is a number that identifies a particular virtual connection, which may be a PVC or an SVC. The DLCI number (or "address") is a label for the virtual connection, but is not the connection

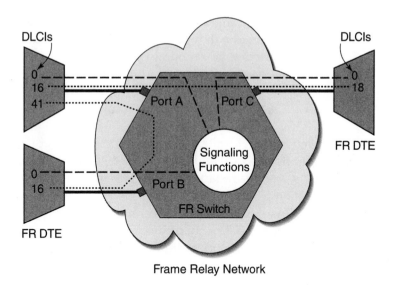

FIGURE 3.6 Data Link Connection Identifiers. *A DLCI makes a local reference to a particular virtual connection.*

itself. In the same way, "325 West Main Street" is an address for a house, but not the actual house itself, even though people often use the terms interchangeably.

DLCIs are represented by 10 bits, so there are 2^{10}, or 1024, different DLCI addresses, whose values range from 0 through 1023. This is enough for practical purposes because DLCIs have only local, not global, significance. Each end of the logical connection assigns its *own* DLCI from the pool of locally unused numbers. The frame relay network (actually the frame relay switch) must map from one DLCI to the other (more about mapping in the next subsection). For X.25, the "virtual circuit numbers" function exactly as DLCIs do for frame relay.

A loose analogy for DLCIs is that "325 West Main Street" can occur in several different cities and yet each address refers to a different house. In the same way, DLCI 16 may be used in several different frame relay DTEs but each one can refer to a different virtual connection.

The alternative to locally significant DLCIs, namely, always using the *same* DLCI at both ends of a virtual connection, is problematic, for the following reasons:

- It would require some sort of *global* management of DLCI values, which could be difficult operationally.

- It would require *many* more DLCI values, hence a larger DLCI field. This in turn would require a larger frame relay header, which would decrease efficiency. It would also lead to interoperability problems with the standard 2-octet header implementations.
- Two end users might not be able to communicate because they would not have a free DLCI value in common!

Thus, even though local DLCIs may seem strange at first glance, they are actually quite practical and efficient. Nonetheless, in a later subsection we describe *global* addressing for DLCIs, which is actually the default DLCI addressing plan for one of the major frame relay service providers.

Figure 3.6 illustrates the operation of a frame relay switch in a situation where several users are directly connected to the same switch over different physical channels. The operation could just as well involve relaying a frame through two or more switches.

The figure also shows the multiplexing function of frame relay. For instance, the three logical connections that leave the DTE attached to port A are multiplexed over the same physical channel to the switch. DLCI 0 is reserved for signaling functions, such as setting up switched virtual circuits, and the LMI functions.

Mapping DLCIs within a Network

The switch contains a **lookup table** that is used to map frames incoming on one physical channel onto frames outgoing on another channel. At circuit provisioning time (for PVCs) or at call setup time (for SVCs), an entry is made in the lookup table. In Figure 3.7, for instance, there is an entry that says, "When a frame comes in on port A with a DLCI of 16, map it to port C with a DLCI of 18." Thus, when the frame arrives at the switch, the switch will change the DLCI in the frame header from 16 to 18 and will pump the frame out on port C. (Note that a port is what a physical access channel attaches to.)

Frame relay virtual connections are typically full duplex. Hence, the DLCI mapping for the "other direction" of the virtual connection can be determined by reading the lookup table in the opposite direction. For instance, reverse traffic coming *in* to the switch on port B, DLCI 16, would be mapped to port A, DLCI 41. Of course, the actual physical implementation of the switch's lookup table is vendor specific.

Note that DLCI number 16 shows up twice in our example. It is associated once with port A and once with port B. This is permissible, since DLCI

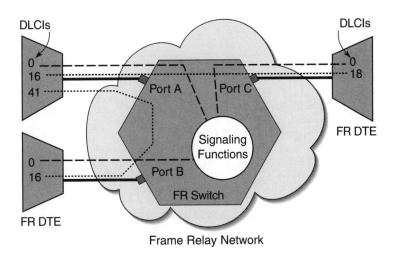

Lookup Table

Incoming		Outgoing	
Port	DLCI	Port	DLCI
A	16	C	18
A	41	B	16

FIGURE 3.7 DLCI Mapping.   *At each port, the frame relay switch maps incoming DLCIs to outgoing DLCIs.*

values have only local significance relative to a single port. They are used merely to distinguish among the frames coming in on a given port.

Lookup tables are also called connection tables, routing tables (a poor choice, since it can be confused with routing tables within a router), mapping tables, cross-connect tables, forwarding tables, or switch tables, depending on the vendor. Internally, packet switches and routers use a somewhat similar table lookup technique, although routers are considerably more sophisticated.

Users do not have all of the 1024 DLCI addresses available to them. According to Table 3.1 [Smith93], only 976 DLCIs are available without conflicting with reserved DLCI ranges. There is no magic about choosing DLCI values for PVCs. Just start with an available number and work

TABLE 3.1 DLCI Values

DLCI Range	Function
0	LMI signaling (SVC setup, link management)
1–15	Reserved
16–991	Available; can be used for both PVCs and SVCs
992–1007	Optional management information (rarely used)
1008–1022	Reserved
1023	Other management functions

upward, or use your own favorite algorithm. One common approach is to start with DLCI 100 and count up by 5s or 10s.

Globally Significant DLCIs

In addition to locally significant DLCIs, which we have been discussing, there is another addressing scheme called **global addressing** or globally significant DLCIs. With this scheme a DLCI is assigned to a globally *unique* location. For instance, in a small corporate network DLCI 100 could mean the headquarters in San Francisco, DLCI 105 might be a branch location in Chicago, and DLCI 110 might be a branch in Atlanta.

With global addressing when the router constructs the header of an outbound frame relay frame, it inserts the DLCI value of the *destination* rather than a locally significant DLCI associated with the virtual circuit. The frame relay switch that receives the frame must be programmed to interpret the DLCI as a destination address. The switch will not overwrite the DLCI field in the header with a new value because the DLCI will not change as the frame is forwarded to the destination.

The major advantage of this scheme is that it simplifies address administration and makes DLCIs more "intuitive." Supporters of global addressing claim that a network technician can look at a DLCI value in a frame and know immediately that the frame is destined, say, for San Francisco. With local addressing, the argument goes, the technician must look up the DLCI value in a large "cheat sheet" to see where the frame is bound.

The major disadvantage of global addressing, as described, is that it only works for small networks because of the limited size of the DLCI field. If the network grows beyond 976 sites, the customer will run out of unique DLCIs.

However, the service providers who use this scheme, notably AT&T, have developed hybrid addressing schemes for larger networks. One variation is to use global addressing for the (few) access circuits that come into the headquarters locations, and local addressing for the traffic that goes out over a specific access circuit to one of the (many) remote sites. Details are vendor specific. This hybrid scheme works best for networks that have only a handful of hubs in a basically hub-and-spoke topology. Another solution is to simply enforce local addressing everywhere within the network.

Another disadvantage of global addressing is that if San Francisco and Atlanta are connected by *two* virtual circuits, the addressing scheme must be modified because it cannot distinguish between them. One approach is to give Atlanta *two* DLCI values, 110 and 111. From the point of view of frames going from San Francisco to Atlanta, DLCI 110 would name one of the virtual circuits to Atlanta and DLCI 111 would name the other one. This is one reason why customers of AT&T usually number their DLCIs by 5s or even 10s.

Many network managers do not realize that there are two DLCI addressing schemes—locally significant and globally significant. In addition, service providers usually do not explain carefully which one they are using. This can be a source of confusion, even for people experienced with frame relay.

Exercises

1a. Break this frame (in hexadecimal) into its component fields:

(beginning)	7E 04 2B 89 AB CD 12 34 7E
Opening flag field	_____ (in hexadecimal)
Header field	_____ (in hexadecimal)
Information field	_____ (in hexadecimal)
Frame check sequence field	_____ (in hexadecimal)
Closing flag field	_____ (in hexadecimal)

1b. Now break the header field into its component subfields:

Upper 6-bits of DLCI	_____ (in binary)
C/R (command/response) bit	_____ (in binary)
EA 0 (extended address 0) bit	_____ (in binary)
Lower 4-bits of DLCI	_____ (in binary)

FECN bit   _____ (in binary)

BECN bit   _____ (in binary)

DE (discard eligible) bit   _____ (in binary)

EA 1 (extended address 1) bit _____ (in binary)

1c. What is the full 10-bit DLCI? _____ (in binary)

_____ (in hexadecimal)

(optional) _____ (in decimal)

Notes

1. A frame-relay-compatible data line monitor will also do this breakdown.
2. The binary equivalents of the hexadecimal digits are shown in Table E3.1.

2. Consider the network topology shown in Figure E3.1 and the switch lookup tables given in Table E3.2. Notice that each port is given a number, 1, 2, or 3, rather than a letter. Conventionally, switch hardware uses numbers like these.

For the virtual connection DLCI 17 that starts at DTE A:

a. Pencil in the path of the connection as it travels to its destination.

b. Where is the other end of this connection? _____

c. What is the DLCI at the other end of this connection? _____

_____

d. Is there any other virtual connection that starts at DTE A?

_____

If so, what are the DLCI values along its path? _____

_____

e. Is the DLCI value 17 used more than once in the network?

_____

If so, where is it used? _____

TABLE E3.1 Hexadecimal Digits—Binary Equivalents

Hex	Binary	Hex	Binary	Hex	Binary	Hex	Binary
0	0000	4	0100	8	1000	C	1100
1	0001	5	0101	9	1001	D	1101
2	0010	6	0110	A	1010	E	1110
3	0011	7	0111	B	1011	F	1111

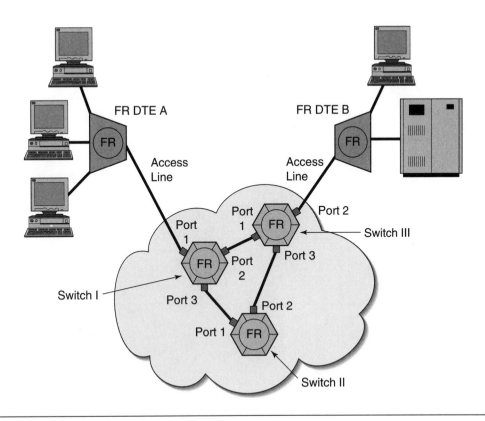

FIGURE E3.1 Network Topology for Exercise 2.

TABLE E3.2 Switch Lookup Tables

Switch I Lookup Table				Switch II Lookup Table				Switch III Lookup Table			
Incoming		Outgoing		Incoming		Outgoing		Incoming		Outgoing	
Port	DLCI	Port	DLCI	Port	DLCI	Port	DLCI	Port	DLCI	Port	DLCI
1	17	3	19	1	19	2	21	3	21	2	23
1	64	2	17	—	—	—	—	1	17	2	65

Chapter 4

Connecting to the Network

This chapter discusses the three major components required for connecting a customer site to a frame relay network:

- Access circuits, which connect the customer's equipment to a port on a frame relay switch located at the edge of the service provider's frame relay network
- Port connections, which provide a physical interface into the service provider's frame relay backbone network and serve as the logical entry point for frame relay virtual circuits
- Frame relay access equipment, which resides on the customer's premises

Three kinds of access circuits are available:

- Traditional leased circuits
- Local frame relay services
- Dial-up access circuits

We consider the characteristics, advantages, and disadvantages of each kind of access. We also discuss how a channelized access circuit can provide integrated access to a frame relay network and the potential advantages of this approach.

We include a list of the physical interfaces that can be used to connect access circuits to customer premises equipment. Along with the physical interfaces, we review the function of **data service units/channel service**

units (DSU/CSUs), which convert local network signals to the format of the wide area access circuits.

We also describe the advantages and pitfalls of Network-to-Network Interfaces (NNIs), which connect two frame relay networks.

Frame relay access equipment, also known as frame relay data terminal equipment (DTE) or frame relay customer premises equipment (CPE), is available in three major varieties:

- Routers
- FRADs (frame relay access devices)
- Interface cards that support frame relay access for PCs and host equipment

We discuss the characteristics, advantages, and disadvantages of each variety and we review how routers behave in frame relay networks, from the point of view of the lowest three layers of the OSI model.

Lastly, we discuss options for recovering from failure of the access circuits and of the frame relay backbone trunks.

Access Circuits

As discussed in Chapter 1, the access circuit connects the customer's frame relay equipment to a port on the service provider's frame relay switch. The access link is a single physical circuit, but it may support many multiplexed virtual circuits. The physical line speed of the access circuit, such as 56 Kbps or 1.544 Mbps, is an important parameter of a frame relay network. Along with the port speed (discussed later), the physical line speed controls the maximum rate at which data can be "pumped" into the frame relay switch from the customer's site.

There are at least three options for access facilities. We outline the options here and discuss them in more detail in subsequent pages.

Leased lines.   This is a very popular option because of the availability, predictability, and manageability of these circuits. The most common leased line speeds used for frame relay access are 56/64 Kbps and 1.544/2.048 (T1/E1). When a fractional T1/E1 is desired, a full T1/E1 is still generally used for access, although the unused portion may transport other traffic. (This is also known as integrated access and is discussed in more detail later.) At the customer's site, a standard DSU/CSU is used to terminate the access circuit.

Local frame relay services.   As intraLATA public frame relay services become more available, this option may become more attractive. (See the Glossary for **intraLATA** and **LATA**.) Consider a long-distance leased line from a customer's site to the nearest **interexchange carrier**'s (IXC's) frame relay switch. It can be replaced with a shorter and less expensive access line to a local frame relay service. The local frame relay service in turn connects to the IXC's broader-reaching frame relay network.

Dial-up/ISDN. This option is more attractive when the customer requires only infrequent access to the frame relay network or when the network manager wants an economical disaster backup solution. The dial-up modem connection or the ISDN connection can provide the temporary physical link from the customer's site into the frame relay network. Note that this is *not* the same as a switched virtual circuit (SVC), because a dial-up connection is only a physical layer (layer 1) connection whereas an SVC is a data link layer (layer 2) connection that "rides over" a layer 1 connection.

The frame relay service provider typically supplies the access link as part of the total service. If the customer purchases frame relay services from an interexchange carrier, the IXC will generally lease the local access circuit from a local carrier on the customer's behalf and provision it for the customer as part of the frame relay service package. However, the customer can instead lease the access link directly from the local provider. If the customer purchases local frame relay services, the local carrier sells and provisions both the frame and access services.

The speed of the access circuit must be matched to the port connection on the frame relay switch. For instance, a 56-Kbps port connection must be accessed by a 56-Kbps line or by a higher speed circuit in which only 56 Kbps of capacity are used for frame relay traffic.

Also, consider a single virtual circuit that goes from user site A to user site B, as in Figure 4.1. The access circuit at A does *not* have to be the same speed as the access circuit at B. This allows users to mix and match so that the speed of an access circuit matches the actual aggregate traffic at that site.

Leased Access Circuits

When accessing a frame relay network, several types of leased line access are common. These local loops are leased from a carrier. The first three circuits are depicted in Figure 4.2.

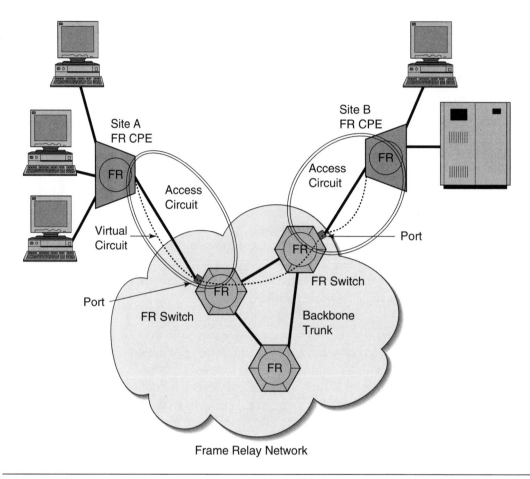

FIGURE 4.1 Access Circuits.   *Access circuits connect the customer's frame relay equipment to the frame relay switch.*

Low-speed DS-0 Circuit.   A popular form of access is a **DS-0** circuit (at 56 or 64 Kbps) connected to a 56/64-Kbps frame relay port. The advantage is that DS-0 circuits are fairly inexpensive, common, and well understood. Also, 56-Kbps connectivity will handle present-day data applications at many remote offices. The main disadvantage is that if the traffic demands grow beyond a 56/64-Kbps port connection, the port connection will have to be upgraded. Also, the DS-0 access circuit will have to be replaced with a higher speed circuit, including a faster DSU/CSU.

Market studies indicate that approximately 60% of all access circuits worldwide are 56/64 Kbps and that the percentage has been slowly decreasing as higher speed access lines have become more popular [DNA-99].

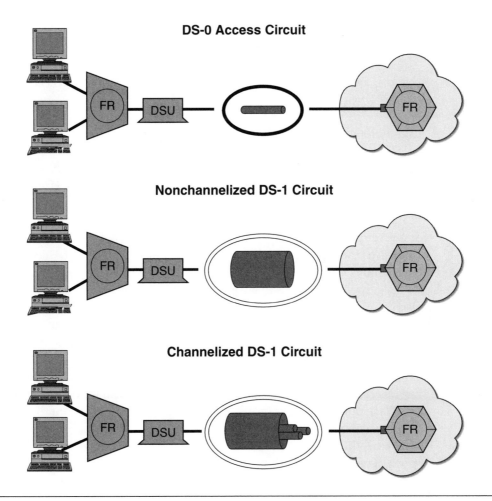

DS-0 Access Circuit

Nonchannelized DS-1 Circuit

Channelized DS-1 Circuit

FIGURE 4.2 Leased Access Circuits.   *Three types of leased line access are common.*

Nonchannelized DS-1 Circuit.   A DS-1 circuit, also known as a T1 circuit (see the Glossary), is useful for higher speed frame relay access. It can be thought of as just a higher speed (1.544-Mbps) version of DS-0 access. DS-1 is used with a 1.544-Mbps port connection (2.048 Mbps in Europe).[1]

---

[1]Sometimes a 1.544-Mbps port connection is known as a 1.536-Mbps port connection, which refers to the maximum capacity actually available to the user (24 channels × 64 Kbps per channel = 1.536 Mbps). The DS-1 framing bit (bit 193) is not available to the user. Similarly, a 2.048-Mbps port connection (E1 speed) may be known as a 1.920-Mbps port connection (30 channels × 64 Kbps = 1.920 Mbps).

"Nonchannelized" means that the entire usable capacity of the circuit is available for frame relay applications. Think of it as a big data pipe.

Market studies indicate that approximately 17% of all access circuits worldwide are full T1 or E1 circuits and that the percentage has been relatively stable [DNA-99].

Channelized DS-1 Circuit.   This type of access gives more flexibility in access rate than the nonchannelized form. "Channelized DS-1" means that the DS-1 data stream at 1.544 Mbps is broken down into 24 DS-0 channels, each operating at 64 Kbps. (In Europe, DS-1 is called E1 and is 2.048 Mbps broken down into 30 DS-0 user channels, plus two signaling and framing channels.) The channelization is performed by a DSU/CSU, a channel bank, or a multiplexer at the customer's location. At the network end of the circuit the carrier typically terminates the circuit in a channel bank or digital cross-connect system that can break out the individual DS-0s.

A channelized DS-1 can support fractional T1 service (FT1), sometimes also known as $n{\times}64$ Kbps service, if the service is available from the carrier. With fractional T1 service the carrier gives the user a group of n consecutive or nonconsecutive DS-0s out of a DS-1 circuit and charges the user less because the full capacity of the T1 is not being used.

One major advantage of channelized DS-1 access is that it allows sub-DS-1 port connections to be supported by a DS-1 local loop. For instance, a 256-Kbps port connection could be supported by 4 DS-0 channels, leaving free the remaining 20 DS-0 channels in the DS-1. Note that in this case the access circuit speed, 1.544 Mbps, is *not* the same as the port connection speed, which is only 256 Kbps. However, it is true that only 256 Kbps of the DS-1 is being used for frame relay traffic to the 256-Kbps port.

A closely related advantage is that channelized access allows **integrated access**, which is the ability to allocate a range of DS-0 channels to frame relay access and the other 64-Kbps bit streams to other applications. We discuss integrated access in more detail later in this subsection.

Market studies indicate that approximately 18% of all access circuits worldwide are channelized DS-1/E1 (fractional T1/E1) and that the percentage has been slowly increasing [DNA-99].

High-speed T3/E3 and $n{\times}$T1 Circuits.   "High-speed" access circuits are available from some carriers. They must be connected to high-speed ports on the frame relay switch. Not all frame relay service providers offer this option, and not all local carriers can supply high-speed local loops. When available, high-speed access circuits may be supported on SONET circuits, on nonchannelized or channelized T3 circuits, or on several parallel T1 circuits combined with an inverse multiplexer.

Market studies indicate that only about 1% of all access circuits worldwide are above T1/E1 speeds [DNA-99], although the percentage will undoubtedly increase.

Emerging Options.　Some carriers are beginning to offer varieties of **digital subscriber line** (DSL) access to customers. As with DSL for Internet access, this option has the advantages of low cost but relatively high speed—up to 1.5 Mbps and beyond for some flavors. However, DSL access is not available in all locations because of distance limitations between the subscriber and the carrier's serving location. Also, the DSL market is still evolving.

Another emerging possibility is frame relay access over a cable TV system with a cable modem. As with DSL access, the cable modem option has the advantage of a very good (low) price-to-performance ratio. However, for frame relay access it is not yet well developed. In addition, the future of this market segment is uncertain, because cable modems are typically targeted at residential customers whereas frame relay services are usually for business customers.

Integrated Access

A channelized DS-1 access circuit allows integrated access. With it the DS-1 loop can be shared among frame relay, voice, and other applications. (See Figure 4.3.)

If a customer wants to obtain frame relay service and has unused DS-0 channels on an existing DS-1 that is carrying, say, voice traffic, these unused channels can provide access into a frame relay network at little additional cost. (Note that the frame relay service provider must offer an integrated access service for the customer to take advantage of this.) Thus, the major advantage of integrated access is the cost savings from not needing separate local loops for different applications.

One disadvantage is that the DS-1 local loop becomes a prospective single point of failure, which could isolate all applications at the site. As usual, this risk has to be evaluated by a network analyst, who will often consider a backup solution, such as dial backup or ISDN.

Another potential disadvantage is that the carrier who provides the integrated access circuit also becomes the default frame relay service provider as well as the provider of the existing voice service, for example.

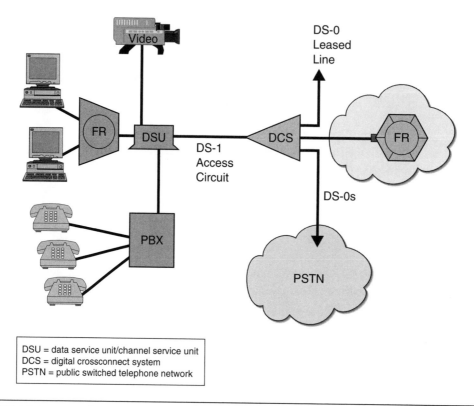

FIGURE 4.3 Integrated Access.   *Integrated access allows a DS-1 access circuit to be shared among frame relay, voice, and other applications.*

A customer might want carrier X to handle its voice traffic but not want carrier X to handle its frame relay traffic because it can get a better deal from carrier Y. In such a case, the customer will likely have to allow carrier X to handle both the voice and the frame relay traffic anyway, or else will need to install a different access circuit to each carrier, thereby losing the advantage of integrated access.

As a last disadvantage, integrated access may require more planning of how the DS-0 slots are laid out in the DS-1. Some applications may need contiguous slotting (in adjacent time slots) in order to minimize delay variation between arriving data across different DS-0s. This is not a major problem, however.

Market studies indicate that approximately 10% of frame relay customers worldwide use integrated access, and that about 6% of customers include voice traffic on their integrated access circuits [DNA-99].

A rough rule of thumb for deciding whether to use multiple DS-0 local loops or one DS-1 local loop is the **three circuits rule**. If a particular location needs three or more DS-0 circuits to support all the data and voice applications at that site, then upgrading to a channelized DS-1 may cost less. The typical breakeven point is about 4 to 8 DS-0s, but this depends greatly on tariffs.

The idea of integrated access also applies to high-speed circuits, such as T3, E3, OC-3, or other SONET circuits.

Multilink Procedures

The Frame Relay Forum recently approved on two Implementation Agreements that will help to bridge the capacity and cost gap between 56/64-Kbps and DS-1 circuits and also between DS-1 and DS-3 circuits. Multilink procedures are similar to the use of several parallel T1 circuits combined by an inverse multiplexer, except that the combining is done within the frame relay access equipment and not in a separate hardware multiplexer. Two DS-1 (T1) circuits in a multilink configuration could support a single frame relay access "channel" of approximately 3 Mbps, for instance. The two Implementation Agreements are FRF.15, *End-to-End Multilink Frame Relay* (previously known as *DTE-to-DTE Multilink Frame Relay*) and FRF.16, *Multilink Frame Relay UNI/NNI*.

Local Frame Relay Services

As intraLATA public frame relay services become more available, this option grows more attractive. The main motivation is economic—both cheaper rates from the local carriers than the IXCs, and simpler network, configurations.

Consider three locations within a single Local Access and Transport Area (LATA), as shown on the left in Figure 4.4. They need to be connected to an IXC **point of presence** (POP) in a different LATA (at the right in the figure). The long-distance provider carries the frame relay traffic to the distant headquarters. Some of the locations also need to be directly connected to each other.

The leased line solution is straightforward. Traditional leased lines allow access to the distant frame relay switch and interconnect the local sites.

In the local frame relay solution, the leased lines are replaced with shorter access lines to a local frame relay service within the LATA. The leased lines that directly interconnect the three sites are not needed at all. The local frame relay service in turn connects to the IXC's broader-reaching frame relay network, usually over a Network-to-Network Interface (NNI).

Leased Line Solution

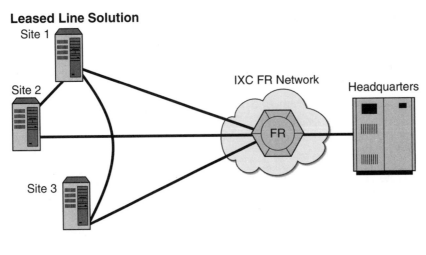

Frame Relay Solution

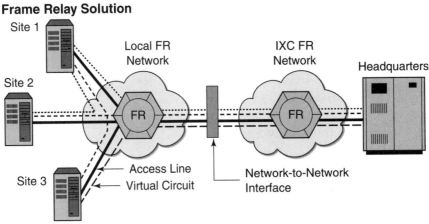

FIGURE 4.4 Local Frame Relay Services.   *A local frame relay service may be more cost effective than a leased line solution.*

In addition to the possible cost advantages of removing the longer distance leased lines, all of the sites in the LATA can share the same NNI into the IXC's frame relay network. They can also share the same port on the IXC's frame relay switch. Note, however, that different sites cannot share the same *virtual* circuit into headquarters; each site must have its own.

A rough rule of thumb for this economic tradeoff is the **three sites rule**: An intraLATA frame relay service will likely be a cost-effective alternative to leased lines if there are three or more sites within the LATA. When mileage-sensitive pricing is in force, the local frame relay alternative may be even less expensive if it replaces a single long access circuit (greater than 10 or 15 miles). This rule of thumb varies greatly by service provider and port speed. As usual, a network designer should evaluate the actual economic tradeoff.

One large potential obstacle to using a local frame relay carrier for access to an interexchange carrier's network is whether the two carriers can connect their networks, generally through a Network-to-Network Interface. Provisioning, installation, accounting, maintenance, and network management procedures must be established between the two service providers before they can offer a high-quality end-to-end service to users. In some cases, the two carriers may not have much experience with this kind of coordination *between* companies. From a technical point of view, having an NNI between the two carriers is not strictly necessary, but it is helpful. However, having an NNI is only part of the coordination issue. We discuss more issues with NNIs later in this chapter.

Another issue that a user may need to investigate is how the local frame relay carrier provides automatic reroute capability in the event of failure in the network. Since a local carrier may have only a few frame relay switches in the network, such backup capability may be limited. However, especially with regard to access circuit failures, the vulnerability may be no worse than that of the traditional leased line solution.

Dial-Up Access

Dial-up access (see Figure 4.5) is the ability to dial into a frame relay network from a customer's site or a mobile location, which means that a dedicated leased access circuit is not needed. As discussed earlier, once dial-up connectivity is established, a PVC or an SVC can be used to provide a path to a remote frame relay port connection.

As in other areas of networking, dial-up access has two major uses. One is to allow occasional, inexpensive, but low-speed, access into a frame relay network. The other is to provide backup for failures in dedicated access circuits. There are several types of frame relay dial access.

Analog.   A modem establishes a standard dial-up analog connection into a **remote access server** (RAS) or modem bank in the carrier's network. The dial-up line may run simple asynchronous (async), **Serial Line IP** (SLIP), **Point-to-Point Protocol** (PPP), or other protocol. The carrier's network terminates the connection with equipment that performs a protocol conversion into the frame relay format. Such conversion equipment is sometimes called a **central office frame relay access device** (CO FRAD). Alternatively,

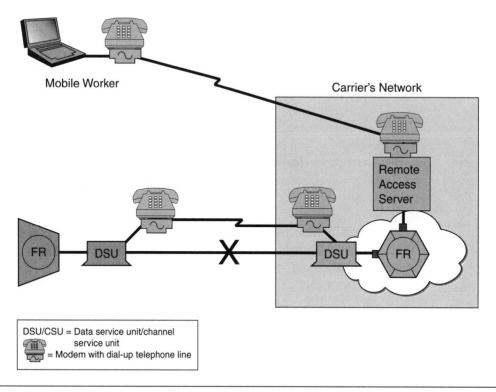

FIGURE 4.5 Dial-Up Access.   *Dial-up access is useful for infrequent access to a frame relay network and for dial backup.*

the carrier may carry the user's data across its own X.25 network or data-oriented VPN until user data reaches the frame relay entry point.

With analog dial-up, the user typically enters an ID and password. The RAS uses this information, and possibly additional information, to establish security and to decide which port connection and PVC (or SVC) should receive and carry the call. Note that the dial-up user must know the telephone number of the RAS that he or she wants to dial into. In addition, the network manager must have already predefined a PVC that can carry the user's call from the RAS through the frame relay network to the customer's data center or other location. Alternatively, an SVC could be dynamically set up to carry the user's call.

Analog dial-up is available up to 56 Kbps, although in practice the speeds are somewhat lower. Hence, it is a lower speed alternative than leased access lines, but it may be useful for infrequent access to a frame relay network, for mobile workers, and for low-speed backup for dedicated access lines.

ISDN BRI. Like analog dial-up, ISDN **Basic Rate Interface** (BRI) gives customers a relatively low-cost way to extend frame relay to small-volume, remote sites. ISDN BRI offers two 64-Kbps channels, called B channels. Because it offers 64 or 128 Kbps of access capacity, it is a higher speed alternative than analog dial-up.

ISDN BRI also enables a simple form of integrated access, since users can partition the bandwidth so that one B channel is used for voice or video and the other is used for data. ISDN is also a solid solution for dial backup. When a dedicated access line fails, an ISDN terminal adapter can automatically set up a replacement ISDN link. However, ISDN lines are not always widely available from carriers, especially outside metropolitan areas.

ISDN PRI. An ISDN **Primary Rate Interface** (PRI) line gives 23 user channels at 64 Kbps each. This makes it faster and more versatile than an ISDN BRI line, but also more expensive and less widely available. Since the 23 channels in an ISDN PRI circuit can be used independently, a PRI link allows even more flexible integrated access than a BRI. A PRI line could be especially attractive for time-of-day-sensitive traffic, such as for a network with heavy voice traffic during the day and heavy data traffic at night.

Switched-56 Kbps. This service can be thought of as a pre-ISDN, proprietary version of digital switched access from a customer's site to a switched-56-enabled carrier's serving office. It tends to be more expensive than other dial access options and is being replaced by ISDN BRI. However, it can be useful in areas where ISDN is not available.

Physical Connections to the Access Circuit

Physical Interfaces

The Frame Relay Forum has approved several physical interfaces for connecting access circuits to customer premise equipment (CPE) [FRF14-98]. In addition, other physical interfaces, such as ISDN and Synchronous Optical Network (SONET), are allowed when appropriate. Interface specifications *between* frame relay switches within the *same* service provider's network are not covered by the Frame Relay Forum and are proprietary to the switch vendor. However, Network-to-Network Interfaces between different carriers' networks can also use the physical interfaces listed here.

The most common interfaces are

- V.35, for data rates up to 56/64 Kbps
- DS-1, for T1 data rates of 1.544 Mbps and for fractional T1 ($n\times64$ Kbps)
- DS-3, for T3 data rates of 44.736 Mbps and fractional T3 (where it exists)
- **High-Speed Serial Interface** (HSSI), for data rates up to 52 Mbps

Other interfaces are not used much in the United States, but are common internationally:

- E1, for data rates of 2.048 Mbps
- E3, for data rates of 34.368 Mbps
- X.21, for lower data rates, depending on the electrical interface used

Data Service Units/Channel Service Units

Data service units/channel service units (DSU/CSUs)[2] (see Figure 4.6) are the termination devices for digital lines on the customer's premises. They convert local network signals to the format of the wide area access circuits and are necessary when using digital circuits. Since almost all frame relay access circuits are digital, DSU/CSUs are a typical part of any frame relay installation, even though they are often not explicitly mentioned. The cost of the DSU/CSUs must be included in the total cost of the frame relay customer premise equipment.

DSU/CSUs can be versatile pieces of equipment. In addition to basic signal formatting and testing, they can often perform the following functions, depending on the product:

- Collect frame relay error and traffic information for performance monitoring. This is especially helpful for supplementing frame relay

---

[2]A note on terminology: DSU/CSUs are often called DSUs, CSUs, or CSU/DSUs. Specifically, the DSU converts digital signals from one format to another. For instance, a particular DSU might convert from the V.35 digital signaling format to the alternate mark inversion (AMI) digital signaling format that is used on T1 lines. The CSU allows loopback testing and other electrical functions for terminating the digital line. Regardless, DSUs and CSUs are usually packaged together. Hence, "DSU," or "CSU," often refers to the whole package. Sometimes (confusingly) DSU/CSUs are called digital modems because they reside in the same place that an analog modem does for an analog phone line.

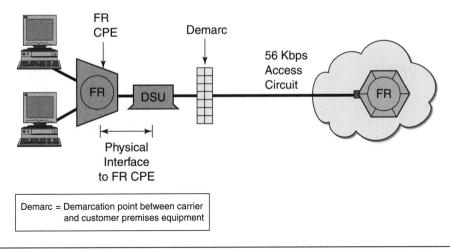

FIGURE 4.6 DSU/CSUs.   *Data service units/channel service units terminate digital lines on the customer's premises.*

management data available from other sources, such as the service provider.

- Continually listen for a "heartbeat" across the access circuit and automatically initiate dial backup procedures if the access circuit fails.
- Allow multiplexing of inputs from various customer sources onto the access circuit. This is quite helpful for the integrated access circuits discussed above.

In addition, a DSU/CSU can be integrated onto the network interface card in a router or FRAD rather than being a standalone box. This form factor is generally less expensive and reduces management complexity for the customer. However, integrated DSU/CSUs may not be able to perform the "intelligent" performance monitoring mentioned above.

Port Connections

A port connection is the entry point into the frame relay network. On the customer's side of the port connection is the access circuit; on the network side is the frame relay switch itself (see Figure 4.7). Physically, the port connection is part of the frame relay switch; however, its purpose is to dynam-

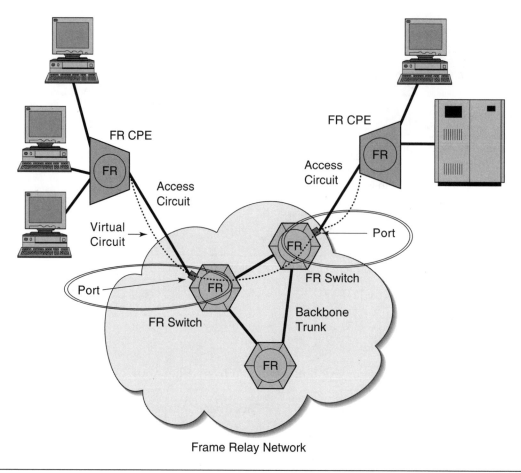

FIGURE 4.7 Port Connections.   *A port connection is the entry point into the frame relay network.*

ically allocate the port's capacity, in real time, to meet the changing needs of the users sharing the network.

The port's capacity is defined in terms of speed. The typical choices for port connection speeds are 56/64 Kbps, 128, 256, 384, 512, 768, 1024 Kbps, and 1.544 Mbps (2.048 Mbps in Europe).[3] Higher speeds, such as 3, 6, 10, 12

---

[3]We repeat our earlier footnote: Sometimes a 1.544-Mbps port connection is known as a 1.536-Mbps port connection, which refers to the maximum capacity actually available to the user (24 channels × 64 Kbps per channel = 1.536 Mbps). The DS-1 framing bit (the "193rd bit") is not available to the user, which accounts for the difference of 8 Kbps between the two port speeds. Similarly, a 2.048-Mbps port connection (E1 speed) may be known as a 1.920-Mbps port connection (30 channels × 64 Kbps = 1.920 Mbps).

Mbps, and beyond, are available from some service providers. Also, some service providers, especially smaller ones, may not offer all of these speeds.

A port connection is typically associated with an individual customer's site, for which, within a given switch, usually only one port connection is needed. However, at the location many different users, applications, and higher level protocols may share this single port connection. The sharing is possible because the single port, just like the access circuit, can handle multiple logical connections (PVCs or SVCs) to many different remote locations.

A network designer will choose a port speed based on the amount of data to be sent to/from the customer's location associated with that port. Chapter 11, Design of Frame Relay Networks, discusses selection of port speed in more detail.

As with the access circuit, the capacity of the port connection can be a bottleneck for the attached location. Data cannot be sent or received faster than the port connection's speed at any given time for that location.

Network-to-Network Interfaces

As we discussed briefly in the earlier section on local frame relay services, an NNI (see Figure 4.8) can be used to "chain together" frame relay networks operated by different carriers. However, support for NNIs is spotty. Network managers should verify that two networks can support an NNI between them, both technically *and* operationally, before committing to virtual circuits that span them.

One disadvantage of using an NNI is the relative lack of management capability across it. An NNI is not much more than a fancy Local Management Interface (LMI). Hence, like the LMI it is more concerned with the existence of PVCs than with their performance or troubleshooting. This makes problem resolution more difficult and finger-pointing between carriers more common. Also, **mean time to repair** (MTTR) may increase for PVCs that cross an NNI. In addition, as happens frequently in all areas of networking, network management features that are unique to a particular brand of switch may not function across an NNI if the switch "on the other side" is not the same brand. This is why the Frame Relay Forum and some DSU/CSU vendors are working on the issues of management of multinetwork PVCs.

In this section we are tacitly assuming that NNIs handle PVCs, because PVCs are far more common than SVCs. However, the Frame Relay Forum

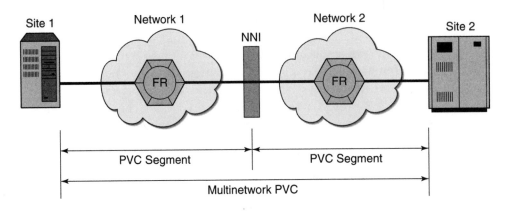

FIGURE 4.8 Network-to-Network Interfaces.   *NNIs can be used to "chain together" frame relay networks.*

has published *FRF.10 Frame Relay Network to Network SVC Implementation Agreement* [FRF10-96], which defines how NNIs should handle SVCs. Support for SVCs over NNIs appears to be even more spotty than for PVCs.

Some regional frame relay providers have formed consortia whose main purpose is to permit NNI interconnection of their individual networks. This allows them to compete more effectively against the large long-distance providers for national customers. On the other hand, some national carriers, notably AT&T, do not allow NNIs at all.[4] Their argument is that the standard NNI [FRF2.1-95] does not allow enough management capability to provide them with an adequate level of service across a multinetwork PVC.

When a long-distance carrier wants to expand its frame relay network internationally, it has two choices:

1. Set up NNI agreements with other existing carriers in the foreign locations
2. Locate its own switches overseas

---

[4]Rumor has it that some of the IXCs that do not allow NNIs unofficially allow selected companies to interconnect the IXC network with a **local exchange carrier** (LEC) network via a simple leased line. The companys' PVCs thus traverse the leased line from the LEC frame relay cloud into the IXC cloud, but without the benefit of an NNI between the two networks. An alternative solution is to have both frame relay clouds meet in the middle at a common router. The common router will have (at least) two WAN ports, one for each cloud.

As might be expected, there are many bilateral agreements in place. However, in general network managers should proceed cautiously when attempting to set up international PVCs.

Access Devices

Routers for Frame Relay Networks

Routers are one of several types of device that allow customers to access frame relay services. They are very popular because they tend to already be in place in customer sites for the interconnection of LANs across local and wide areas.

Depicted in Figure 4.9, routers interconnect LANs and other networks. They operate at layer 3, the network layer, of the OSI model, transparent to the layer 2 protocol in use.

Routers are more sophisticated than bridges or LAN switches, which are interconnection devices that operate at layer 2. For that reason, they are also more expensive and need more configuring than bridges or LAN switches. Routers work most naturally with routable protocols like TCP/IP, Novell IPX, and AppleTalk, but most also have bridging or encapsulation features to deal with nonroutable protocols. Routers are particularly useful in wide area networks, where routable protocols are common and bandwidth is expensive.

Most routers include frame relay as one of the standard layer 2 protocols they handle. If not, a router can usually be upgraded easily because of the similarity of frame relay to traditional packet switching, such as X.25.

When a frame-relay-capable router receives an incoming packet destined for a remote site on a frame relay network, it encapsulates the packet in a frame relay header and trailer and then routes it appropriately into the frame relay network. The steps are

1. The packet—say, an IP packet—enters the router. As usual, the packet comes wrapped in a layer 2 protocol header and trailer, which make up, say, an Ethernet frame.
2. After stripping off the Ethernet header and trailer, the router reads the destination IP address in the packet header to determine where the packet is to be sent. It looks up the IP address in a routing table to decide which frame relay DLCI and which outbound router port should be used for the frame that will carry the packet.

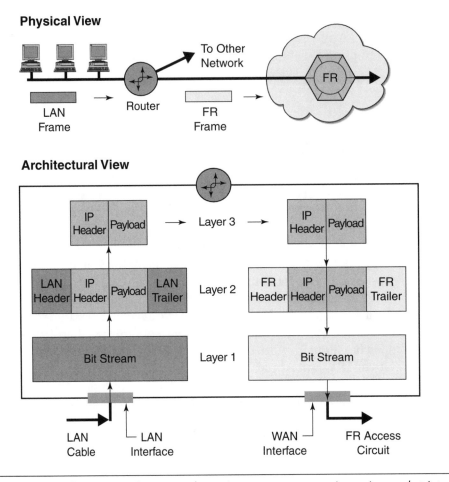

FIGURE 4.9 Routers for Frame Relay Networks.   *A router converts an incoming packet into frame relay format and sends it into the frame relay network.*

3. The router constructs the frame relay header and trailer that encapsulate the TCP/IP packet. The proper DLCI value is inserted into the DLCI address field.
4. The router sends the frame over the proper frame relay access circuit, via the appropriate outbound router port, into the frame relay network.
5. The frame relay switch at entry to the network reads the DLCI on the incoming frame to determine where to send the frame next. By using

the DLCI, the switches send the frame along the predetermined PVC or SVC path.

6. At the destination frame relay equipment, which is also likely a router, the frame header and trailer are stripped off, and the enclosed TCP/IP packet is eventually delivered to the receiving host's TCP software.

From an architectural point of view, notice that the use of a frame relay network, versus, say, a leased line network, is transparent to the higher layer protocols, such as TCP/IP. *Any* higher layer protocol can be carried over a frame relay network. This is one of the strengths of frame relay.

Frame Relay Access Devices

Frame relay access devices (FRADs), shown in Figure 4.10, are specifically designed to allow non-frame-relay protocols to gain access to a frame relay service. Like frame relay switches, FRADs operate at layer 2, so they typically do not offer routing functions except as add ons. FRADs are also known as frame relay assemblers/disassemblers. The term "FRAD" comes from the packet switching market, where **packet assembler/disassemblers** (PADs) have been performing a similar function for X.25 networks for years.

FRADs typically provide intelligent local functions, such as local device polling, in order to offload some of the network overhead and hence increase the user's response time. These local functions may also provide optional error detection and correction between the two FRADs. This can be especially useful for interactive asynchronous traffic that is traveling over the frame relay network. Voice FRADs handle voice traffic over a frame relay network (see Chapter 12, Voice over Frame Relay).

A FRAD may be a standalone device, or it may be an integral function of a frame relay switch. In either case, the user data enters the FRAD and is wrapped in a frame relay protocol envelope with an appropriate DLCI. It is then transported across the frame relay network to a remote FRAD, where the unwrapping takes place.

A FRAD consists of two major functions: a multiprotocol handling function and a frame relay interface component. Since the FRAD should be transparent to the end user, the multiprotocol handler must act as if the user is directly connected to the destination, and it must deal with the device-to-network link level issues. So, for instance, the module for handling SNA should "spoof" polling for the local SNA devices. The frame relay

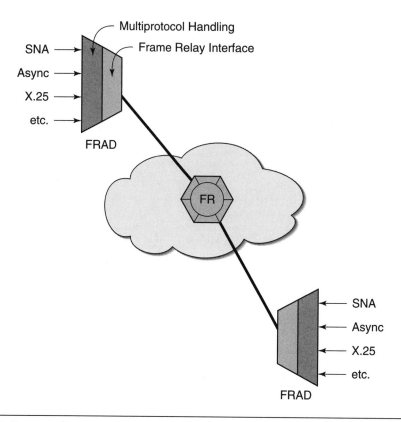

FIGURE 4.10 Frame Relay Access Devices.   *FRADs allow non-frame relay protocols to gain access to a frame relay network.*

interface component of a FRAD wraps the output of the multiprotocol handler in a frame relay frame.

Data communications trade magazines note that large internetworks with FRADs may be less expensive than comparable branch office (low-end) router networks, by a factor of 20%. In addition, FRADs typically have better congestion control and traffic prioritization than small routers, although there is considerable variation across vendors.

The desirable features on a FRAD are

- RFC 1490/FRF 3.1 compliance for encapsulating SNA, IP, and IPX traffic (Multiprotocol encapsulation is discussed in Chapter 13, Internetworking with Frame Relay.)

- Congestion control for throttling back traffic in the event of encountering FECN or BECN bits. (See Chapter 6, Traffic Management, for discussions of FECN and BECN.)
- Prioritizing multiprotocol traffic, especially to give SNA traffic high priority without starving other protocols

Other Interfaces for Frame Relay Access

Some host equipment can support direct frame relay connections. For instance, IBM AS/400 computers, IBM 3745 Communications Controllers (front-end processors), and IBM 3174 Network Processors (cluster controllers) can include frame relay interfaces (see Figure 4.11). Essentially, the

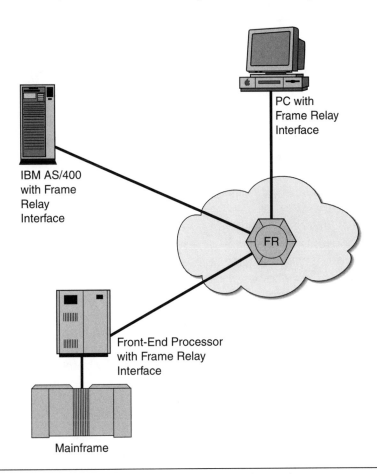

FIGURE 4.11 Host and PC Frame Relay Interfaces.   *PCs and some host equipment can also support direct interfaces to a frame relay network.*

IBM equipment implements an onboard FRAD capability rather than an external frame relay access device. Such interfaces tend to be expensive, but can provide a seamless connection to inexpensive frame relay services.

Although not common, frame relay adapter cards are also available for PCs. These boards connect the PC directly to a frame relay network over an access circuit. Some of the boards also contain ISDN interfaces. Essentially, a frame relay card brings the FRAD function right into the PC. Using a frame relay PC adapter card might be helpful for a network designer who wants to use a PC as a low-cost gateway from a LAN into a frame relay WAN.

Recovery from Physical Circuit Failures

Failure of the Access Circuits

Sometimes access circuits fail. When considering this possibility, a network designer can choose among several options, depending on the cost and risk of failure.

One common option is to use some form of dial backup for the failed access circuit. As discussed earlier in the section on dial-up access, the network designer can use an analog dial-up modem, ISDN BRI, ISDN PRI, or possibly a switched-56 service.

An expensive, but convenient, option is to use a physically diverse SONET ring[5] as an access circuit. The advantage of SONET is that its **automatic protection switching** (APS) feature can provide self-healing in a very short time, about 50 milliseconds or less. To make this cost effective, the SONET ring also has to act as an integrated access circuit for other traffic from the customer premises.

A third option is to route traffic over some alternate network if a frame relay access circuit fails. Thus, a network designer might use dial backup to bypass the entire frame relay network and dial directly to the remote site. Or he or she might use a data VPN as an alternative to the frame relay network. Many possibilities exist, although for branch offices alternate networks may be too expensive.

---

[5]"Physically diverse" means that the SONET ring enters through one location and exits through another in the customer's building. It also means that the two parts of the SONET circuit never share the same physical conduit outside of the building. Thus, no single cut in the ring can isolate the customer's building.

A last, and cheapest, option is to simply wait for the access circuit to be repaired. This may be the most appropriate solution if the cost of network downtime is low.

Failure of the Backbone Trunks

The backbone trunks in the frame relay carrier's network can also fail. If the carrier's network is based on SONET rings, SONET automatically provides a self-healing capability, as mentioned above. Carriers typically also have proprietary methods for quickly recovering from failures in their networks. Some are based on automatic or manual procedures in digital cross-connect systems (DCS).[6]

Network managers may want to discuss with prospective frame relay carriers just how the network recovers from physical circuit failures and what the availability and MTTR statistics are.

---

[6]Digital crossconnect systems are often referred to as DACS boxes, although "DACS" (Digital Access and Crossconnect System) is actually an AT&T term.

Chapter 5

Frame Relay Virtual Circuits

In this chapter we explain the concept of virtual circuits. First, we compare physical circuits to virtual circuits in general, then discuss frame relay virtual circuits in particular. We mention frame relay switches, which are the network devices that implement virtual circuits. This leads into the differences between the two types of frame relay virtual circuits, namely, permanent virtual circuits (PVCs) and switched virtual circuits (SVCs) (see Figure 5.1).

Next we discuss switched virtual circuits at some length. We include signaling specifications for setting them up, their advantages and disadvantages, and a remark about how SVCs are not the same as switched physical access circuits. We close with comments about recovering from virtual circuit failures.

Physical versus Virtual Circuits

For networking in general, there are important similarities and also important differences between physical and virtual circuits. Physical circuits, sometimes also called "real" circuits, have been in use for many years, especially by the telephone companies. Examples are telephone local loops, trunks between central offices, ISDN lines, and leased line networks based on time division multiplexing. Virtual circuits originated with X.25 packet switching and with the dynamic bandwidth allocation done by statistical multiplexers.

Similarities
- Connect two endpoints
- Deliver traffic in order
- Occur in a switched or permanent form
- Can allocate capacity (bandwidth, bits/second)

Differences

	Physical Circuits	Virtual Circuits
How capacity is allocated	Reserved for each user	Shared among active users
How idle capacity is treated	Wasted	Allocated to other users
Nature of circuit delay	Constant	Variable
Data format	None (transparent transmission)	Specified by a protocol; uses VC identifier

FIGURE 5.1 Physical versus Virtual Circuits.   *The similarities and differences between physical and virtual circuits are shown here.*

Similarities between physical circuits and virtual circuits follow:

- Both are connections between two end points.
- Both deliver traffic in order.
- Both can occur in a switched or a permanent form.
- Both have capacity (also known as bandwidth, rate, speed, or bits per second) that can be allocated among several users (or sometimes just one).

However, physical circuits differ from virtual circuits in that they have a fixed amount of capacity reserved for each user. If the user does not use the reserved capacity, it is "wasted" and unavailable to any other user. For physical circuits such as trunks, once all the capacity has been allocated the circuit cannot support any more users.

Physical circuits do have advantages, though. The delay over a physical circuit is constant and hence predictable. Also, physical circuits are transparent in the sense that whatever data the user presents to them is simply transmitted to the other end of the circuit, in order, regardless of the data format. Hence, physical circuits are "simple" and act merely as data pipes. These characteristics ease the network management burden.

For the case of virtual circuits, each user is allocated a virtual circuit for his or her own use. However, the total capacity of the underlying physical link is shared only among the *active* users. Hence, if a given user is idle, it will not be wasting capacity on the physical link and its unused capacity will be available to other users. As the capacity of the underlying physical link is used up, more active users can be squeezed onto the physical link, but each user will receive a smaller share of the capacity and congestion will result.

Thus, a large number of active users results in one of the disadvantages of virtual circuits, which is variable and unpredictable network delay. However, **quality of service** (QoS) mechanisms can decrease the variation in delay. We discuss QoS in more detail in Chapter 6, Traffic Management.

Another complexity of virtual circuits is that information must be presented to them in a defined format, using an appropriate protocol. Thus, the customer premise equipment has a more complex job than in the case of physical circuits. The network equipment also has a more complex job. It must switch traffic from each virtual circuit to the correct destination by using lookup tables. The lookup procedure is the same one described in Chapter 3, Frame Relay Architecture.

In addition, the different virtual circuits must be distinguished. Their labeling is done through a virtual circuit identification field in the protocol header. For frame relay, the identification field contains the data link connection identifier (DLCI). For X.25, the identification field contains the virtual circuit identifier, also known as the logical channel number, which functions in a similar way to the DLCI.

Nonetheless, virtual circuit networks have important advantages. Because capacity is shared rather than reserved, the service provider can make more efficient use of the underlying physical circuits. This in turn can reduce the price to the end user. A second advantage is that a virtual circuit can be configured, and reconfigured, more easily than a physical circuit, since it is essentially just software entries in lookup tables. Another advantage is that since many virtual circuits can share a single physical access circuit, their port costs can be significantly reduced. Lastly, network monitoring equipment can usually collect statistics about virtual circuits, especially permanent ones, more easily than about physical circuits, since the network switches often collect such information for their own uses.

An analogy may help explain the difference between physical and virtual circuits. A physical circuit is similar to a private driveway. The maximum number of cars it can hold is small and fixed (fixed capacity). Even if the driveway is empty, no one else will use it (for long). The delay time to drive down the driveway is short and predictable. A car does not need a license plate to be driven on a private driveway. On the other hand, a virtual circuit is similar to a highway. The capacity of the highway is shared among all the cars that are being driven on it. More cars can always be squeezed onto the highway (up to a point), but congestion and delay will result. Cars must be licensed and in good working order (defined format) to be legally driven on the highway. Drivers must obey rules of the road (protocols). Each car has a path (virtual circuit) that it follows to its destination. The highway contains interchanges and traffic lights (switches) so that traffic can get to its destination. And highways are much more cost effective than private driveways for long distances!

Virtual Circuits

We now apply the preceding discussion of physical versus virtual circuits to frame relay networks. As mentioned earlier, the logical components of a frame relay network are the virtual circuits (see Figure 5.2). The virtual circuits allow the frame relay DTEs to communicate with each other.

The communication takes place across the physical combination of access circuits, frame relay switches, and backbone trunks. A single physical path may contain many virtual circuits. The frame relay equipment along the path can distinguish one virtual circuit from another because each virtual circuit has a different DLCI. Thus, multiple logical channels can exist across a single physical link. This type of multiplexing, called statistical multiplexing or logical multiplexing, is similar to X.25 multiplexing and is an important advantage of frame relay.

A virtual circuit is "virtual" in that it does not physically take up space on the port connection, or in the network, until information needs to be sent across it. Because it does not take up capacity when it is idle, this capacity is available to be allocated to other virtual circuits that are active and may need additional bandwidth. This allows the other virtual circuits to "burst," which is discussed in Chapter 6, Traffic Management.

A frame relay virtual circuit is connection oriented rather than connectionless, which means that it has a connection establishment phase, a data transfer phase, and a connection termination phase. This is true for both PVCs and SVCs, even though for PVCs the establishment and termination phases are not dynamic, but occur because of provisioning in advance by the network provider.

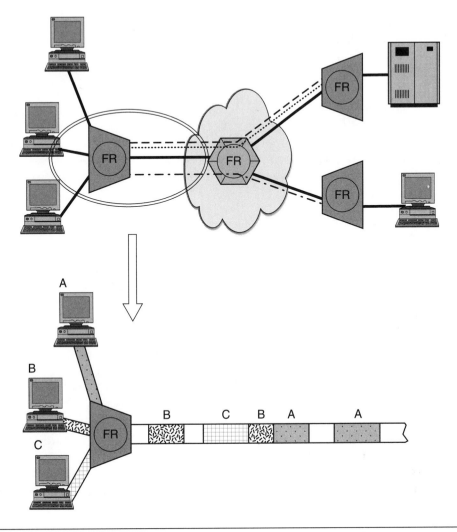

FIGURE 5.2 Frame Relay Virtual Circuits.   *Frame relay multiplexing is efficient.*

Since frame relay virtual circuits are connection oriented, they are also often called virtual connections or logical connections or just frame relay connections.

The frames traveling on a virtual circuit will in general take the same path each time. The primary exception to this happens when a major network failure occurs along the path. In that case, the network will likely attempt to automatically reroute the virtual circuit over an alternate physical path. For many frame relay service providers the reroute may take only a few seconds. However, there is much variability in how carriers handle reroutes. In addition, some proprietary carrier implementations may send "overflow" frame relay traffic over alternate physical paths. Again, the details are highly vendor specific.

Since the frames traveling on a virtual circuit normally have a constant path, they will also flow in sequence, meaning that they do not have to be reordered at the far end. Even if a frame is discarded for some reason along the path, the remaining frames can still be delivered to the upper level protocol at the far end. In any case, the frame relay header does not contain a sequence field, so resequencing the frames is impossible at the frame relay level.

Switches

Frame relay switches are the heart of a frame relay network (see Figure 5.3). They handle, among other issues:

- Switching of frames through the network
- Conformance with frame relay protocols
- Implementation of congestion control mechanisms

The switching equipment may be a specialized frame relay switch, an I/O card on a T1/E1 multiplexer, or a packet switch that supports frame relay. Any piece of equipment that implements the standard frame relay interface and is capable of switching information received in frame relay format can function as a frame relay switch. Since frame relay is closely related to packet switching, many frame relay switches are just modified X.25 packet switches.

However, since frame relay switches are often third-party devices, each manufacturer may interpret the frame relay standards differently, which can give rise to many problems. For instance, the exact details of congestion control are vendor specific and are usually not the same from one vendor's switch to another. We expand on these issues in Chapter 7, Engineering of Frame Relay Networks.

To make matters more confusing, when a customer buys frame relay services from a carrier, he or she might not be told what kind of switch the carrier is actually using in its network. This is an area where careful investigation may bring long-term benefits.

All the details not specified in the frame relay standards or in the Frame Relay Forum's Implementation Agreements have to be worked out by the

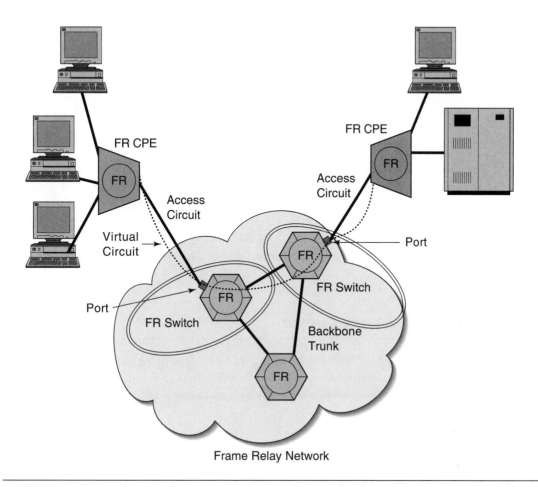

FIGURE 5.3 Frame Relay Switches. *Frame relay switches are the "heart" of a frame relay network.*

frame relay switch designers . Thus, two different vendors' switches may both be frame relay compliant, but might not be compatible in the features they offer. This problem of equipment conforming to standards but still not being interoperable occurs throughout the networking industry.

A frame relay switch must offer a frame relay compliant interface to the user. However, *within* a frame relay network, there are several options for transmitting the frames. In general, for a public network the user has little control over which option is used:

- Pass frames to other switches using the frame relay standards.
- Break frames into fixed-length cells and pass the cells to other switches using the ATM standards or other cell-based methods.

- Use some other proprietary scheme to pass traffic from the entrance port (ingress) to the exit port (egress) of the frame relay network.

Of these options, ATM backbones are very common among the larger frame relay carriers. Some observers estimate that 80% of all frame relay traffic actually rides over an ATM backbone for some part of the connection.

Public service providers offer frame relay services by deploying frame relay switching equipment, backbone trunks, and network management infrastructure. Both private frame relay access equipment and private frame relay switching equipment may be connected to services provided by a carrier. The service provider maintains access to the network via the standard frame relay interface and charges for the use of the service. The alternative to using a public service provider is to install a private frame relay network. More about this in Chapter 11, Design of Frame Relay Networks.

Differences between PVCs and SVCs

For frame relay networks, there are two types of virtual circuits: PVCs and SVCs. Their differences are described here (see Figure 5.4).

Permanent Virtual Circuits

The characteristics of PVCs are as follows:

- PVCs are permanent connections between a pair of frame relay DTEs. They are set up by the network operator and typically remain in place for days or months. Hence, they are also called semipermanent. The network operator may use manual or semiautomatic tools for the configuration.
- PVCs have no call setup. Transmission parameters, such as maximum frame size and throughput, are negotiated at the time of service establishment (also known as subscription or provisioning time).
- Since a PVC is a virtual circuit, the frames on it will take the same path each time.
- A PVC has no call completion. It remains permanently available as long as it is in place.
- PVCs are the frame relay equivalent of traditional dedicated point-to-point physical circuits.

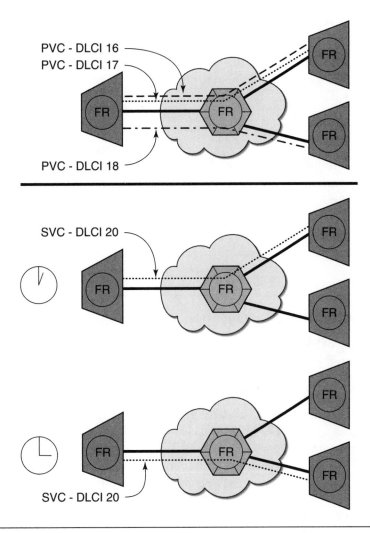

PVC - DLCI 16
PVC - DLCI 17
PVC - DLCI 18
SVC - DLCI 20
SVC - DLCI 20

FIGURE 5.4 PVCs versus SVCs. *PVCs are "permanent" connections, but SVCs are temporary.*

Switched Virtual Circuits

In contrast to PVCs, SVCs have the following characteristics:

- SVCs are temporary connections between a pair of frame relay DTEs. The network sets up an SVC on demand, in physical time, at the request of a frame relay DTE. An SVC may remain in place for only seconds or for hours or longer.

- The originating DTE submits an explicit call request to the frame relay network. It asks the network to set up a frame relay connection to a particular destination. The network and the DTE dynamically negotiate the transmission parameters of the connection.
- The frames traveling on a given SVC will take the same path each time and will arrive in order.
- SVCs do have a call completion process. Once an SVC is torn down, the connection is gone. At a later time, the originating DTE may request setup of another SVC, which might even have the same DLCI as the old connection. The new SVC may take an entirely different path to an entirely different destination.
- SVCs are the frame relay equivalent of traditional switched telephone calls. The SVC call setup process is the equivalent of dialing a call.

More on SVCs

SVC Signaling Specifications

Setup of SVCs is handled by special call control protocols, which are implemented cooperatively by the customer's frame relay equipment and the frame relay switch (see Figure 5.5). The protocols are rather complex, which is one reason that vendors have been slow to implement SVCs.

Details of the call control protocols can be found in ITU-T Recommendation Q.933 [ITU-Q.933-92, ITU-Q.933-95].[1] In addition, the Frame Relay Forum has, as usual, issued an Implementation Agreement, *FRF.4 User-to-Network SVC* [FRF.4-94], which defines the parts of Q.933 that should actually be implemented and those that should be ignored. ANSI also has a specification, ANSI T1.607 [ANSI-T1.607-91], which is quite similar to Q.933 but does not form the basis for FRF.4. The books by Smith [Smith93], Black [Black96], and Stallings [Stallings95] also contain explanations of the protocols.

SVC Signaling Architecture

The signaling messages that request setup and teardown of SVCs are passed from the customer premise equipment to the frame relay network as layer 3 messages [ITU-Q.931-92]. Thus, they are contained in data link

---

[1]Q.933 is a subset of Q.931 [ITU-Q.931-92] specifically for frame relay. As is typical for standards, the text in Q.933 makes reference not only to Q.931 but also to other frame relay and ISDN standards as well. Q.933 is sometimes referred to as Q.933/931. The ITU-T updated and simplified Q.933 in 1995.

SVC Call Control Messages

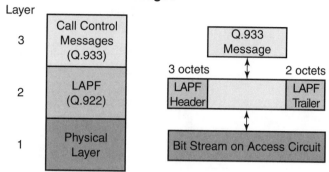

SVC Data Transfer (for comparison)

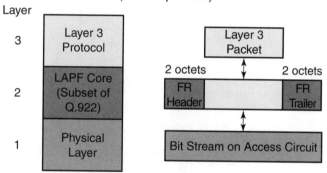

FIGURE 5.5 SVC Signaling—at the CPE. *SVC call control messages are contained within LAPF frames.*

layer (layer 2) frames. In particular, FRF.4 specifies that the signaling messages must be carried in Q.922 frames [ITU-Q.922-93], which use the full, not just the core, LAPF. In addition, all signaling messages use DLCI 0 to control the call rather than PVCs that transfer data.

The entire SVC control frame has a number of fields, as indicated in Figure 5.6.

- The flag field is the usual frame relay and HDLC flag. Its value is 01111110 in binary.
- The **frame relay header** is the usual 2-octet header used for data transfer. The DLCI value is 0, as is that of the FECN, BECN, DE, and C/R flags. The other name for this header is the LAPF Core protocol header. See Chapter 3, Frame Relay Architecture, for more details on this header.

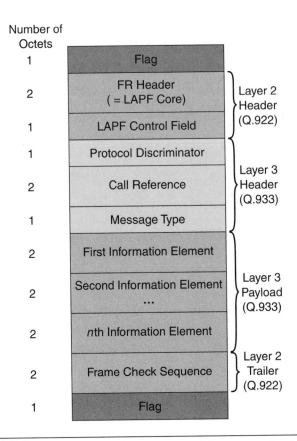

FIGURE 5.6 SVC Control Frame Format.　*The SVC control frame contains fields for the LAPF (layer 2) and Q.933 (layer 3) protocols.*

- The **LAPF control field** indicates that the data link layer is the full, rather than the abbreviated, LAPF Core protocol. This field is the same as the 1-octet control field in HDLC. It has value 00000011 in binary, which indicates that the SVC control frame is a LAPF/HDLC **Unnumbered Information** (UI) frame. UI frames provide a "reliable" link layer, but do not allow for sequencing or flow control since there are no sequence numbers associated with the frames. A related purpose of this field is to provide ISDN compatibility.
- The **protocol discriminator** is the first octet of the layer 3 call control message. Its value is 00001000 in binary, which indicates that the layer 3 message is actually a user-to-network call control message rather than some other kind of layer 3 protocol. It provides compatibility with ISDN frame relay procedures.

TABLE 5.1 SVC Call Control Message Types

Grouping	Message Type	Meaning
Call Establishment	SETUP	Caller requests an SVC.
	CALL PROCEEDING	Network acknowledges the SETUP request.
	CONNECT	Called user accepts the SETUP request.
Call Clearing	DISCONNECT	Request to clear an SVC.
	RELEASE	Accept DISCONNECT.
	RELEASE COMPLETE	Acknowledge RELEASE.
Miscellaneous	STATUS ENQUIRY	User requests status information.
	STATUS	Network gives status information.

- The **call reference** field uniquely identifies each call across the access circuit. This is important so that multiple SVCs can be set up simultaneously across the same frame relay User-Network Interface. In spirit, the call reference is similar to the DLCI, which uniquely identifies each PVC or SVC across the physical access circuit. Like the typical usage of DLCIs, the call reference has only local, not global, significance. It is a 2-octet field when used for the usual call establishment and call clearing.[2]
- The **message type** field indicates whether the control frame contains a call establishment message, a call clearing message, or a miscellaneous (status) message. See Table 5.1 for more information about message types. The message type is a 1-octet field.
- The **information element** fields contain the parameters for setting up SVCs and for tearing them down. Each information element contains one parameter or a group of related parameters. Each type of information element has a defined format for encoding the parameters. See Q.933 for more details [ITU-Q.933-95].
- After a variable number of information elements, the **frame check sequence** field, which is the usual LAPF/HDLC checksum, occupies the 2 octets of the frame relay trailer.
- The control frame ends with the closing flag, which is the same bit pattern as the opening flag.

---

[2]LMI messages are essentially just another type of call control signaling message, which can report status for both PVCs and SVCs. For LMI messages, the call reference field is only 1 octet and has value 0.

SVC Signaling Procedures

The process of setting up and tearing down frame relay SVCs is typical of dynamic circuit establishment in other areas of networking. As mentioned earlier, frame relay draws heavily on concepts and standards from ISDN.

As Figure 5.7 shows, the frame relay user initiates SVC call establishment with a SETUP message directed across the access circuit to the frame relay network. We discuss the negotiation of the setup parameters in the next subsection. The network acknowledges the SETUP message by returning a CALL PROCEEDING message back to the user. The network also conveys the SETUP message to the called user; the network responds with a CONNECT message if it accepts the SVC request. The network then con-

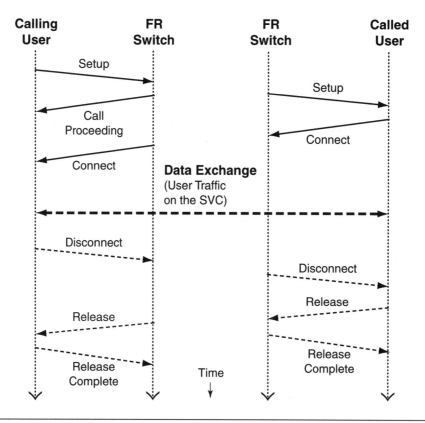

FIGURE 5.7 SVC Signaling—in the Network. *The users and the network exchange call control messages to set up and tear down SVCs.*

veys the CONNECT message back to the originating user. At that point the SVC has been established and is ready for use by the end users.

The user and network use DISCONNECT, RELEASE, and RELEASE COMPLETE messages to tear down the SVC. Either the user or the network itself can initiate the call-clearing process. The DISCONNECT message contains a cause information element that indicates why the disconnection is occurring.

The STATUS ENQUIRY and STATUS messages allow the customer premise equipment to request SVC status information from the network. These message types are the same ones used for PVC status information and are discussed in the section on the Local Management Interface (LMI) in Chapter 8, Network Management.

SVC SETUP Parameters

The SETUP message for establishing SVCs is the most complex of all SVC call control messages. It contains several parameters, in the form of information elements, that must be negotiated between the user and the network so that the SVC can be set up. The most important parameters are mentioned here.

Data Link Connection Identifier.   The calling user may request a particular DLCI value for an SVC. If the network can grant the request, it will use that DLCI and so notify the caller. If the network cannot grant the request, or the caller has not specified the DLCI value, the network will assign a suitable DLCI to the SVC. From the called user's point of view, the network simply informs the called user of the assigned DLCI.

Link Layer Core Parameters.   This information element consists of a group of throughput and size parameters that need to be negotiated for the SVC. These are the same parameters that must be negotiated for a PVC, but in that case the negotiation is carried out by humans, or perhaps higher layer software. Each parameter may be negotiated separately for each direction if the service provider allows it. Details of the negotiation process are given in Q.933 [ITU-Q.933-95].

> **Maximum frame relay information field size** is measured in octets. It is the size of the payload of the data transfer frames.

> **Throughput** is the average number of payload bits per second that will be carried across the SVC. It is equivalent to the committed information rate (CIR), discussed in Chapter 6, Traffic Management.

Committed burst size indicates the maximum number of bits the network will transfer over a measurement interval. It is equivalent to B_c, the committed burst size variable (see Chapter 6).

Excess burst size indicates the maximum number of "uncommitted" bits that the network will attempt to deliver over a measurement interval. It is equivalent to B_e, the excess burst size variable (see Chapter 6). Within a measurement interval, if more data bits are sent than the committed information size allows, but fewer than the excess burst size "cap" specifies, those extra bits are burst data and may be marked discard eligible by the network.

Called Party Address.   This information element gives the specific address of the called user to the network and indicates which numbering plan to use. FRF.4 states that the international numbering plan ITU-T E.164 is preferred, but ITU-T X.121 is also acceptable. E.164 is the international evolution of "normal" telephone numbers and is also used by ISDN and ATM networks. X.121 is the international numbering plan for public data networks and is used by X.25 networks. The service provider determines which numbering plan will be used.

Advantages and Disadvantages of SVCs

Switched virtual circuits have a number of potential advantages. An obvious one is obtaining bandwidth on the fly. SVCs are useful for applications needing infrequent connectivity to a given network site.

Another advantage is the ability to establish new circuits without entering service orders. This can include changing CIR (throughput) just by tearing down the old SVC and setting up a new one with a different CIR. It can also include automatic time-of-day reconfiguration of virtual circuits through the use of SVCs rather than PVCs.

SVCs also scale better to large networks. Large frame relay networks typically need to be more highly meshed than small hub-and-spoke (star topology) networks, but large highly meshed PVC networks are prohibitively expensive. SVCs potentially provide a way to achieve more meshing as needed without huge costs.

From the carrier's point of view, SVCs allow easier management of moves, adds, and changes, especially for large networks. With PVCs, network technicians typically need to be more intimately involved in the details of changes.

However, switched virtual circuits also have disadvantages. For SVCs to become more popular, their pricing needs to be less than that of comparable PVCs [Taylor97]. (Also see Chapter 9, Frame Relay Service Pricing.) Otherwise, there will be little economic incentive to change from PVCs to SVCs. At the time of this writing, only one major carrier offers SVCs, and the pricing model is too immature to make long-term predictions about what SVC prices will be.

Carriers have been very slow to offer SVCs, even though adequate standards have been in place for years. The standard joke in the industry is that most carriers say they will offer SVCs two quarters from "now" and have been saying it for years. Some carriers cite a lack of customer demand as the reason for not offering SVCs.

Some analysts also suggest that the router vendors have been slow to adopt frame relay SVCs because routing protocols prefer stable interrouter circuits, such as PVCs, and tend to have difficulty with SVC links that can appear and disappear quickly.

Lastly, the signaling protocols for setting up SVCs are indeed more complex than those for establishing PVCs, at least from the customer's point of view. In addition, customers have traditionally had the mindset that frame relay is simply a cheaper replacement for leased lines. Frame relay SVCs do not fit this mindset, since they are switched rather than permanent.

Switched Physical Access and SVCs

An SVC is *not* the same as a dial-up access line into a network. In order to establish a frame relay SVC, the frame relay DTE must *already* have a physical (OSI layer 1) access connection into the frame relay network (see Figure 5.8). The physical link may be a dedicated circuit, a dial-up line, or an ISDN line, but the process of establishing the access connection must come *first*, before the SVC can be established.

Recovery from Virtual Circuit Failures

Chapter 4, Connecting to the Network, discussed how users can attempt to recover from failures in the physical access circuits and how carriers can recover from failures in their backbone trunks. Virtual circuits can also fail. A virtual circuit will fail if any of its underlying physical links go down for too long—for instance, if the LMI heartbeat across the access circuit is

Stage 1: Establish the physical access connection.

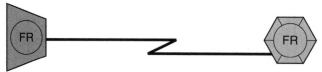

Stage 2: Establish the SVC over the access connection.

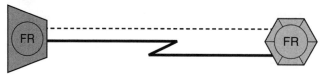

FIGURE 5.8 Setting Up an SVC.   *An SVC must be set up in two stages.*

interrupted. A virtual circuit can also fail because of equipment malfunction, even if the underlying physical circuits are intact. Recovery depends on which equipment notices the failure.

If a PVC or SVC failure occurs in the carrier's network, the network switches can attempt to rebuild the DLCI lookup tables on the fly. This reroutes the affected virtual circuits over other physical circuits and away from failed components or lines. A carrier might be able to reroute in seconds or less. However, such action is very much carrier dependent and varies from carrier to carrier.

For an SVC failure in the carrier's network, the carrier has the simpler option of just redialing the call internally within the network. Similarly, if the user detects a failure in an SVC, it can redial the call itself.

If a customer's router detects a PVC failure, the router can use standard routing protocol procedures to attempt to find an alternate route to the destination machine that does not use the failed PVC. Alternatively, the router can wait for the PVC to be fixed by the carrier.

Chapter $\boxed{6}$

Traffic Management

Now that we have discussed the physical components and virtual circuits in a frame relay network, we look at how a frame relay network manages traffic.

We introduce the important idea of **committed information rate** (CIR). We explain CIR from the user's point of view and then show how the standards documents define it. We show how CIR is related to the concepts of bursting, capacity allocation, and oversubscription. We also describe the advantages of asymmetric PVCs.

Then we discuss how a frame relay network handles congestion. We explain the techniques of frame discarding and explicit and implicit congestion notification. We show how the DE, FECN, and BECN bits are used with these techniques. We also describe where congestion can occur in a frame relay network and remedies for the different cases that can occur.

Lastly, we point out the considerable limitations of congestion management for frame relay networks. We also debunk the myth that the DE bit can guarantee transmission priority. Through an example, we show that customer use of the DE bit is "weak" and does little to improve performance.

Committed Information Rate

The User View of CIR

The committed information rate for a frame relay virtual circuit is the rate at which the network agrees to accept data from the user over that virtual circuit, measured in bits per second. (See Figure 6.1.) Any data transmitted in excess of the CIR is vulnerable to discard if congestion occurs in the network. Thus, the CIR for a virtual circuit should reflect the expected average traffic volume between the circuit's two end points.

For a permanent virtual circuit (PVC), the CIR is set at the same time the connection is agreed upon between the user and the network. For a switched virtual circuit (SVC), the CIR is negotiated dynamically when the circuit is set up, as discussed in Chapter 5, Frame Relay Virtual Circuits. The CIR is not always easy to estimate when a frame relay network is first being designed, but some guidelines are given in Chapter 11, Design of Frame Relay Networks.

Virtual circuits are often able to exceed the rate set forth by the CIR via a technique called bursting, which is discussed later in this chapter.

In spite of the use of the word "committed," there is no guarantee that the CIR will be met. When the network is suffering extreme congestion, it may be forced to give a connection less throughput than the connection's CIR specifies. However, with proper design of the user network, this should be quite rare. In addition, if the customer has negotiated a **service level agreement** (SLA) with the carrier, the carrier must pay a penalty for missing a CIR commitment, which tends to make carriers careful about meeting CIR commitments. (More on SLAs in Chapter 10, Procurement of Frame Relay Services.)

If a network is suffering congestion and must discard frames, the frame relay switch will typically choose frames on connections that are exceeding their CIR before frames on connections that are within their CIR (often called CIR frames). Thus, the CIR provides a crude method for being fair

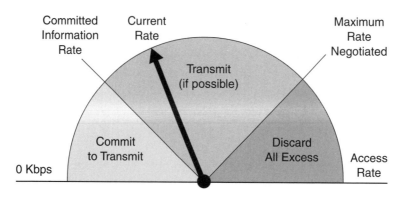

FIGURE 6.1 Commited Information Rate—The User View.   *The CIR meters the traffic on a virtual circuit.*

when allocating limited capacity. Details of exactly how the switch chooses which frame to discard is proprietary to the switch vendor, although some vendors claim special "fairness algorithms."

Many switch vendors go a step farther. If the transmission rate exceeds a previously agreed upon maximum, all frames beyond that maximum will be discarded automatically, even if there is no congestion. This maximum rate is sometimes called the excess information rate (EIR), although that term does not appear to be used in the standards documents. However, not all switch vendors implement a maximum rate, and some have variations on it. This maximum rate is actually determined by the excess burst size, which is discussed in the next subsection.

Service providers typically offer CIRs from 0 to 1.536 Kbps. The usual offerings are several sub-64-Kbps choices plus any multiple of 64 Kbps.

Note that the CIR for a virtual circuit cannot be set higher than the transmission rate of the access circuit over which the virtual circuit travels, which will be the same as the speed of the port to which the circuit is attached. For example, if an access circuit is at T1 speed (1.536-Mbps available data rate), then no PVC or SVC over that access circuit can have a CIR greater than 1.536 Mbps. Even so, it makes sense for there to be several 64-Kbps CIR virtual circuits over that T1 link.

Generally, a higher CIR, since it represents more capacity, costs more money. When the user has a known amount of traffic to send, say 32 Kbps, choosing a lower CIR, such as 16 Kbps, will cost less but will make the traffic more vulnerable to frame discards and transit delays. However, not all frame relay service providers charge by CIR. This will be discussed more fully in Chapter 9, Frame Relay Service Pricing.

The Standards View of CIR

In the previous subsection we discussed in general terms how a frame relay network controls the user's access to it. The ITU-T and ANSI standards documents give more detail about how this should be done. However, *not all switch vendors implement these recommendations*, and not all of them implement these recommendations the same way.

From the viewpoint of the standards documents, there are three interrelated parameters that must be negotiated between the user and the service provider. All three of these parameters depend on a particular time interval T, which is supposed to be computed separately for each virtual circuit. However, most switch vendors simply set T to a fixed value, often 1 second, or 1/40th of second in the case of one major vendor. The following are the three interrelated parameters.

Committed information rate (CIR), the rate at which the network agrees to accept data from the user, as discussed earlier. The CIR is intended to be an average throughput over the time interval T.

Committed burst size (B_c), the maximum amount of data (in bits) the network agrees to carry under "normal" conditions, during time interval T. This data may appear in one or several frames. Think of B_c as the quota of bits that can be transmitted during the time interval T.

Excess burst size (B_e), the maximum amount of data (in bits) by which the user may exceed the committed burst size B_c, during the interval T. The network will *attempt* to deliver this uncommitted data. Data sent between the committed burst size and the excess burst size may be marked discard eligible by the network—that is, the DE bit is set to 1. (The DE bit is discussed later in this chapter.) Sending excess data this way is often called simply **bursting**, because, in effect, it is over and above the CIR. Again, think of B_e as the quota of bits that can be transmitted beyond B_c.

CIR and B_c are related as described by the formula CIR $= B_c/T$. The standards state that the measurement interval T is supposed to be calculated by this formula. However, as discussed earlier, many switch vendors just fix T, for simplicity. In this case, specifying CIR automatically specifies B_c. So once T has been fixed, the parameters CIR and B_c (committed burst size) essentially become synonymous. The user needs to negotiate only one of the parameters, not both, when setting up a frame relay virtual circuit.

Figure 6.2 shows how all of these quantities are related. Note the following:

- The vertical axis is *bits*, not a rate. The CIR and the speed of the access circuit are shown as *slopes* because they are *rates* (units are bits divided by time). The formula for the committed burst size is $B_c = $ CIR $\times T$.
- The heavy line plots how the amount of transmitted data changes over the time interval T.
- When a frame is being sent, the heavy line is parallel to the access rate because when a frame is actually being transmitted on the access circuit, the entire capacity of the access circuit is momentarily dedicated to it. When no frame is being transmitted, the heavy line is horizontal because no data is flowing.
- In the upper diagram of Figure 6.2, during the transmission of the first frame the actual transmission rate temporarily exceeds the CIR. This doesn't matter, because the switch is concerned only with the cumulative number of bits transmitted over the entire interval T.

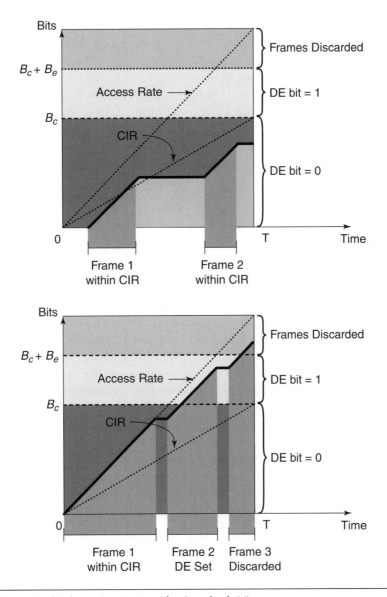

FIGURE 6.2 Commited Information Rate—The Standards View.

The determination of whether a traffic stream is exceeding the CIR is calculated independently for each time interval T. Thus, the traffic stream might be within the CIR for one interval because the quota B_c was not used up. But in the very next time interval, the traffic might be over the CIR because that interval's quota was exhausted during the interval. In general, B_c

quotas do not carry over from one interval to another. Thus, if a B_c quota is not exhausted during one interval, the unused portion cannot be added to the B_c quota of the next interval. However, at least one switch vendor has a (confusing) scheme for allowing credits for not bursting.

In their marketing literature, some carriers stress that the CIR is the *minimum* data rate that a customer's PVC will receive. For instance, MCI's tariff [MCI97] states, "Each PVC is assigned a committed information rate, which is the average minimum [*sic*] data rate the network will allocate to the PVC under normal operating conditions." The intent is to point out that the user will be able to burst above the CIR when there is adequate excess capacity.

Capacity Allocation

Bursting

Bursting, depicted in Figure 6.3, can occur on a virtual circuit when a large quantity of information must be transmitted and when the associated access circuit has excess capacity. In this case, "bursting" really means "bursting above the CIR" because transmitting information at or below the CIR is standard operating procedure for a virtual circuit.

Bursting is helpful because it allows data to be sent across the network more quickly, which improves the response time of the application using frame relay. Bursting will *not* occur if

- The maximum burst rate (as determined by the excess burst size, B_e) is set only at the CIR. In this case, the switch will simply discard all frames above the CIR. This is not a typical occurrence. Actually, the maximum burst rate is often set at the highest possible value, the access rate, to allow for the largest possible bursts.
- Excess capacity is not available at the port connection (on the access circuit). This can happen if other virtual circuits sharing the port are also active.
- The switch itself is congested or other switches in the network are congested. This can happen because of heavy traffic on other port connections or on the backbone trunks.

As discussed earlier, the frame relay standards specify that frames transmitted in excess of the CIR should be marked as discard eligible. **Discard eligible** (DE) means that the DE bit in the frame relay header is set to 1

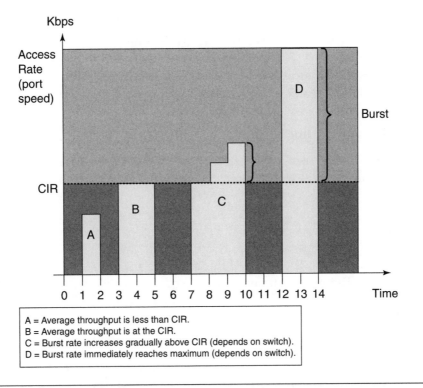

A = Average throughput is less than CIR.
B = Average throughput is at the CIR.
C = Burst rate increases gradually above CIR (depends on switch).
D = Burst rate immediately reaches maximum (depends on switch).

FIGURE 6.3 Bursting.   *A virtual circuit can burst above the committed information rate if excess capacity is available on the access circuit and the network.*

by the switch. If congestion then occurs in the network, these frames are the first to be discarded.

Figure 6.3 is a simplification in that it ignores the effect of serialization at the port and the effect of flow control imposed by higher layer protocols. Nonetheless, it provides a useful model. For this diagram, we assume the maximum burst rate is set as high as possible, namely, at the access circuit rate (which is the same as the port speed). Time is in units of the measurement interval T, often 1 second.

Depending on its design, the switch may or may not allow sustained bursts. Some switches allow the throughput to immediately rise to the maximum burst rate, which is usually just the access rate. Others only allow the throughput to rise in a gradual stepping fashion, by buffering traffic, or by simply discarding frames.

If congestion does begin to occur in the network, the ability of virtual circuits to burst above the CIR will be quickly scaled back. Again, the details depend on the switch vendor.

Bursting is useful, but it is a risky way to get something for nothing. In general, it is best to set the CIR to meet the average expected needs of the associated application. Some network managers, though, prefer to gamble by setting the CIR deliberately low and then using performance reports to verify that frame discards and delays are within acceptable limits.

Dynamic Allocation

How a port connection allocates capacity (Figure 6.4) can be explained by means of an example. First, some assumptions for the example:

1. The frame relay access device (often a router) is sending frames over the access circuit to the port connection on the switch. The frames are being sent at the port connection speed of 256 Kbps, which is the same as the speed of the access circuit.
2. The access circuit is carrying four virtual circuits (PVCs or SVCs), named VC1, VC2, VC3, and VC4. Each has a CIR of 64 Kbps.
3. The switch uses a time interval, T, of 1 second to measure the CIR. (This is often true, but depends on the switch design.)
4. The port connection allows each virtual circuit to burst up to the maximum possible speed, which is the port speed, 256 Kbps. The switch also allows the burst throughput to rise immediately rather than in a gradual stepping fashion.
5. To make this example simpler, the fact that input to the port connection is actually serial rather than simultaneous is ignored, as is the effect of flow control imposed by higher layer protocols.

For this scenario, Table 6.1 explains what happens during each time interval. Another way to view the scenario is that at time interval $t = 1$ all four virtual circuits are 100% active, each at its CIR of 64 Kbps. (Lowercase "t" represents a variable; uppercase "T" represents a fixed amount.) At $t = 3$, no other virtual circuit needs the capacity of the port connection, and the network congestion is low, so VC1 can burst up to the entire capacity of the port. At $t = 6$, VC3 needs only half of its CIR to transmit its file, so that is what it receives. Also, frames transmitted in excess of CIR, such as the "upper" three-fourths of VC1 during $t = 3$, are marked as discard eligible.

Oversubscription of Port Connections

Oversubscription of a port connection is a technique to allow more cost-effective network connectivity. It is illustrated in Figure 6.5.

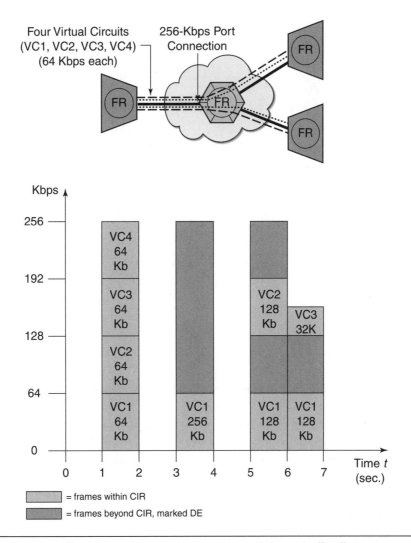

FIGURE 6.4 Capacity Allocation. *The port connection can dynamically allocate capacity depending on need.*

Data connections are used intermittently. In fact, most leased line connections between two locations have an average utilization of 30% or less, which allows a network designer to play the averages by assigning more virtual circuits and a higher *total* CIR to a port connection than the port connection's speed allows. This is the same principle that makes statistical multiplexers better at handling "random" data traffic than standard synchronous time division multiplexers. It is also similar to overbooking

TABLE 6.1 Time Intervals

Time	Requirement	Response
t=0	No information needs to be sent.	The port connection is idle.
t=1	Each VC needs to send a 64 Kbit-file (8 Kbytes), as a series of frames.	The port capacity is divided equally among the four VCs.
t=2	No information needs to be sent.	The port connection is idle.
t=3	VC1 needs to send a 256-Kbit file.	The entire port capacity is allocated to VC1 during this time interval.
t=4	No information needs to be sent.	The port connection is idle.
t=5	VC1 and VC2 each need to send a 128-Kbit file.	The port capacity is divided equally between the two VCs.
t=6	VC1 needs to send a 128-Kbit file, and VC3 needs to send a 32-Kbit file.	Half of the port capacity is allocated to VC1. Enough capacity is allocated to VC3 for its needs.

airline flights and hotel rooms, although overbooking has a somewhat negative connotation in these contexts.

What does this give the network designer? One advantage is that more virtual circuits can be supported by oversubscribing a given port connection. Alternatively, a given number of virtual circuits could be supported by a lower speed port connection. This could save on the cost of both the access circuit and the port connection.

Another advantage is that oversubscription may allow the network designer to set up a direct PVC between two remote sites that cannot cost-justify a direct connection in a leased line network. This could reduce the complexity of sending low-volume traffic through intermediate user sites, which in turn could improve response time for those direct PVCs. More about this in Chapter 11, Design of Frame Relay Networks.

What is the risk of oversubscription? If *all* of the users of the virtual circuits attempt to send frames concurrently at their assigned CIRs, then the port connection will not have enough capacity to accommodate them all. Some of the virtual circuits will not have their CIR met and will not be able to send their frames as fast as expected. However, for typical data applications the chances of this happening are low. Nevertheless, some

No Oversubscription
(100% subscription)

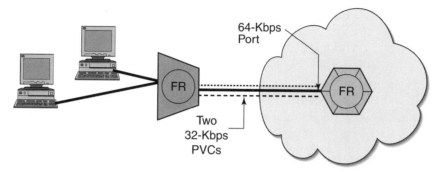

Oversubscription
(200% subscription)

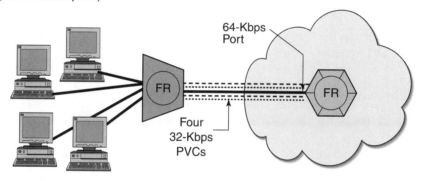

FIGURE 6.5 Oversubscription.   *Oversubscription allows a port connection to support additional virtual circuits, which can reduce costs.*

engineering is called for in order to choose an appropriate level of oversubscription.

Oversubscription is usually measured by percentages. Thus, *four* 32-Kbps PVCs (total CIR of 128 Kbps) attached to a 64-Kbps port give a 200% subscription (which may be excessive). Only *two* 32-Kbps PVCs attached to a 64-Kbps port give 100% subscription, which is no oversubscription at all.

Note that oversubscription as we are discussing it here applies only from the customer premises to the edge of the network. It does not apply within the frame relay network itself. It is not the same as "overengineering," which is a marketing term that some carriers use to tout their network capacity. Some people use the term "oversubscription" to mean that too many customers have subscribed to the frame relay service, but that is not the way the phrase "oversubscription of the port connection" is used here.

Different frame relay service providers may restrict the use of oversubscription. For instance, one major carrier restricts oversubscription to a maximum of 200%, although for SNA traffic they recommend a maximum of 150%.

The **bottom line** is that oversubscription may be able to reduce costs *and* possibly improve responsiveness.

Asymmetric PVCs

Normally, frame relay is a full duplex service. Furthermore, the CIR is normally exactly the same in both directions of a virtual circuit. Some service providers, however, allow *asymmetric* virtual circuits, especially asymmetric PVCs.[1] In this case, the PVC has a different CIR in each direction, better reflecting actual traffic patterns, which allows the network designer to pay only for needed capacity.

For example, in Figure 6.6, the PVC from west to east has a CIR of only 16 Kbps, but the same PVC from east to west has a CIR of 32 Kbps. This type of asymmetrical PVC might be useful, for instance, if the western user is typically sending small frames requesting database services, but the eastern database server is responding with large frames.

Asymmetric PVCs are often implemented as two simplex PVCs, one in each direction. In particular, some service providers price an asymmetric PVC as two completely separate simplex PVCs, each with its own CIR. This can be a source of confusion when reading tariff tables. Many providers offer neither simplex nor asymmetric PVCs.

Market studies indicate that few customers are making use of asymmetrical PVCs. Distributed Networking Associates reports that only about 4% of PVCs worldwide are asymmetrical [DNA-99].

Note that the port connections at either end of a PVC do *not* have to be the same speed. For instance, in Figure 6.6 the west port is 56 Kbps, but the east port is 384 Kbps. This is easily justified if the east port connection to the host must support traffic aggregated from a number of locations. In any case, the CIR for a PVC or an SVC cannot exceed the speed of the port connection at *either* end of the virtual circuit.

---

[1]In this case, the word "asymmetric" is used the same way as in "asymmetrical digital subscriber line" (ADSL), meaning that the capacities are different in each direction.

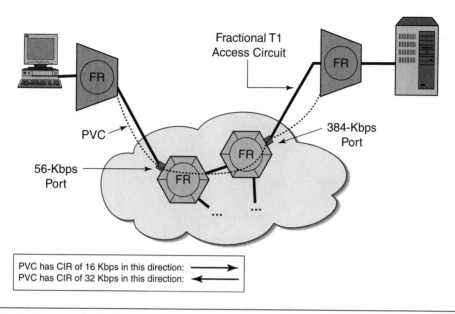

FIGURE 6.6 Asymmetric PVCs. *Asymmetric PVCs allow the assignment of different CIRs in each direction of a permanent virtual circuit.*

Also note that access circuits, and port speeds, of 56/64 Kbps are very common in frame relay networks because they have enough capacity to support most branch offices and are relatively inexpensive.

Congestion Management and Flow Control

Before discussing how a frame relay network handles congestion, we make a distinction between congestion control and flow control. Congestion control has to do with making sure that the network is able to carry the offered traffic. It is a global issue, involving the behavior of all the hosts, the access equipment, and the network nodes. Unmanaged congestion can become a severe problem (see Figure 6.7). Bursty networks are inherently vulnerable to congestion, but it can usually be controlled within acceptable levels.

Within a frame relay switch, the main symptom of congestion is that the memory buffers within the switch begin to overflow. This may be caused by frames arriving faster than the switch can handle them or by frames stacking up for output on a channel.

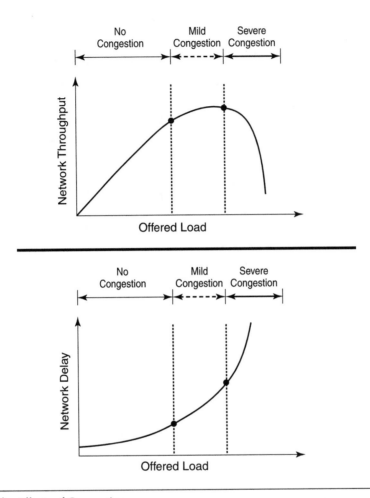

FIGURE 6.7 The Effects of Congestion.

Flow control, in contrast, relates to the point-to-point traffic between a given sender and a given receiver. Its job is to make sure that a fast sender cannot continually transmit data faster than the receiver can absorb it. Flow control nearly always involves some direct feedback from the receiver to the sender to tell the sender how things are going at the other end. Nearly every off-the-shelf protocol, such as TCP/IP, IPX, DECnet, and SNA, has mechanisms for controlling the flow of information across the network.

The higher layers, such as TCP at layer 4, typically do end-to-end flow control. For them the sender and receiver will simply be the end systems on the customer premises. The higher layer protocol will not be implemented by the layer 2 or layer 3 network components (switches and routers) at all. But flow control can also be exercised between switches in a network, usually at lower layers, on a hop-by-hop basis. This type of internal network flow control is often proprietary and not very visible to the end users, but it can be helpful for reducing network congestion.

One reason that congestion control and flow control are sometimes confused is that flow control is only one of several methods of congestion control. Other methods can also be used, such as preallocation of buffer space or simply discarding packets.

Within the frame relay network, each carrier has its own methods for controlling congestion. These methods are typically *not* visible to users, and it may in fact be very difficult to get reliable information about how the network (that is, the switch) is actually engineered. Nonetheless, how the network handles congestion internally can be an important issue for users.

Generally, frame relay networks employ three methods for controlling congestion, none of them perfect. These are discussed on the following pages.

Frame discarding, a method of last resort, uses the DE bit.

Explicit congestion notification, a congestion avoidance technique, uses the FECN and BECN bits.

Implicit congestion notification, a congestion recovery technique, uses flow control in the higher layer end-to-end protocols.

Frame Discarding and the Discard-Eligible Bit

One method of congestion control that is specifically permitted by the frame relay standards is for the network to simply discard frames when it encounters congestion that it cannot handle in any other way (see Figure 6.8). The network starts by discarding frames that have the discard-eligible (DE) bit set. If congestion persists, the network will begin throwing away the remaining frames that have the DE bits cleared (set to 0). The details of this technique are all vendor specific and are not described in the standards.

The DE bit may be set by the network *or* by the user. If set, it will never be cleared by the network. As discussed earlier, the DE bit *will* be set by the network if the amount of user traffic exceeds the committed information rate. However, it *may* also be set by the user before the frame enters the frame relay network, in an attempt to indicate that the frame is less important than a frame with the DE bit cleared.

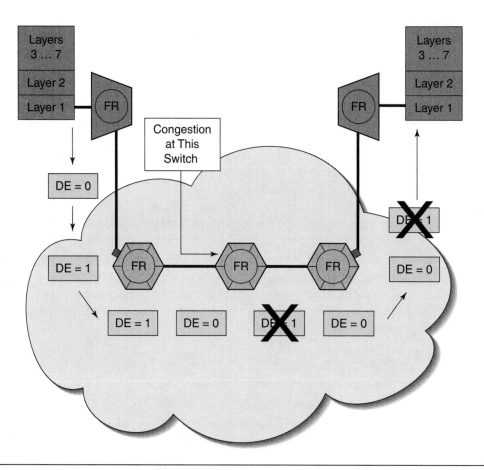

FIGURE 6.8 Frame Discarding.   *The method of last resort for controlling congestion is to discard frames; frames with the DE bit set are discarded first.*

Two notes about discarding frames:

- It is a self-defeating "method of last resort" for handling network congestion. The discarded frames will potentially have to be retransmitted, adding to the problem. Hence, public carriers typically work very hard to *avoid* congestion in their network because they know that once congestion has started it can snowball.
- If a frame *is* discarded by the network, it is not lost forever. The higher layer end-to-end user protocols, such as TCP, will detect that the frame has been lost and eventually retransmit it. However, this

process of timing out and retransmitting will negatively impact performance. In particular, frame delay times may increase dramatically during retransmission.

Explicit Congestion Notification Using the FECN and BECN Bits

Frame relay networks have another method for attempting to handle congestion—notifying end users that network congestion is occurring and then trusting that the sending end users will be able to slow down the rate at which frames are delivered to the network. This method is helpful in principle, but since it relies on the "good citizen" behavior of equipment outside the frame relay network proper, it is not very dependable.

Notification is implemented by use of the forward explicit congestion notification (FECN) and backward explicit congestion notification (BECN) bits in the frame relay header (see Figure 6.9). The network switch sets the FECN bit (to a binary 1) to notify the end user that congestion was experienced for traffic in the direction of the frame carrying the FECN indication. The switch sets the BECN bit to notify the end user that congestion may be experienced by traffic moving in the opposite direction of the frame carrying the BECN indication. FECN and BECN are set only by the network, not by the users, and there is *no* obligation for the end systems to take any regard of either bit. The exact algorithms used to determine when congestion is occurring are vendor specific, although an appendix to ANSI T1.618 gives suggestions (which are usually ignored).

In addition to the BECN bit, the switch may also use a special **Consolidated Link Layer Management** (CLLM) message to indicate to a sender that a set of logical connections is experiencing congestion. (More about the CLLM in Chapter 8, Network Management.) The CLLM technique can be used when congestion occurs at a network node, but no reverse traffic is available to carry the BECN indication. The CLLM message is carried over a separate control DLCI, number 1023. Not all switch vendors support CLLM, and it is not required by the User-to-Network Implementation Agreement FRF 1.1. In practice, CLLM is rarely used.

Implicit Congestion Notification

When a frame relay network discards a frame, the missing frame will eventually be detected by the receiving end user at a higher, end-to-end layer, such as TCP or SNA. This is because higher layer protocols, such as TCP, use sequence numbers to detect missing data. When this situation occurs,

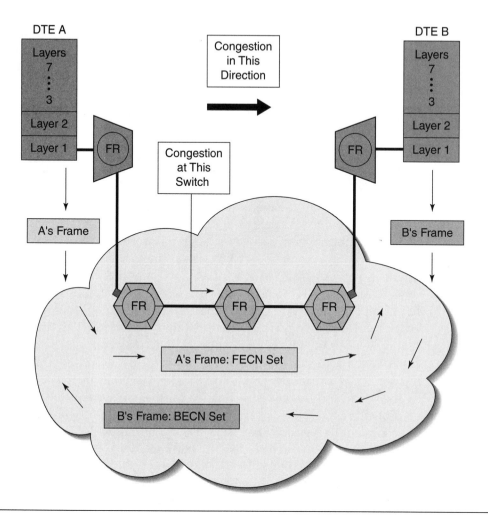

FIGURE 6.9 Operation of FECN and BECN.   *The FECN and BECN bits tell the end user that congestion is occurring in the network.*

the end-user software may deduce that congestion is occurring. This is *implicit* congestion notification (see Figure 6.10).

Once congestion is detected, the higher layer protocol can use end-to-end flow control to recover. For example, for sliding-window-based protocols, the receiver can reduce the window size in order to throttle the flow of frames from the sender.

Some protocols are even proactive about congestion recovery. For instance, TCP goes a step farther than just waiting to detect discarded frames. It continuously measures the effective throughput of the layer 4

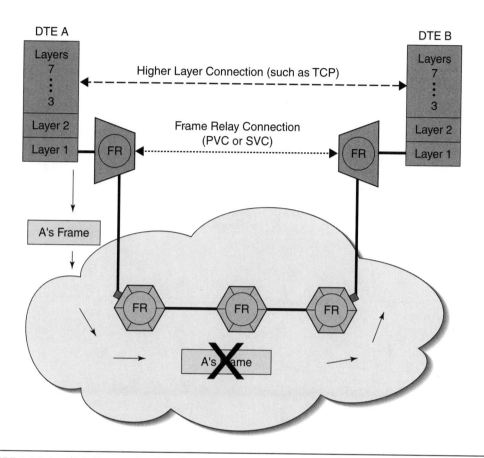

FIGURE 6.10 Implicit Congestion Notification. *When a frame is discarded, the missing frame will eventually be detected by the receiving end user at a higher layer.*

connection by monitoring timeouts. If the throughput drops, likely because of congestion, TCP will reduce the window size. This puts fewer frames into the network, which should help with the problem. SNA has a somewhat similar proactive technique, called pacing.

Where Congestion Can Occur

Congestion can actually occur in several places within a frame relay scenario (see Figure 6.11). Generally, the observable symptoms are delay of and possibly loss of frames. We examine where congestion can occur in the context of sending traffic from a local frame relay CPE to a remote CPE.

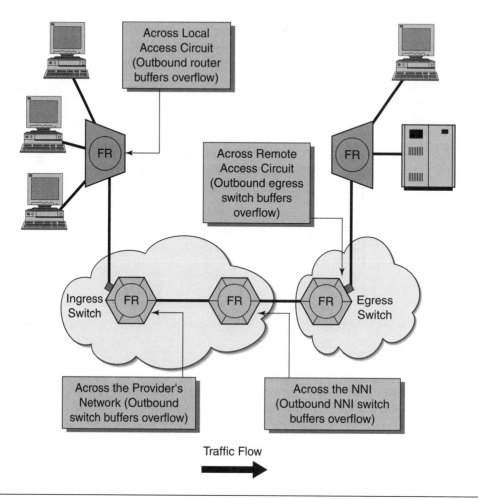

FIGURE 6.11 Where Congestion Can Occur.   *Congestion can occur in four major places in a frame relay network.*

Congestion across the Local Access Circuit

Symptom.   The outbound router (or FRAD) buffers overflow.

Cause.   The local access circuit does not have enough capacity to support the amount of traffic coming out of the router. This type of congestion does not depend on CIR settings because the router doesn't pay attention to CIR. Instead, it is due to the aggregate amount of traffic across all PVCs on the access circuit.

Remedy.   Increase the port speed, which might also necessitate changing the access circuit from a 56-Kbps line to a T1, for instance. Or decrease the traffic flow for the peak periods, which might be possible by load-shifting some of the traffic to an off-peak period. Chapter 13, Internetworking with Frame Relay, discusses some router-based methods, such as random early detection and fair queueing, that can help with congestion.

Congestion across the Provider's Network

Symptom.   The frame relay switch buffers overflow. The carrier notices this, but the customer may not be able to observe it directly.

Cause.   The backbone trunks between switches, or possibly the switches themselves, do not have enough capacity to support the total amount of traffic flowing through that part of the network.

Remedy.   The service provider needs to upgrade the frame relay network. Depending on where the undercapacity is, the provider may need to increase the capacity of the backbone trunks, the switch's buffers, or the switch's processing speed, or reroute PVCs through less-utilized parts of the network.

From the customer's point of view, increasing the CIR for a given PVC will likely improve the performance of that PVC relative to other PVCs, but it will not help the root problem of network congestion.

Note, however, that transient congestion can occur even in a well-designed network if too much traffic from too many sources temporarily shows up at a switch. Think of Mother's Day in the public telephone network. The problem needs major attention only when the congestion is chronic.

Another practical remedy for congestion across a provider's network is for the customer to start evaluating alternative service providers' offerings. This will do two things. First, it will put pressure on the incumbent frame relay provider to expedite the required upgrades to the network, at least to meet the needs of that customer. Second, it will provide the research for changing the service provider, if necessary. Since upgrades to a provider's network infrastructure may take years, purchasing services from an alternative carrier may well be the best way to increase the performance of critical business applications. In the event that the incumbent provider's congestion exists in many locations, changing providers often is the best business decision. Additionally, a competitive frame relay provider will often absorb the costs of the changeover in order to win the frame relay contract.

Congestion across the Network-to-Network Interface

Symptom. The buffers overflow at the frame relay switch on the "local" side of the Network-to-Network Interface (NNI). Symptoms are similar to the case of congestion across the provider's network.

Cause. The physical circuit that underlies the NNI does not have enough capacity to support the traffic between the two networks. Possibly, the switches at each end of the NNI do not have enough internal capacity.

Remedy. As in the case of internal network congestion, the two service providers need to upgrade the NNI. This may mean a faster physical circuit, more powerful switches, or setting up an alternative NNI for load balancing. Again, the customer may want to increase the CIRs on affected PVCs so that the PVCs receive better treatment.

Congestion across the Remote Access Circuit

Symptom. The outbound buffers at the egress frame relay switch overflow. (The egress switch is the last frame relay switch before the frame reaches the remote CPE.)

Cause. The remote access circuit does not have enough capacity to support the amount of traffic coming out of the egress switch. Or, possibly, the remote router (or FRAD) is too slow to handle all the traffic coming across the access circuit.

This type of congestion is due to poor capacity planning on the customer's part rather than on the carrier's part. Hence, a carrier may exclude it from a service level agreement (SLA), since the carrier has no real control over this type of insufficient capacity.

Remedy. Increase the egress port speed, which might also necessitate upgrading the type of access circuit, for instance, from 56 Kbps to T1. As mentioned earlier, increasing the CIR for a given PVC will likely improve the performance of that PVC relative to other PVCs, but it will not help the root problem of limited bandwidth on the access circuit.

Limitations of Congestion Management

Proprietary Implementations of CIR and the DE, FECN, and BECN Bits

As said earlier, the frame relay standards documents describe the "standard" way of implementing CIR and the congestion management bits DE, FECN, and BECN. However, especially for the congestion management bits, many frame relay switch vendors choose to implement their own proprietary versions. For instance, one major vendor is reputed to pass the FECN and BECN bits through the frame relay cloud but not use them for any internal control purposes. And its switches don't use the DE bit at all, because its internal, proprietary flow control software makes no use of it. Another switch vendor does not use the FECN or BECN bits within the frame relay cloud, but sets them appropriately as the frame exits the cloud at the customer premises.

Proprietary implementations of published standards are nothing new in the networking industry.

The Customer's Inability to Respond to the FECN and BECN Bits

Practically, what can the receiving end system do if it receives frames with the FECN bit set? At the frame relay level, the end system, which is often a router, can count the number of such frames and possibly signal the network management system if the percentage goes over a preset threshold. However, the end system cannot directly slow down the received traffic, nor can it notify the sender that there are congestion problems, because there are no frame relay mechanisms for doing that. Furthermore, along with being unable to *react* effectively to the FECN, the end system cannot handle the congestion "coming at it" *proactively* because it cannot detect the congestion building up in advance.

What can the *sending* end system do if it receives reverse traffic with the BECN bit set? First of all, it may not even receive the BECN if the congestion is too severe or if there is no reverse traffic. If the frame relay sender, which is often a router, does receive a BECN, it should slow down the frame relay traffic it sends into the network. But layer 2 in a LAN has no flow control mechanism, so there is no direct way for a router to signal the originating computer system to throttle its flow of data. The router can buffer up frames in an attempt to slow the flow into the network, but there are limits on router memory.

Thus, one of the best uses of the FECN and BECN bits is simply to indicate the general load on the virtual circuits. If a connection is repeatedly suffering congestion, the CIR can be increased for it. Although not sophisticated, this is a useful technique.

Theoretically, it would be good if the layer 2 frame relay FECN and BECN bits could somehow be fed to the higher layer protocols on the end systems. Then the higher layer protocols could institute tighter flow control based on direct information from the frame relay layer rather than wait for implicit notification. Unfortunately, there are no procedures in place at this time for translating FECN and BECN bits into higher layer flow-control policies. Furthermore, any such feedback from layer 2 to higher layers would violate the strict layering guidelines of the OSI standards, although many vendors are paying less attention to OSI layering these days.

Note that the frame relay protocol itself can do nothing about flow control across the User-Network Interface (UNI) because it has no mechanisms for it.

Use and Misuse of the DE Bit

Some network analysts believe that the DE bit can be used to guarantee that one type of traffic will be transmitted before another type of traffic. Loosely said, they want to use it to indicate "priority (see Figure 6.12)"[2] The DE bit cannot do this, as the following example shows.

Consider a large frame relay network in which two PVCs send data from location A to location B. Each PVC has a CIR of 32 Kbps and similar traffic patterns. The access circuit is 64 Kbps. The network analyst wants the data on PVC1 to have priority over the data on PVC2. Thus, he sets up the frame relay access equipment at location A to keep the DE bit cleared (DE = 0) on frames traveling over PVC1. The access equipment sets the DE bit (DE = 1) on frames that are sent over PVC2. The analyst thinks that PVC1 will then have priority over PVC2 because the frames on PVC2 are more likely to be discarded.

What will actually happen? If there is no congestion, which is the normal operation, all the frames on PVC1 and PVC2 will be delivered just fine. Each PVC will receive a CIR of 32 Kbps on average. The DE bit has *no* effect.

If there is moderate congestion at the switch, PVC1 will receive a CIR of 32 Kbps, but frames on PVC2 will be discarded. Hence, the network analyst

---

[2]This use of the DE bit is similar to the use of IP precedence bits in layer 3 IP networks.

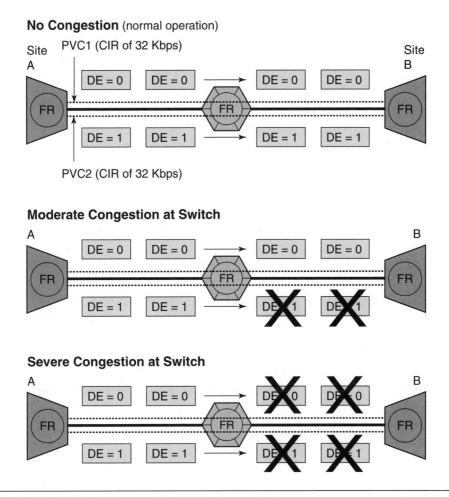

No Congestion (normal operation)

Moderate Congestion at Switch

Severe Congestion at Switch

FIGURE 6.12 The DE Bit Fallacy. *The DE bit does not indicate transmission priority.*

will have paid for a CIR of 32 Kbps on PVC2 but may receive no throughput at all on it. The DE bit *does* have an effect, but it is not the effect the analyst wants. (Note that, depending on the switch design, PVC2 may suffer frame discard even if it is not causing the congestion in the switch.)

If there is severe congestion at the switch, then both PVC1 and PVC2 will suffer frame loss. On PVC1, frames above the CIR will be thrown away first, but if the congestion is severe, frames within the CIR will also be thrown away. For PVC2, since all of its frames have the DE bit set on entry to the switch, all of its frames will likely be discarded. The DE bit has little effect, and certainly not the effect the analyst wanted.

Note that the DE bit has a possible use when two traffic streams are sharing the same PVC (likely using *RFC1490 Multiprotocol Encapsulation*). If one of the streams—for instance, voice traffic—is considered more important than the other stream—for instance, LAN traffic—the DE bit could be set for the less important traffic, which then would be sacrificed if there were any congestion problems on the PVC. A better solution, though, from a performance standpoint, would be to give each traffic stream its own PVC.

The moral is that if turning on the DE bit has a noticeable effect, the network design is wrong. But then what should the network analyst do?

- Use frame relay access equipment, such as a router, that allows explicit prioritization of its output queues based on type of traffic or other parameters.
- Keep the DE bit cleared when sending frames into the frame relay network.
- Be aware that even if traffic is prioritized going into the network, the switches within the network will usually *not* prioritize traffic on their outbound queues.
- Make sure that each PVC has a CIR adequate for carrying its traffic.
- Obtain assurance that the frame relay network itself is well engineered. This might take the form of a service level agreement with the provider, as discussed in Chapter 9, Frame Relay Service Pricing.

Chapter 7

Engineering of Frame Relay Networks

This chapter discusses the internal engineering of frame relay networks, in particular, the architecture of the frame relay switches and how that influences the services that public carriers can offer. Even for private frame relay networks, the switch architecture can have a major impact on how traffic is transported.

First we survey the switching platform landscape and note which switches the major carriers use. Next we contrast two major families of first-generation frame relay networks. For our discussion we call these two families **non-CIR** and **flow-controlled**. Then we describe features of second-generation frame relay switches.

Lastly we discuss the zero CIR controversy, an ongoing argument within the industry about the advantages and dangers of zero CIR PVCs. We follow up with a discussion of the worldviews of the opposing sides.

Frame Relay Switch Families

Carriers typically buy their switches from third-party vendors and then customize them by setting configuration parameters. For instance, AT&T buys Cisco/StrataCom switches. As we will see, the type of switch a carrier deploys can have a great impact on such issues as how congestion is managed, how CIR is actually defined, and how services are priced.

There are about two dozen vendors of frame relay switches, of which only a handful sell to the larger frame relay service providers. In the next pages, we discuss two major families of networks built on these switches, within which there are many variations. One family is the non-CIR networks, for which the representative switch is the Alcatel Data Networks 1100 TPX. The other is the flow-controlled networks, for which the representative was the StrataCom IPX, later upgraded to the StrataCom BPX. Note that "non-CIR" and "flow-controlled" are not industry-standard terms but merely handles used here. Also note that not all frame relay switches fall into these two families, as they have characteristics of both. These two families present different approaches to the design of a frame relay switch.

This chapter uses the term "ingress switch" to mean the frame relay switch that first receives frames from, say, a router. It is also known as the entry switch or source switch or originating switch. The "egress switch" is the last switch in the frame relay network before the frame travels across the access channel to the customer's receiving frame relay device. It is also known as the exit, or destination, switch. These definitions assume traffic flow in only one direction, from ingress to egress. For traffic flowing in the reverse direction on a virtual circuit, what was previously the egress switch for the virtual circuit becomes the ingress switch for the reverse flow.

Typically, a backbone network of some sort will connect the ingress and egress switches. It might be composed of more frame relay switches, or it might well be an ATM network. Note that the ingress switch may also be the same as the egress switch. This can happen, for instance, with two frame relay customer sites within the same LATA exchanging data via a single (ingress and egress) switch in the LATA.

Public Service Provider Switches

As indicated in Table 7.1, AT&T is now using Cisco BPX switches, which are broadband multiservice switches originally developed by StrataCom. AT&T upgraded its frame relay network from StrataCom IPX switches to support ATM backbone trunks at T3 speeds rather than the IPX's T1 speeds.

The MCI portion of MCI WorldCom has used Bay Networks Baystream BNX switches, which are based on Bay's Backbone Concentrator Node routers. However, Nortel, which bought Bay, is discontinuing production of the Baystream line, although it will continue product support for several years. In response, MCI is considering adding Lucent/Ascend/Cascade CBX 500 switches to its existing frame relay network.

The WorldCom portion of MCI WorldCom uses Cisco/StrataCom switches mainly within the United States and Lucent/Ascend switches internationally. At the time of this writing, the MCI and WorldCom frame

TABLE 7.1 Frame Relay Switches Used by Carriers

Carrier/Service	Primary Frame Relay Switch
AT&T Interspan	Cisco/StrataCom BPX
Sprint Frame Relay	Alcatel Data Networks 1100 TPX, Nortel Magellan Passport
MCI HyperStream (of MCI WorldCom)	Nortel/Bay Networks Baystream BNX
WorldCom (of MCI WorldCom)	Lucent/Ascend/Cascade B-STDX 9000, Cisco/StrataCom

relay networks have not been closely integrated. However, MCI World-Com has built four Network-to-Network Interfaces (NNIs) in the United States to move MCI's domestic frame relay traffic onto WorldCom's global frame relay network.

Sprint uses switches from a joint venture of Sprint and Alcatel, called Alcatel Data Networks. The Alcatel Data Network 1100 TPX switches are updates of the X.25 packet switches originally developed by Telenet, bought by Sprint some years ago. However, Sprint has also installed a parallel frame relay network based on Nortel Magellan Passport switches, which are broadband multiservice ATM/frame relay switches. The Nortel Passport switch provides class-of-service differentiation, so that, for instance, SNA traffic can be guaranteed lower latency than LAN traffic. New customers are placed on the Nortel network, and existing customers have the option of migrating to that network from the Alcatel network.

Many of the smaller frame relay service providers use Lucent/Ascend/Cascade and also Newbridge frame relay switches.

Since service providers and vendors seem to be constantly merging, the landscape described here will undoubtedly have evolved by the time you read this.

The Non-CIR Approach

As noted earlier, "non-CIR" is not an industry-standard term, but refers to a family of frame relay switches that do not use CIR as one of their primary traffic management parameters. The ancestors of this particular representative non-CIR network are packet-switched rather than circuit-switched networks, which is one reason that the concept of bursting at the full channel speed is so firmly established. Figure 7.1 depicts non-CIR networks.

PVC Services and Bursting

Two services are available: a zero CIR service and (much less commonly) a reserved service with a subscribed CIR. The zero CIR service defines no minimum committed information rate, but does allow sustained bursting

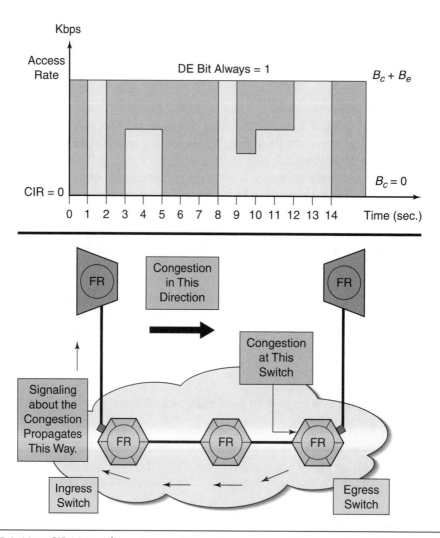

FIGURE 7.1 Non-CIR Networks. *A zero CIR service in a non-CIR network can burst up to the full access channel rate, and it can signal when congestion is occurring.*

up to the full access channel rate for at least 1 second, if capacity is available. Because of the (mostly undeserved) negative connotations of a zero CIR, the marketing literature often uses terms like "Burst Express" service instead. The reserved service reserves bandwidth over the network based on the subscribed CIR. It also allows bursting up to the full access circuit speed. The data sent within the CIR level is given a higher priority than data sent above the CIR. Since the reserved service is essentially a virtual dedicated line rather than a statistically multiplexed virtual connection, it is more expensive than zero CIR service.

Capacity Planning

The carrier constantly monitors utilization on the backbone trunks and targets a peak utilization around 50%. If peak utilization exceeds 70%, the carrier adds additional physical capacity. The 70% threshold ensures a statistically nonblocking network. The access channels must be adequately sized at subscription time.

Traffic Handling

Between switches, the network uses a variation of cell relay. The cells, called subframes, are a maximum of 124 bytes of user data plus 8 bytes of overhead. The switch uses **cut-through** or **data pipelining**. The ingress switch will immediately begin to segment an incoming frame into subframes before the end of the frame has arrived and then pipeline the subframes across the network. The egress switch reassembles the subframes into the original frame. Cut-through tends to reduce delay. It also upgrades relatively easily to ATM.

Congestion Management

For each PVC, the network monitors queues at every switch along the PVC's path. When a queue threshold has been exceeded, indicating congestion, that switch immediately signals the upstream switch to slow down the flow of traffic. After receiving the signal, the upstream switch buffers data until notified by the congested switch to speed up again. If congestion thresholds are then reached in the upstream switch, the switch signals its upstream neighbor (backpressure). When the ingress switch is reached, it sets the FECN and BECN bits on the affected PVC's data frames. If the traffic flow from the customer equipment does not slow down, the ingress switch will start to discard incoming frames. Since the congestion avoidance is per PVC, a misbehaving PVC will not starve other PVCs, even on the same access circuit. This method of handling congestion is some-times called **open-loop flow control**, which means that traffic is allowed into the network without any guarantee that there is enough capacity within the network to ensure its delivery to the destination.

Summary

A non-CIR network may not behave internally the way one would expect from reading the frame relay standards. However, if well engineered, it can perform quite well, from the user's perspective. For instance, for the network just discussed, the performance objective is delivery of 99.64% of all traffic offered to the network.

The Flow-Controlled Approach

Like "non-CIR," "flow-controlled" is not an industry-standard term, but refers to a family of frame relay switches that use a flow control mecha-nism as one of their primary traffic management methods (see Figure 7.2). This technique has a circuit-switched mentality. That is, if you can get onto the network, you're fine, but you may get a busy signal and will have to try again later.

PVC Services

A CIR-based service is available. There is no zero CIR service. The flow control mechanism, called ForeSight by one vendor, operates from ingress switch to egress switch within the network. It is somewhat like pacing in SNA networks, relying on the originating (ingress) switch receiving mes-sages from the destination (egress) switch to confirm that there is sufficient capacity along the path. This is an example of **closed-loop flow control**, in which there is explicit feedback to the ingress switch about whether the network has enough capacity to ensure delivery of the traffic to its desti-nation. The flow control mechanism combined with correctly sized access circuits will support the subscribed CIR level quite well.

Capacity Planning

The capacity of the network is engineered to support the underlying CIRs, with "extra" capacity for bursting and backup. The carrier monitors uti-lization to ensure that the capacity remains adequate.

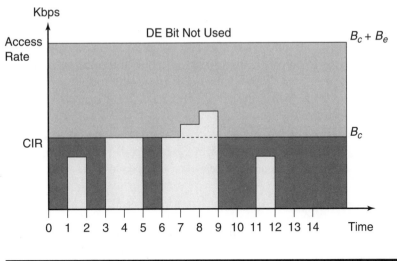

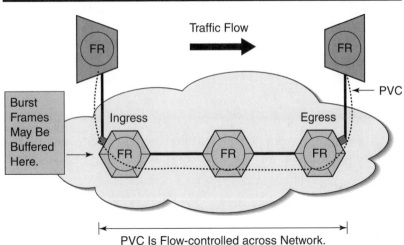

FIGURE 7.2 Flow-Controlled Networks. *A flow-controlled network increases the burst rate in small increments and controls entry into the network.*

Traffic and Burst Handling

Burst traffic is admitted into the network only if there is sufficient capacity along the path. If bursts are allowed in, the flow control mechanism allows the PVC's throughput to increase above the CIR only in small, steady increments, even if excess capacity is available. With some carriers the PVC rate can increase all the way to the access rate. With others it can increase only to 150% of the CIR. (These are configuration parameters set by the carrier.) If congestion occurs, the PVC is throttled back to the CIR or (configurably) to a value such as 50% of the CIR. The burst frames are then delayed in buffers at the ingress switch. If the buffers fill up, the incoming frames are discarded. Since there is no distinction within the network between burst and nonburst traffic, the DE bit is not needed and not used by the network.

The frame relay service is migrating to ATM as a backbone network. Thus, frames will be broken into 53-byte cells for transport across the backbone to the destination switch.

Congestion Management

As discussed above, a CIR-based flow control mechanism is set up for each PVC. Since the mechanism carefully controls traffic flow at the boundary of the network, there is essentially no congestion *within* the network itself. However, the ingress switch may buffer and eventually discard burst traffic (above the CIR). If this happens, the switch will set the FECN and BECN bits on the affected PVC's data frames. Since flow control is done per PVC, a misbehaving PVC will not starve other PVCs.

Summary

A well-engineered flow-controlled network will usually give the user throughput up to the CIR and *may* allow bursting even higher than the CIR.

Comparison of the Non-CIR and Flow-Controlled Approaches

Frame relay networks built with non-CIR switches tend to have advantages different from those of networks built from flow-controlled switches. However, these are just general tendencies. The ultimate performance of a frame relay network depends heavily on the carrier's engineering and capacity planning, not just on the capabilities of the switch platform. A comparison of network families is given in Table 7.2.

Advantages of Non-CIR Networks

As discussed earlier, non-CIR networks typically support bursting up to the full rate of the access circuit. If the carrier allows sustained bursts at the access rate, overall throughput can be significantly higher than for flow-

TABLE 7.2 Comparison of Network Families

Advantages of non-CIR networks	Advantages of flow-controlled networks
• Greater burst capability	• Less congestion *within* network
• Overall capacity and price	• More consistent throughput and delay
• Good for file transfers, IP internetworking	• Good for interactive traffic, for example, IBM's SNA

controlled networks. Even if the carrier allows bursts of only limited duration, throughput can still be improved.

For this reason, non-CIR networks tend to make efficient use of their capacity, which can lead to lower prices. However, many other factors besides switch architecture influence value.

Because of their ability to burst, non-CIR networks tend to do well with traffic that is bursty but that tolerates some delay. Examples are file transfers and most IP internetwork traffic.

Advantages of Flow-Controlled Networks

Flow-controlled networks have look-ahead congestion management schemes that ensure that frames are not sent into the network unless there is bandwidth available to deliver them out the other side. (This is also called a closed-loop architecture.)

Thus, flow-controlled network providers can truthfully say that once a frame enters their network, it is unlikely that it will be discarded. For instance, they may make claims of 99.995% frame delivery for *accepted* traffic. However, frame discard may occur at the network boundary (at the ingress switch) if there is congestion anywhere along the frame's path within the network. Neither frame delivery percentages for *offered* traffic nor boundary frame discard statistics are typically published by the providers of flow-controlled networks.

Because of their flow control mechanisms, these networks tend to have more consistent throughput and delay than non-CIR networks. End-to-end network delay (sometimes called network latency) especially tends to be more uniform. Independent, but proprietary, benchmark studies have noted these results.

Hence, flow-controlled networks tend to do well with interactive traffic that is low volume but needs relatively short and consistent delays. An example is most interactive SNA traffic.

Second-Generation Frame Relay Switches

As vendors and service providers have gained experience with frame relay, first-generation frame relay switches have evolved into what can be loosely called **second-generation** platforms. Examples of first-generation platforms include the Cisco/StrataCom IPX and the Alcatel Data Networks 1100 TPX discussed above. Examples of newer platforms include the Nortel Magellan Passport and the Lucent/Ascend/Cascade B-STDX 9000 (often combined with the Lucent/Ascend/Cascade CBX 500 at the core).

We will discuss a few second-generation features that first-generation switches do not have. (As usual, different vendors' products vary considerably, new features are constantly being added to product lines, and the term "second-generation" is *not* standardized in the industry.) Second-generation switches typically have the following features:

- Quality of service support
- Greater speeds and scalability
- Improved traffic routing

Quality of Service Support

Second-generation frame relay switches have support for **quality of service** (QoS), sometimes also known as **class of service** (CoS), **traffic classes**, or **differentiated service**. This feature works well in combination with an ATM backbone, which can provide guaranteed traffic delivery within the core of the frame relay network. Thus, second-generation switches tend to have ATM interfaces to the backbone trunks.

One major carrier uses a second-generation platform to provide three classes of service:

- Voice traffic, which needs low delay variance (more about this in Chapter 12, Voice over Frame Relay)
- SNA traffic, which needs low delay (or high performance)
- Inter-LAN traffic, which receives just plain-vanilla frame relay service

Another carrier uses a different platform to provide three other classes of service. These three classes have been named using ATM terminology and are targeted at somewhat different types of traffic.

- Variable frame rate real-time class of service, which takes priority over other types in case of congestion and is designed for SNA traffic
- Variable frame rate non-real-time class of service, which has ordinary priority and is designed for inter-LAN traffic
- Unspecified frame rate class of service, which is lower priority and is suitable for best-effort applications

Quality of service on the public frame relay network can be a blessing for customers trying to send high-priority traffic, such as SNA or voice, over the public network. As usual, though, public network providers make their own decisions about which features of a switch platform they will actually implement, and market forces often drive these decisions.

Greater Speeds and Scalability

Second-generation switches typically have access speeds up to DS-3 (45 Mbps) and trunk speeds with ATM backbones up to OC-3c (155 Mbps) or beyond. They are scalable to networks with hundreds of switches and hundreds of thousands of ports. The internal capacity is in the low-Gbps range. They also have improved end-user reporting capabilities and a range of billing options.

Improved Traffic Routing

Second-generation switches can include a variety of traffic routing improvements. In part, these enhancements are the vendors' proprietary responses to the weaknesses of the standards-based frame relay congestion control mechanisms.

Some borrow OSPF-like routing concepts from the router community so that the network can "self-learn" its topology. This lessens the need for manual input and updating of the backbone trunk configuration.

Many newer switches can reroute traffic within the network more quickly when trunks or switches fail. Some divert traffic surges by sending frames across an overflow route during peak traffic conditions. This overflow routing allows load sharing of traffic over trunks and decreases the number of frames that might otherwise be discarded because of congestion.

Needless to say, all of these possible features are proprietary and may be implemented in different ways, or not at all, by different vendors.

The Zero CIR Controversy

Although the zero CIR controversy has been fueled by marketing departments trying to outshout each other's claims of superior services, there is a basis for it. We will attempt to examine the viewpoints of the opposing camps, shown in Table 7.3.

Since a zero CIR service gives no commitment to supporting any particular data rate over the virtual connection, *all* frames are sent as burst traffic and are marked discard eligible. However, the service usually allows sustained bursts right up to the access channel rate (port speed) if there is sufficient network capacity.

On the face of it, a zero CIR may sound like a bad idea. However, in practice the best-faith effort of a well-engineered zero CIR service may be quite good—better than 99% delivery of frames. Also, zero CIR services tend to be less expensive than fixed CIR, and zero CIR may provide for much higher burst throughput, depending on network load. Discomfort with zero CIR stems from the lack of guarantees, since the actual delivered data rate depends greatly on network load and on the carrier's capacity planning.

TABLE 7.3 A Simplified View of the Opposing Camps on Zero CIR

	Zero CIR	**Fixed CIR**
"Commitment" to VC throughput	None	At CIR
Typical throughput	Higher, but less consistent	Lower, but more consistent
Capacity planning on	Access circuit speeds	CIRs
Slogan	"Zero CIR is useful."	"Zero CIR is too risky."
Associated with	Internet, LANs	SNA
Worldview	Packet switching (Net-heads)	Circuit switching (Bell-heads)
"Natural" switch family	Non-CIR switches	Flow-controlled switches
Motivation	Get lots of bandwidth cheaply	Keep response time consistent

Some of the carriers that offer zero CIR have attempted to counter its negative image by offering service level guarantees. One such guarantee is that the carrier will deliver 99% of the customer's frames or, if it cannot, will move a customer to a CIR-based service at no additional charge.

Across the global marketplace, about 15% of frame relay PVCs are zero CIR [DNA-99]. Zero CIR has often been marketed as an inexpensive way to provide backup service.

The controversy about zero CIR underscores more fundamental differences between the two opposing camps in the frame relay arena. Put simply, the zero CIR camp believes that zero CIR is useful, whereas the fixed CIR camp believes that zero CIR is too risky. However, the zero CIR camp tends to be associated with the Internet community and LAN networking and sees the world in terms of packet switching. (People with this orientation are sometimes called Net-heads.) Since the non-CIR family of switches arose out of this environment, it is quite natural for the non-CIR frame relay networks to offer a zero CIR service. The underlying motivation is to get as much bandwidth as cheaply as possible and tolerate the inevitable variations in response time.

The fixed CIR camp is often familiar with IBM's SNA and tends to see the world in terms of circuit switching. (People with this orientation are sometimes called Bell-heads.) Hence, the CIR-based frame relay networks are seen as a natural evolution, so it is not surprising that the design of the typical CIR-based switch does not even allow for a zero CIR service. The underlying motivation is to keep response time consistent hour by hour and also month by month as the network grows.

For this reason, a carrier may be pushed toward a philosophy about zero CIR just because of the type of frame relay switch it buys. In turn, the marketing department will have to compensate for these switch constraints.

Having said all this, the ultimate question about zero CIR is still simply whether the user is satisfied with the quality of service.

Chapter 8

Network Management

This chapter discusses management of a frame relay network, including the functions of a general management system and management of frame relay networks in particular.

We begin with an overview of the five functions of network management systems. Following this, we describe where frame relay management data can be obtained within a network—namely, from switches, routers, protocol analyzers, and enhanced DSU/CSUs.

Briefly, we describe how frame relay standards for network management are an important but small part of a full-blown system for managing a frame relay network. Then we go into more detail about each of the frame relay standards useful for network management. The first standard is the **Local Management Interface** (LMI), which allows a frame relay switch to directly transmit a limited set of management information to the customer's equipment. The LMI is one of the low-level support functions for managing a frame relay network. The next standard is the **Consolidated Link Layer Management** (CLLM), which allows a frame relay switch to notify the end user about congestion in the network. Finally, two frame relay-related **Management Information Bases** (MIBs) are used to store management data collected by frame relay switches and routers. Along the way, we also survey the **Simple Network Management Protocol** (SNMP), which is the major infrastructure tool for managing all types of data networks. Although it is indeed (relatively) simple in its functions, SNMP is widely used and widely available for supporting network management systems.

Then we outline three major approaches to frame relay management, which are user-based monitoring, carrier-based monitoring, and managed network services. We follow this by naming a few network management systems available in the marketplace.

Next we discuss the five major functions of a network management system in the specific context of frame relay. We describe each, showing how it is related to SNMP, and compare alternatives for performing the function.

Lastly, we explain more about the main alternative to building a customer-operated management system—managed network services. With this alternative, the carrier provides comprehensive management of both the frame relay network and the customer's equipment. This may be an attractive alternative for some customers.

Network Management System Functions

The "Holy Grail" of network management is for a company to have a single, integrated system that handles everything. Such a system would be available on a single workstation (with backup) and would handle the three major data networking domains:

- The wide area network, which for us is the frame relay network
- The IBM SNA applications and equipment
- The LAN applications and equipment

In reality, a customer will typically need to strike a balance between

- Integrated systems that provide overall monitoring, especially fault monitoring
- Specialized systems that provide detailed configuration, fault, and performance management, especially in a particular networking domain

Thus, a customer will typically need several management systems, each targeted at a different aspect of the network and each collecting data from different locations in the network.

Before investigating management of frame relay networks in particular, we review the five functions of network management systems in general.

Configuration management. Setup and ongoing management of equipment and connections at both the physical layer and higher layers.

Fault management. Detecting, tracking, and responding to network alarms. It is sometimes also known as "putting out brushfires."

Performance management. Collecting and interpreting information about quality of service and performance, both for individual components and for the network as a whole. Performance management is sometimes also known as statistics gathering or as trending.

Accounting management. Charging customers for the use of the network. For some internal networks, accounting management may not be necessary.

Security management. Authorization, protection of information and resources, and such issues as encryption and passwords. It may be relatively minimal, or it may be a major effort.

Management Data Sources

Frame relay management data, especially fault and performance data, comes from several possible locations within a network. As we will see later, this raw data is typically gathered at a physical device and then sent to a higher layer management software package, where it is summarized and reported to the network operators.

Data from Switches

Frame relay switches can be a very valuable source of information about a frame relay network, because the switch software typically collects data in order to manage the virtual circuits and handle congestion. However, this information may or may not be accessible by the end user, depending on whether the carrier chooses to make the information available and, if so, what type.

Data from switches typically has limitations. The major limitation is that switches focus on the per-port statistics they contain. Thus, it is difficult for them to report on the behavior of PVCs (such as delay) from the ingress port all the way to a distant egress port. A related limitation is that switches cannot report on PVC behavior across the access circuit, because that is outside the frame relay network from the point of view of the carrier. Also, the switches in a carrier's network will typically not report on anything that occurs on the other side of an NNI, in another carrier's network.[1]

Data from Routers

Routers (and FRADs) are another important source of management information, especially for the data that comes into the router across the LMI (discussed later).

However, routers, too, typically have limitations. They usually pay no attention to CIR or bursting and hence do not report such data to the end user. Also, a router that is suffering internal congestion can distort PVC delay measurements. Since routers are not under the control of the carrier, unless the carrier is providing managed network services, router-based measurements will be of help to end users but will not be accessible by the carrier. Lastly, routers are not primarily protocol analyzers and have a lot of work to do other than reporting detailed statistics.

Data from Protocol Analyzers

Protocol analyzers, often also called network probes, can provide a wealth of detailed information about a frame relay network. A protocol analyzer typically has a hardware interface—the network probe—which inserts into the access circuit. The protocol analyzer then analyzes the traffic monitored by the probe and reports its findings to a network technician. Because of its expense, an analyzer is often used for reactive monitoring, troubleshooting, rather than for continuous monitoring. Protocol analyzers are particularly helpful for diagnosing problems and collecting statistics about access circuits.

Data from Enhanced DSU/CSUs

Enhanced DSU/CSUs, also called frame-monitoring DSU/CSUs, are becoming popular for monitoring frame relay networks. These devices are a combination of a DSU/CSU and a built-in network probe. They often work

---

[1]However, at least one of the second-tier long-distance frame relay service providers, Intermedia Communications, Inc., has developed software for its Lucent/Ascend/Cascade switches that allows performance monitoring of multicarrier frame relay networks [NW97APR21]. Since second-tier providers often make NNI arrangements with other providers, such multicarrier tools can be a useful marketing advantage.

in concert with reporting software built by the DSU vendor. Or they may simply be the hardware collection point for a third-party reporting tool.

In some sense, DSUs are a natural data collection point because they are on the customer's premises but on the network side of the router. Hence, they can get a good look at PVCs that cross the frame relay network just before the PVCs terminate at the router. Customers, and some carriers, are using DSU-based management systems to verify service level agreements (SLAs), especially the SLA's end-to-end parameters. We will say more about "smart" DSU/CSUs' features shortly.

Frame Relay Standards versus Proprietary Network Management Systems

Parts of the frame relay standards relate to network management. These are the Local Management Interface, the Consolidated Link Layer Management, and the two frame relay Management Information Bases, all of which we will discuss in the next section. However, these standards are somewhat primitive and are only a part of what is necessary for a useful frame relay network management system. For that reason, the bulk of any commercially available network management system will be proprietary (although the vendors will describe the system as "open," as discussed later).

Some network management vendors use a two-tier architecture for their systems. The lowest layer, sometimes called the element layer, uses SNMP agents (see later) or proprietary probes to collect information within the network. The upper layer, sometimes called the application layer (but not the same as the OSI application layer), summarizes and reports the lower layer information to the network operator. The upper layer assists the operator in the configuration, fault, and performance aspects of managing the network.

Many other network management vendors use a three-tier architecture. In this case, the middle layer—called the mediation layer, the archive manager, or by other names—contains the configuration and performance database together with tools for analyzing the database. Then the upper layer becomes just the man-machine interface. The three-tier architectures appear to have advantages for flexibility and for scalability to large networks [NC98JUN15].

In any case, the complete network management picture available to the customer depends on what data the management system vendor can collect, how the vendor can analyze it, and what data the carrier will make accessible to the customer.

Note that as the number of networking elements monitored grows, so does the management data collection traffic. An important network design issue is to understand the management traffic generated by the monitored elements and to adjust the polling intervals and amount of data collected to minimize the effect of the data collection traffic on the application traffic. Additionally, as the number of networking elements becomes large, intermediate data collection points may be required to consolidate the management traffic from a group of elements before it is passed on to a central network management station.

Frame Relay Standards in Network Management

Here we describe the frame relay standards that are specifically related to network management, namely, the LMI, the CLLM, and the two frame relay MIBs. We also review SNMP, which is a very common way to collect management data within a network.

The LMI gives basic management information about the physical access circuits and the DLCI values for the PVCs that cross the access circuit. It is much more useful for configuration and basic fault management than for performance management. The CLLM can show congestion on the PVCs. The two frame relay MIBs store standardized management data that is collected by frame relay switches and routers.

The Local Management Interface

As mentioned in Chapter 3, Frame Relay Architecture, the Local Management Interface (shown in Figure 8.1) helps to ensure the valid operation of the local frame relay User-Network Interface (UNI). Thus, for instance, a frame relay-compliant router can interact with the frame relay switch at the other end of the access circuit about the following:

- Which virtual circuits (VCs) *exist* across the access link, and, of the existing VCs, which ones are *active* (can accept data frames).[2] (There

---

[2]The active status of a PVC is indicated by a bit in the PVC's status information element. This is sometimes called the **A-bit**. Standard practice for carrier switches is to set/clear the A-bit to inform the router of the active/inactive status of the PVC. The carrier also implements similar procedures for the New Indicator bit.

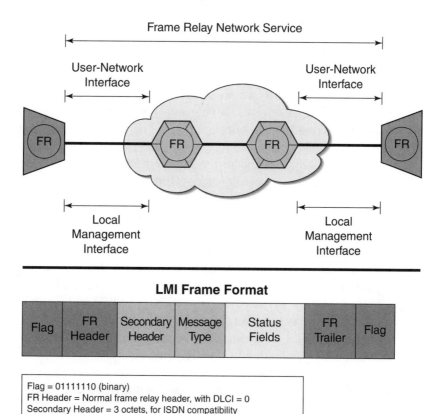

FIGURE 8.1 The Local Management Interface. *Frame relay access equipment can use the LMI to obtain status information about the virtual circuits that cross the User-Network Interface.*

might be existing but inactive VCs because they have not been fully set up.)

- Whether any *new* VCs have been configured across the access link and, if so, whether they are active or inactive
- Whether the physical access link itself is alive and well[3]
- Establishing, clearing, and accessing the status of switched virtual circuits (SVCs)

---

[3]The periodic polling procedure that monitors the access circuit is also known as the link integrity, keep-alive signal, or heartbeat.

The frame relay user can gather the above status information by means of a periodic polling procedure (heartbeat). In its basic form, the frame relay access device sends a simple STATUS ENQUIRY message to the frame relay network every few seconds (the default is 10 seconds). The network responds with a simple STATUS message to verify that the access link is working properly. During every sixth polling cycle (the default value), the access device sends a full STATUS ENQUIRY message, to which the network responds with a full STATUS message containing the DLCI, the active/inactive status, and the new/old status for *every* virtual circuit configured on the frame relay access link.

The LMI message format has the same header and trailer as other frame relay frames, except that the DLCI is 0. However, the first part of what would be the frame relay payload is devoted to a "secondary header" and a message type field. This makes the LMI message more closely aligned with the ISDN LAPD packet signaling protocol. The remaining part of the payload is given over to the various status information elements. More details can be found in the books by Smith [Smith93] and Black [Black96].

The frame relay user can also handle establishing, clearing, and accessing the status of SVCs by means of several types of LMI-formatted messages on DLCI 0. By design, the LMI status messages and the SVC signaling messages have identical formats, except for different message type values and for a call reference value of 0 in the LMI status messages. Chapter 5, Frame Relay Virtual Circuits, discussed setup of SVCs.

Note that since the frame relay frame format has no field in the header to indicate whether the frame is a control or a data frame, all control frames must be sent "out of band" on a separate channel. This is why all LMI frames use DLCI 0 instead of a virtual circuit that is transporting user data frames. (The old Frame Relay Forum LMI standard used the incompatible DLCI 1023.) Also note that the LMI messages, like DLCIs, apply only to the user's interface into the frame relay network. LMI messages are not end to end.

As mentioned earlier, there are several versions of the LMI:

- ANSI T1.617a Annex D, the most common, which uses DLCI 0 for the LMI. This is often called the **ANSI LMI** or **LMI Annex D**.
- ANSI T1.617 Annex D, the older, but similar, version of ANSI T1.617a.
- ITU-T Q.933 Annex A, which is closely aligned with T1.617a Annex D. It is often called simply **LMI Annex A**.
- The Frame Relay Forum's first-generation LMI, which uses DLCI 1023 and is now largely outdated

Also as noted earlier, "LMI" is a de facto, but common, term. In the Frame Relay Forum, the mechanics of the LMI are referred to as control procedures, signaling procedures, or management procedures.

When choosing frame relay access equipment, such as routers, it is important from the point of view of network management to have LMI capability. For example, if a PVC is added between two sites, the routers at the two sites will be automatically notified of its presence. Without LMI enabled, the routers must be manually updated. Nearly all routers do have LMI capability.

Consolidated Link Layer Management

As mentioned in Chapter 6, Traffic Management, a frame relay switch may also use a special Consolidated Link Layer Management message to indicate to a sending DTE that a set of logical connections is experiencing congestion. The CLLM technique can be used when congestion occurs at a network node but no reverse traffic is available to carry the BECN indication back to the source router or FRAD. The CLLM message is carried over a separate control DLCI, number 1023, to separate it from user or LMI traffic.

Use of the CLLM is optional. It may be used in place of "missing" BECN bits or in addition to them. Not all switch vendors support CLLM, and the User-to-Network Implementation Agreement FRF 1.1 does not require vendor support. Furthermore, many routers will neither recognize nor act on CLLM messages. For these reasons, CLLM is rarely used.

The CLLM message is a type of control frame (an exchange identifier, or XID, HDLC frame) in the full LAPF protocol. (See Chapter 5, Frame Relay Virtual Circuits, for more details on LAPF.) The body of the control frame contains a list of DLCIs that are suffering congestion and a cause for the congestion. The cause field indicates if the congestion is due to excessive traffic, equipment failure, or maintenance action, or if the cause is unknown. Several books give more detailed explanations of the CLLM [Smith93], [Black96], [Stall95].

Review of the Simple Network Management Protocol

The Simple Network Management Protocol is a useful, relatively "simple," and widely available tool for network management. It was originally

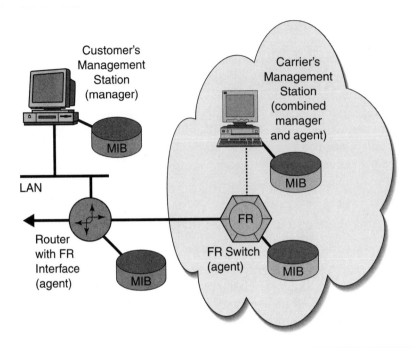

FIGURE 8.2 SNMP.   *The SNMP management station collects management information from all the SNMP agents in the network.*

developed by the IETF to help manage TCP/IP networks and has proven quite popular. SNMP consists of four parts (see Figure 8.2):

- A **management station**, or **manager**, which collects the management information from the network and stores it in a central database.
- **Agents**, which are software modules in routers, switches, and the like. An agent collects management data from its associated device and stores it in a local database for later interrogation by the manager.
- **MIBs**, which are the tree-structured and standardized databases for the management data (known as objects) mentioned above.
- A **network management protocol**, which links the manager and the agents. SNMP is basically a request/response protocol that runs on top of the **User Datagram Protocol** (UDP), which in turn is part of the TCP/IP protocol suite.

SNMP is an "infrastructure" rather than a full-blown management system. It does *not* include the management applications for data analysis, fault recovery, and so forth, or the user interface for the human network manager. These are available from various vendors or can be written in house by the customer.

The SNMP includes

- A **GET** message, which allows the management station to get management data from an agent's MIB
- A **SET** message, which allows the manager to set the values of variables (objects) in a MIB
- A **TRAP** (or alarm) message, which allows the agent to send an unsolicited message to the manager about some abnormal network condition

Normally, the management station simply polls the agents in turn, collects the managed objects from the agents' local MIBs, and stores the collected information in its own central MIB for use by the management applications.

With most public frame relay services, the carrier runs its own SNMP system and provides the results in a MIB that can be accessed by the customer. The MIB is partitioned so that the user organization can see only its own data and not that of other companies. This service, combined with the customer's own SNMP system on its own equipment, can be a valuable tool for overall management of a frame relay network. However, because the SNMP SET command is so limited, vendor-specific management tools still typically perform the more complex configurations for frame relay equipment.

Most management platforms use SNMP, version 1 (SNMPv1). A few use portions of SNMPv2; however, since the IETF SNMP working committees cannot agree on its complete specifications, especially security, SNMPv2 has essentially stalled. Recently, work has begun on SNMPv3, which promises improved security features, additional message types for bulk data collection, and other improvements.

Note that although SNMP is very common in enterprises, many service providers prefer a more versatile, though complex, network management platform, **Common Management Information Protocol** (CMIP), for managing their own networks.

The Management Information Base for Frame Relay Service

The Frame Relay Forum and the IETF jointly developed a standard MIB for frame relay service. The details are in *RFC 1604, Definitions of Managed Objects for Frame Relay Service* [RFC1604], which is also attached as Annex

B to FRF.6 [FRF6-94]. This MIB includes information on performance statistics, alarms, and virtual circuit status. It allows a customer's network management station to monitor its PVCs, UNI ports, and NNI ports. Most frame relay vendors support this standard MIB, but many also add proprietary extensions for information not included in it.

The major limitations of the frame relay service MIB are these:

- It does not monitor the physical layer. Other existing MIBs, such as the DS1 MIB and MIB II, do.
- It does not monitor internal aspects of the network, such as switching elements, line cards, and network routing tables. These internal details are vendor proprietary.
- It is not implemented on user equipment, such as routers or FRADs. (Instead, the **frame relay DTE MIB** [RFC1315] should be used to manage those devices, as it is adequate for managing frame relay ports on routers. However, the DTE MIB is rather rudimentary with respect to network management and as such is not included in any Frame Relay Forum Implementation Agreement.)
- It does not cover SVCs, although they may be added in the future.
- It covers only a single frame relay service offering from one network. A multinetwork PVC must be managed by polling a network agent in each network and then piecing together the results for an end-to-end view of the PVC.
- The customer management station must have a separate PVC to the SNMP agent in the network, or else use proprietary methods to piggyback the SNMP messages onto a customer's data PVC.

Frame Relay Management Approaches

The main approaches for customers seeking frame relay management capability are not exclusive; it often makes sense to use them in combination.

User-Based Monitoring

The customer's management system can gather information from equipment on the customer's premises and then display it with a management platform. This is a very common approach.

Hardware-Based

One option for user-based monitoring is to install a hardware-based management system. In this case the vendor of the system will rely on hardware probes or DSU/CSUs that it also manufactures (or resells). This option tends to be especially good for fault management and reporting of real-time alarm conditions detected by the hardware.

For data collection, hardware probes tend to be more versatile and have more storage capacity than DSU/CSU-based systems. Probes also are more likely to be able to collect **Remote Monitoring** (RMON) information, which is used to analyze the activity of the upper-layer protocols running over the frame relay network.

On the other hand, enhanced DSU/CSUs are often simpler, cheaper, and quite sufficient for collecting useful management information. As we mentioned earlier, DSUs reside at "natural" monitoring locations in the network, just before the transmitted frames leave the customer's premises and enter the frame relay cloud. Enhanced DSUs are becoming more popular with customers and also with carriers who want to verify service level agreements.

Enhanced DSU/CSUs have some interesting features:

- Some vendors' DSUs can correlate frames traversing the PVC if the customer has an enhanced DSU at each end of the PVC. This allows accurate measurement of delays across the PVC, which is quite helpful for verifying the delay portion of an SLA. Correlation of frames is typically more accurate than "pinging," which is commonly used for delay measurement when DSU-based measurement is not available. Ping measurements can be distorted by congestion-induced delays within the device that is trying to turn the ping around and send it back to the source.
- Some enhanced DSUs can recognize network (layer 3) protocols so that they can report PVC traffic flows by protocol.
- Enhanced DSUs may or may not use SNMP to report their data to the vendor's associated analysis and display software, but most DSU analysis software can provide SNMP-compliant data to higher level management platforms.
- As noted earlier, enhanced DSUs report their data to their associated software packages via a separate management PVC, by piggybacking on an existing user data PVC (using proprietary methods), or with a LAN interface.

Software-Based

An alternative to buying data collection hardware and analysis/display software from the same vendor is to buy only the management software from a vendor. With this approach the vendor's software will collect information from various third-party sources, including, perhaps, network probes, enhanced DSUs, and routers. This type of software is either a general-purpose monitoring package that has been modified for frame relay or an enterprise-wide management platform that includes frame relay as one of the protocols it handles.

The software-based approach tends to be good for performance management and historical trend analysis, as opposed to the hardware-based approach, which tends to be better at fault management. Some companies use both types because they complement each other well.

Carrier-Based Monitoring

In place of, or in addition to, user-based monitoring, a customer can use a carrier-provided network management application. This application may be integrated into the customer's existing management platform. It may also be provided as a stand-alone turnkey solution on a separate workstation, or it may be Web based. In some cases the carrier may partner with an existing monitoring vendor, such as AT&T partnering with Visual Networks, to provide a monitoring solution for the customer.

Usually, carrier-based monitoring is read only. Thus, customers can use it for network monitoring and real-time (or near-real-time) statistics collection, but not for configuring equipment or services. However, a few carriers allow limited configuration, such as changing CIR within prescribed limits.

Managed Network Services

A last approach is to contract with a carrier or third-party network management firm that will provide comprehensive managed network services. This is discussed later, along with other, related topics.

Open Network Management Systems

For general-purpose enterprise management, major platforms are HP OpenView, Cabletron Spectrum, Tivoli TME 10, and IBM NetView/6000. For the SNA domain, the major platform is IBM NetView. Some companies that specialize in performance monitoring, especially through the use of network probes, are Concord Communications, DeskTalk Systems, and Kaspia Systems. One company that has pioneered the use of enhanced

DSU/CSUs for performance monitoring is Visual Networks, although there are others in this area.

Most of these vendors would describe their product architecture as open rather than proprietary, because their tools can accept and process standard SNMP messages generated by *any* element in the network being monitored.

Some enterprise management systems, or "managers of managers," can monitor system components beyond networking. They can monitor non-network elements that collect performance statistics from computing platforms, databases, middleware infrastructures, and even business applications. This overall system visibility can help isolate a troubleshooting problem to the appropriate domain. Too often problems are immediately associated with the network when in fact the culprit may be another component in the overall system.

Low-end, PC-based general-purpose management systems start in the low $1,000s. Higher end workstation-based management systems start in the $10K range and go up into the $100K+ range. However, the more sophisticated systems have *considerably* more capability for gathering and storing performance data, prioritizing alarms, displaying configuration information, and customizing the management system.

Frame Relay Network Management Functions

Having discussed the general functions of a network management system, we now examine these same functions in the context of frame relay.

Configuration Management

Configuration management means managing both equipment and connections, at both the physical and the logical level (see Figure 8.3). For a frame relay network, this includes managing

- DLCI assignment
- Sizing of port connection and virtual circuits
- Moves, adds, and changes (also known by the acronym **MAC**)
- Configuration of routers, FRADs, and so forth
- Planning and optimizing the network

To properly manage the configuration of a network, the network operators need the following:

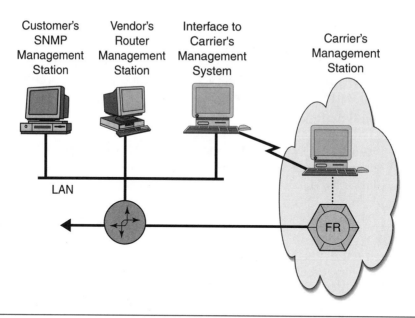

FIGURE 8.3 Configuration Management.   *Configuration management can include a combination of customer, vendor, and carrier management systems.*

Information about the current configuration, including performance. A customer-operated, SNMP-based management system can supply much of this information, especially for the customer's equipment. A carrier-provided management system can also give additional insight into the network configuration.

Tools for modifying the configuration in response to the information collected. The SET command of an SNMP system can be useful for simple configuration of customer equipment, but anything more complex will likely need to be handled by a vendor's proprietary tool. For instance, remote router configuration will almost certainly need to be handled by a tool that the router vendor provides.

For a public frame relay service, the carrier is usually able to provide a management system that shows the status of the customer's portion of the frame relay network. Such a system will often have a **graphical user interface** (GUI) with windowing that includes the capability to "drill down" into the details of the network. The carrier's management system may be based on a carrier-provided MIB, on the carrier's own proprietary management system, or on a hybrid.

An application can directly establish and configure an SVC in real time. However, most PVC configuration needs to be handled indirectly through the carrier. Some carriers are working on tools to allow more direct user control over PVCs, such as changing the CIR.

Fault Management

Fault management means collecting, keeping track of, and responding to network alarms (see Figure 8.4). For a frame relay network, alarms include

- Circuit failures
- Equipment failures
- Error rates that exceed predefined thresholds

An SNMP agent can be programmed to generate alarms if predefined thresholds are crossed. For instance, if the number of discarded frames goes above a certain number per minute, the agent that notices the condition can signal an alarm. Such alarms are sent as unsolicited TRAP messages by the agent to the SNMP management station. Alarms can be

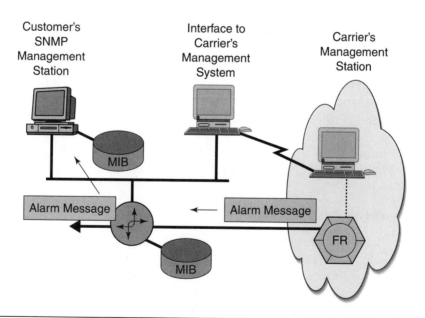

FIGURE 8.4 Fault Management. *Fault management depends on alarms sent from the customer's devices and/or carrier management systems.*

generated by SNMP agents in the customer's own equipment or by the carrier's management system.

Thus, a customer's SNMP-based management system can be a very useful tool for fault management. Alternatively, for public frame relay services the carrier can often provide a management system to collect and report alarms. Such a system may be combined with the carrier's configuration management system, discussed earlier. A carrier's management system may also have a direct link into the carrier to report and resolve problems. As usual, a carrier's system relieves the customer of having to build its own system, but it may not be readily customizable to meet the customer's unique needs.

The best approach for the customer may be to use *both* its own SNMP-based fault management system *and* one provided by the carrier. The customer's system can give an overview of the *entire* network, not just the frame relay portion. The carrier's system can give more detailed information and a direct link into the carrier. It may even be possible to integrate both systems onto a single workstation, such as an X-station or a Windows-based system.

Regardless of which fault-reporting tool is used, the responsibility for prioritizing and processing alarms is the customer's, unless the customer purchases managed network services from the carrier (discussed later). Many customer network management departments already have a history and procedures for handling network problems.

Assuming that the customer wants to access the carrier's management system in some way, the customer must decide whether to use an inband or out-of-band connection. An **inband connection** would typically be a PVC that accesses the carrier's SNMP or proprietary system. An **out-of-band connection** would be a dedicated leased line, an X.25 connection, or some other access method supported by the carrier. It might provide more safety in case of PVC outages but at a higher price. A good compromise might be to use a PVC with dial backup capability.

Performance Management

Performance management means collecting, interpreting, and judging information about the quality of service, the performance of individual frame relay components, and the performance of the whole network. Performance management can lead to proactive network management, especially the anticipating of network problems before they become network outages. Performance management can also be valuable for resizing virtual circuits and generally for network optimization and redesign.

Depicted in Figure 8.5, performance management is based on collecting large numbers of raw performance statistics and then summarizing them as more user-friendly performance measures that describe the health and growth of the network. Some of the more important measures are

- Frame counts and octet counts on entrance to and exit from the frame relay network, for each port connection, and across different time periods
- Number of discarded frames, for each port connection, in different time periods
- Utilization of each virtual circuit, as a percentage of CIR, across different time periods, including both average and peak utilization
- Congestion and discard information for each virtual circuit, including the number of frames marked discard eligible (DE bit set to 1)
- Statistics on which are the peak traffic periods
- Network availability
- One-way delay through the network

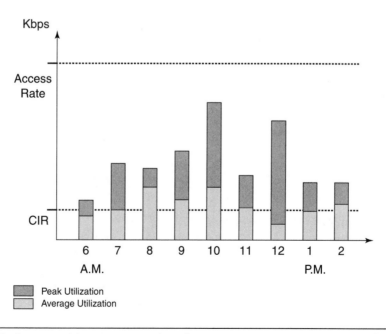

FIGURE 8.5 Performance Management. *A performance management system can display data useful for optimizing network design. This graph shows utilization of a PVC for a given day.*

The Frame Relay Forum has published FRF.13, *Service Level Definition Implementation Agreement*, which should help when comparing measurements taken by different tools.

As with configuration management and fault management, the measures mentioned above can be derived from three sources. A customer may want to use all three sources because each has a somewhat different view of the network.

- The customer's own SNMP-based management system, with access to the MIBs in the customer's own frame relay devices
- The customer's SNMP-based management system, but with access to the frame relay service provider's MIB
- A carrier-provided performance management system

However the raw performance statistics are obtained, the customer will need tools for storing, analyzing, aggregating, and displaying the performance results. These tools are applications that run on top of SNMP or other network management protocols and are not strictly a part of SNMP itself. As usual, the customer has four choices: build its own, customize an existing package, buy a plain-vanilla package, or depend on the service provider for performance information.

There is a trade-off between the amount and frequency of raw performance statistics collected (a more complete view of the network) and the amount of SNMP traffic generated (possible network congestion). Similarly, there is a trade-off between the value of establishing trends from historical performance data and the space the data takes.

Service Level Agreements

Acceptable levels of performance are often specified by a service level agreement (SLA). The carrier will usually offer an SLA to the customer with provisions for service credits if the terms of the SLA are not met. (Note, though, that service credits rarely make up for lost business due to extended downtime!) From the customer's point of view, verifying that service levels have actually been met can be difficult and may require the use of special monitoring equipment, such as enhanced DSUs.

SLAs usually specify parameters such as maximum delay time through the network (often 60 milliseconds or less), frame discard rate (often 0.1% or less, at or below CIR), network availability (99.9% or higher), and sometimes other measures [Wexler99]. However, the definitions and conditions for the parameters are usually complex.

SLAs have improved recently. One reason is advances in switching equipment. (See the section Second-Generation Switches in Chapter 7, Engineering of Frame Relay Networks.) A second reason is increasing use of ATM backbones, which automatically provide strong quality of service (QoS). (See Chapter 14, Frame Relay and ATM, for more details.)

Accounting Management

A carrier typically provides a company with enough accounting information that it can charge back to the individual departments if it chooses. Of course, the carrier may well charge for this service. The format of the accounting records is carrier proprietary. In practice, it may be a major headache to change frame relay service providers because of the consequent change in accounting procedures.

Security Management

Most companies do not bother much with security management for their frame relay networks beyond what they already have in place for their application programs. Because PVCs are private and typically run over dedicated access lines, most companies consider them secure enough. If necessary, companies can use end-to-end encryption of the data sent across PVCs or SVCs.

Managed Network Services

A frame relay customer may opt for managed network services. This means that the carrier provides comprehensive management services in addition to its transmission services. Alternatively, an independent management services firm may provide the managed network services. Such services may be an attractive option when the customer's existing network management staff do not have the resources, time, or expertise to manage the "new" frame relay network. Also, the use of managed network services may be part of a company's policy of outsourcing their noncore businesses.

Managed network services typically include most of the following elements (see Figure 8.6):

Initial network design. The carrier handles circuit layout, sizing, backup, and all aspects of the network design.

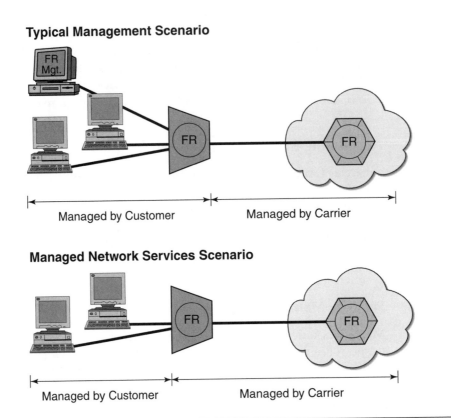

Typical Management Scenario

Managed by Customer   Managed by Carrier

Managed Network Services Scenario

Managed by Customer   Managed by Carrier

FIGURE 8.6 Managed Network Services.   *With managed network services, the carrier provides comprehensive management of the customer's frame relay devices and the network.*

Selection, configuration, and installation of frame relay equipment. This includes all the routers, DSU/CSUs, FRADs, and dial backup modems necessary for accessing the frame relay service. Router configuration by itself can be a headache.

Implementation plan.   The carrier typically works with the customer to develop a complete plan for the network and equipment installation. The document defines what the customer is responsible for and what the carrier is responsible for.

Fault detection and correction.   Various grades of network monitoring service may be available, from 7×24 to just business-day monitoring.

Maintenance.   The carrier maintains the hardware at the customer's sites. This may include an onsite spare parts inventory.

Ongoing configuration management. This includes handling moves, adds, and changes, especially for the router tables.

Performance reporting. The carrier provides performance summaries. These may be available from an online system or as hardcopy.

Performance evaluation. The carrier interprets the performance reports and makes recommendations for changes to optimize the network. This can be a very important and sometimes overlooked part of managed network services.

Planning for the future. The carrier works with the customer to plan for future growth and changes in the network.

Customer organizations may or may not be comfortable with buying managed network services. There is an element of uncertainty when an "outside" company is brought in to manage part of an organization's overall network. In the right situations, however, managed network services can be a wise business decision.

Chapter 9

Frame Relay Service Pricing

This chapter outlines pricing of public frame relay services. First we survey the general pricing structures used by carriers. We discuss how the FCC's decision to tariff frame relay services has affected the frame relay marketplace.

Then we examine the three major components of pricing that are typically used by all carriers:

- Access circuits
- Port connection charges
- Virtual circuit charges, including zero CIR versus fixed CIR

We show a generic tariff that indicates some "typical" prices and the relationships between port speed and CIR.

Next we describe a number of variations in pricing structures that are used by different carriers. These include usage-sensitive pricing, distance-sensitive pricing, simplex versus full-duplex pricing, and related issues.

We briefly survey pricing of SVCs and of international circuits. Then, lastly, we outline the ancillary services that most carriers can provide. These services are in addition to the basic data transport service and can be quite attractive to customers using a frame relay network.

Pricing Structures

Not only are the prices different for different carriers, but so are the pricing structures. There are some similarities in structure, and many variations. The main similarities are the three major components of pricing listed previously, discussed in more detail in the next section (Figure 9.1).

Most PVC services are priced as a flat monthly fee for each location connected to the frame relay network. However, there are many variations, such as zero versus fixed CIR, usage-sensitive pricing, distance-sensitive pricing, simplex or duplex connections, and limits on oversubscription. We explore these variations later in this chapter.

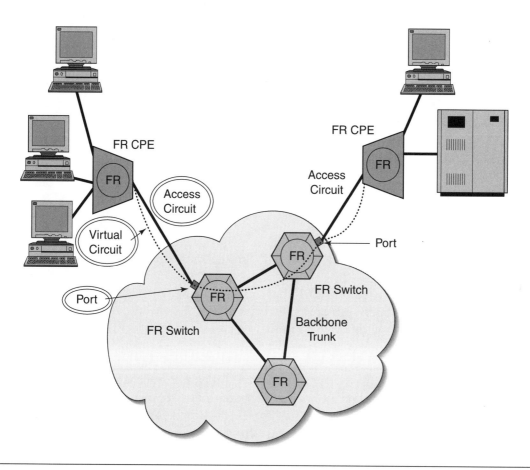

FIGURE 9.1 Pricing Structures.   *Frame relay pricing structures have three major components.*

Almost all carriers also offer volume and term discounts. For instance, a three-year contract could bring the price down by 10% to 15%. A combination of volume and five-year-term discounts could bring the price down by as much as 30%, and discounts are typically negotiable, especially for larger customers. However, there is risk associated with a long-term contract if market prices for frame relay services should drop, as they often have. To minimize these risks, business-savvy customers include price protection clauses in their contracts to ensure that their contracted price will decrease if market prices decrease. (More about this and related issues in Chapter 10, Procurement of Frame Relay Services.)

As usual, most of the charges have both a nonrecurring component (for installation and configuration) and a monthly recurring component. However, the one-time components can sometimes be reduced or waived depending on the size of the contract and the customer's negotiating skills.

In February 1996 the Federal Communications Commission (FCC) began to require tariffs of long-distance frame relay services as basic services. This has pushed the interexchange carriers (IXCs) away from confidential pricing and toward more uniform pricing structures. As a result, comparison between carriers has become easier, but it is still far from simple. The FCC is considering a long-term policy of eliminating *all* tariffs. If this happens, we may see a move back to confidential pricing.

Some industry analysts argue that without tariffing, we would have seen a drop of 10% to 30% in market prices over three years. But with tariffing, they argue, list prices become "sticky" as carriers "legally collude." Others argue that market forces will continue to push actual bottom lines for service contracts down as more package discounts and ancillary services are negotiated. Also, since networks that include protocol conversion are not basic services, but enhanced services, they legally do not have to be tariffed. Thus, strictly speaking, pricing for a network that does SNA-to-frame-relay conversion could still be confidential.

In fact, list prices for frame relay services have dropped somewhat, and negotiated prices have dropped even further, because of competitive pressures (sample prices are shown in Table 9.1).[1]

PVC Pricing

Three major pricing components for PVCs are common to all carriers: access circuit, port connection, and permanent virtual circuit charges.

---

[1]Prices vary considerably among carriers. This is only a generic sample of recurring charges.

TABLE 9.1 Sample Tariff—Monthly Charges

CIR (Kbps)	Port Speed (Kbps) and Cost ($)				
	56/64	128	256	384	1544
	$150	$275	$380	$500	$1500
16	$23*	$23	$23	$23	$23
32	$27	$27	$27	$27	$27
48	$37	$37	$37	$37	$37
64	$42	$42	$42	$42	$42
128		$72	$72	$72	$72
192			$105	$105	$105
256			$140	$140	$140
320				$174	$174
384				$210	$210
448					$245
512					$276
. . .					. . .
1024					$550

*Thus, a 64-Kbps port costs $150 a month, and one PVC with 16-Kbps CIR costs $23 a month, for a total cost of $173 a month for frame relay transport, exclusive of access circuit charges.

Access Circuit Charges

As discussed in Chapter 4, Connecting to the Network, there are actually several methods for connecting the customer's frame relay devices to the frame relay network: leased lines, local frame relay services, and dial-up access. Leased lines are by far the most common, so we focus on them here. Typically, the leased lines are available bundled or unbundled. **Bundled** means that the cost of the access lines is included as part of the frame relay service package. For bundled service the customer will likely not distinguish between the access charge and the port charge; together, these charges simply represent the fee for connecting to the network. **Unbundled** means that the access circuits are purchased separately, out of their own tariffs. An unbundled package may be more appropriate if the customer already has access circuits in place that are going to be converted to frame relay or if the customer intends to integrate other non-frame relay traffic over the access circuit (see Chapter 4, Connecting to the Network).

Normally the access circuit only needs to be provisioned to the frame relay carrier's nearest point of presence (POP). If the frame relay switch is not actually located at the carrier's POP, the carrier assumes responsibility for backhauling the circuit to the nearest frame relay switch. Backhauling is not uncommon, especially for IXC carriers, who may have widely scattered frame relay switches. Local carriers, however, sometimes charge for backhauling, although long-distance carriers usually don't.

The cost of access circuits is heavily dependent on local exchange carrier (LEC) local loop tariffs and on the length of the local loops. However, some LECs now offer flat-rate (distance-insensitive) local loops, which simplifies pricing computations. Because of the vagaries of LEC pricing for access circuits, this entire component is sometimes dropped in a comparison of two carriers' pricing structures. Note that an access circuit typically needs a DSU/CSU, although it may be purchased as CPE rather than leased.

By various estimates, 60% to 65% of frame relay leased access lines are 56/64-Kbps circuits. These speeds are adequate for most branch office applications. The other leased lines are almost all T1 or fractional T1 (FT1), with the remainder (1%) T3 or other high-speed lines [DNA-99].

Port Connection Charges

The port charge is a flat fee that covers the cost of the hardware port on the frame relay switch. The price varies with the bit rate supported. The lowest port speed available is 56 Kbps, which can be as inexpensive as about $75 a month from local carriers. The highest common port speed is 1.544 Mbps (sometimes labeled as 1.536 Mbps), which can be as much as $2,500 a month. Port speeds up to 45 Mbps (DS-3) are relatively rare and cost in the range of $5,000 to $15,000.

Depending on the carrier, port connections are also known as just ports, port speeds, access channels, or access rates. However, the terms "access channels" and "access rates" can easily be confused with the "access circuits" described earlier. The only relationship is that the port connection speed has to be less than or equal to the physical access circuit's speed (the physical circuit's clock speed).

Permanent Virtual Circuit Charges

This component of price is based either on the number of PVCs or on the CIRs of the PVCs. Zero CIR services (see Chapter 7, Engineering of Frame Relay Networks) base prices only on the number of PVCs because there is no CIR involved. Fixed CIR services include the CIR as part of the pricing structure, especially since the capacity engineering of the network is based on CIRs rather than port speeds. Fixed CIR is also known as assigned CIR, positive CIR, or non-zero CIR. Also, in their tariffs carriers sometimes refer to PVCs by the slightly misleading term "DLCIs." (See Chapter 3, Frame Relay Architecture, for the actual differences between PVC and DLCI.)

Note that different carriers put different weights on port charges and PVC charges. For instance, AT&T emphasizes port charges as compared to other carriers. This type of pricing structure tends to encourage a more highly meshed network because the additional cost of adding PVCs to an existing network is relatively low.

Variations in PVC Pricing

In addition to the three major pricing components discussed earlier, different carriers often have variations in their frame relay pricing structure (see Figure 9.2).

Usage-Sensitive Pricing

Some carriers vary their PVC charges by how much traffic the PVC transmits. The amount of traffic may be measured in bits, bytes, frames, or fixed-length interswitch cells, depending on the carrier. Usage-sensitive pricing is common for zero CIR PVCs, but is also sometimes available for fixed CIR PVCs. Most often, usage-sensitive pricing is simply linear, but with a minimum and with a cap that is reached quickly, even for relatively low traffic volumes. For instance, the customer might be charged $8 a month for an unused PVC, but might reach a cap of $75 a month with only router keep-alive (LMI) traffic on the PVC. This type of pricing is attractive for backup PVCs.

For a usage-sensitive zero CIR PVC, the cap is usually a fixed dollar amount. For a usage-sensitive fixed CIR PVC, the cap is often a percentage, such as 100% or 120%, of the corresponding non-usage-sensitive PVC charge for that CIR.

Distance-Sensitive Pricing

A few carriers, especially local ones, vary their PVC charges by distance, although most prefer the simplicity of non-mileage-sensitive pricing. As expected, longer PVCs cost more. At least one carrier uses mileage bands for the calculation. Customers with geographically concentrated networks might be attracted to distance-sensitive pricing. This variation, when it occurs, may be used by ILECs that provide the access circuit and then bun-

Usage-Sensitive Pricing

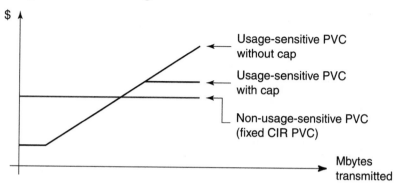

Distance-Sensitive Pricing

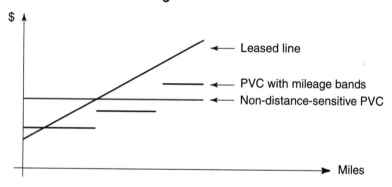

FIGURE 9.2 Variations in Pricing Structures. *Some carriers have usage-sensitive or distance-sensitive pricing for PVCs.*

dle its charge with the PVC charges. Also, some IXC carriers use distance-sensitive pricing for PVCs that cross an international border—for instance, from the United States to Canada.

Other Pricing Variations

Descriptions of some of the other SVC pricing variations follow.

Enhanced PVC service. A few carriers offer enhanced frame relay services that have "tighter" service level agreements (SLAs) and hence give higher quality of service. Often, one type of enhanced service is targeted at SNA traffic and another type at voice traffic. Enhanced services are noticeably more expensive, sometimes 50% more than plain-vanilla frame relay service. However, they may provide necessary quality of service for particular traffic types. In addition to enhanced PVC service, carriers typically offer many other ancillary services, which are discussed later in this chapter.

Simplex versus full duplex.   Many carriers offer the option of purchasing a PVC on a simplex, or unidirectional, basis. Thus, a normal full-duplex PVC could consist of two simplex PVCs, one in each direction. Furthermore, each direction could have a different CIR, which could be advantageous for customers with asymmetric traffic flows.

A few carriers also charge for each end of a PVC rather than treat the PVC as a single, end-to-end, chargeable item. This is sometimes called pricing by DLCI rather than by PVC. It is not necessarily the same as simplex pricing because it may not allow different CIRs in each direction.

Quantity discounts.   A few carriers have lower rates per PVC when there are many PVCs out of a port. For instance, the first five PVCs might be $15 each, the next five $10 each, and any additional ones only $5 each.

Oversubscription.   No carriers appear to charge for oversubscribing a port connection. However, some put limits on the amount of oversubscription allowed, such as 4:1 (400%), 2:1 (200%), or no oversubscription at all (1:1 or 100%).

Burst charges.   On usage-sensitive fixed CIR PVCs, some carriers charge slightly less for burst traffic than for traffic within the CIR. A variation is to charge a flat rate for traffic within the CIR and additional usage-based charges for burst traffic. However, discriminating in pricing between burst and nonburst traffic is not widespread.

LEC versus IXC carriers.   Local and some regional carriers often have simpler and very aggressive pricing, but they may lack fine granularity in port speeds and CIR. In particular, local carriers' prices may be 50% or less of the most expensive IXC carrier prices. Also, many local carriers, especially incumbents (ILECs), routinely bundle the access circuit charge *and* one "free" PVC into the frame relay price.

SVC Pricing

At the time of this writing, only a few public service providers offer SVC services; MCI was the first to venture into this arena. Thus, the ultimate pricing structure for SVCs is still unclear. However, in addition to the three pricing components for PVCs described before, SVCs will probably factor in connect time (holding time).

From the carrier's point of view, billing for SVC connect time is considerably more complex than billing for PVCs. This is one likely reason why MCI's initial announcement for SVCs was flat rate (not time sensitive).

We discussed advantages and disadvantages of SVCs in Chapter 5, Frame Relay Virtual Circuits.

International Issues

International frame relay services are typically much more expensive than their U.S. counterparts. Port and PVC charges may be 5 to 25 times U.S. averages; leased access circuits may be 2 to 5 times as expensive as in the United States and may have long lead times or not be available at all. Often much less capacity is engineered into the frame relay network. In some countries the connection to the customer's premises must be made with a local frame relay or X.25 network. And, of course, tariffing, availability, and local customs vary widely from country to country.

Ancillary Carrier Services

In addition to basic data transport over a frame relay network, carriers typically offer a number of ancillary services, for which pricing is quite variable. Many of the services can be quite valuable to a customer. Some of these services were discussed in Chapter 8, Network Management. Not every carrier offers all of the following services.

SNMP management capabilities.   SNMP-savvy customers can take more responsibility for monitoring the health and performance of their network, in near real time. This may also include the use of carrier-provided network probes or enhanced DSU/CSUs so that customers can better monitor whether carriers are complying with SLAs.

Network performance reports.   Monthly reports provide a snapshot of all data traffic in a variety of formats. They allow for detailed analysis of the data traffic on the network.

Full network management support.   Carrier-provided, full-service 7×24 network management support can reduce or replace the need for in-house monitoring, maintenance, and installation. Full support can include managing customer premises equipment, especially routers.

Consulting and design services.   The carrier can provide consulting and design expertise, especially for large or complex networks.

One-stop shopping.   The carrier can provide not only network design and network management but also selection and installation of hardware and circuits. Equipment can include routers, FRADs, and DSU/CSUs. The carrier can help with the customer's decision to purchase or lease equipment.

As an aside, a lease can be economical and can avoid the problem of getting locked into obsolete equipment. In a field that changes rapidly, such as networking technology, avoiding obsolescence can be vital.

Disaster recovery capabilities.   The frame relay carrier can design and provide redundancy in four areas: access circuit LEC backup, port connection backup, frame relay switch and backbone backup, and host disaster recovery.

Native protocol support.   The carrier's frame relay network can accept protocols such as X.25, asynch, and SDLC directly from the customer's site. The conversion to frame relay format is provided within the network itself rather than by the customer's equipment. Essentially, a FRAD function is built into the frame relay switch rather than being on the customer's premises. Alternatively, the FRAD may be a separate box, called a CO FRAD, on the carrier's premises.

Gateway access.   The carrier can also function as an **internet service provider** (ISP), providing access to the Internet or to other networks.

Service level agreements.   The frame relay service contract can provide for credits or other allowances if the carrier does not meet specified service levels. For instance, one carrier offers credits of 5% of the total monthly cost for failure to meet a frame delivery rate guarantee of 99% for zero CIR PVCs, or 99.9% for fixed CIR PVCs. A service level agreement can be a useful assurance that the carrier will engineer the network well. SLAs were discussed more fully in Chapter 8, Network Management, and they are touched on again in the next chapter.

Interworking with ATM.   The carrier can provide network or service interworking with ATM. See Chapter 14, Frame Relay and ATM.

Chapter 10

Procurement of Frame Relay Services

This chapter discusses procurement of frame relay services. First we outline the steps a customer might follow to make the procurement process go more smoothly. Next we elaborate on several of the steps of the methodology. In particular, we describe the objectives that a customer might have when considering procuring services. We also survey criteria for evaluating carriers and their proposals. We then outline the contents of a customer's **Request for Proposal** (RFP).

We include several tips for contract negotiations and close with comments on monitoring the contract.

The RFP Process

Typically, a customer will procure frame relay services by issuing an RFP to various carriers, evaluating their proposals, and selecting a carrier based on that evaluation. However, there are many other steps in the process to make it successful. We outline the steps here and elaborate on several of the more complex ones in succeeding sections. The assumption here is that the customer has already completed a feasibility study indicating that public frame relay services would be an appropriate part of its network.

1. Organize the customer team that will handle the RFP process. Often both the WAN manager and the Telecom manager should be included.
2. Set the objectives of the entire RFP process. (See the next section for more details.)

3. Determine the evaluation criteria that will be used to select the winning carrier (elaborated on in a later section).

4. Decide the overall methodology, which may be a modification of the steps in this outline.

5. Determine which carriers might be able to respond and then contact potential bidders.

6. Draft the RFP. (An outline for the RFP is given in a later section.)

7. Review preliminary material from carriers in order to decide on an appropriate bidder pool.

8. Send out the RFP to the carrier bidder pool.

9. Make visits to carrier facilities and contact references. Preferably, the carrier facility visited should be a network operations center. This will provide insight into the overall operation of the frame relay service. It is helpful to make site visits early so that the selection process does not drag on.

10. Respond to questions from carriers and distribute important clarifications to all other carriers.

11. Review proposals for completeness as they come in. Timely review by the customer helps avoid holes farther along in the evaluation process. Missing or incomplete responses can be discussed with the carrier during the next step, meeting with the carrier.

12. Conduct a meeting with each carrier to assess its "bench strength," discuss any issues that showed up in the proposal, and allow the carrier to further explain alternative network designs.

13. Evaluate each carrier's response, including the proposal, the meeting, the references, and any other information gathered about the carrier.

14. Develop a short list with remaining issues.

15. Gather additional information to resolve the remaining issues with each carrier.

16. Select the winner and notify the other carriers.

17. Refine and execute the implementation plan.

Objectives

Customers will have many objectives when considering frame relay services. This section outlines the typical ones.

- Strategic objectives, which include how the company expects to benefit from the upgraded network.

- Scope of project, which includes which part of the existing network will be upgraded and the extent of services provided. For instance, responsibility for procuring and managing the routers and DSU/CSUs must be clearly defined.
- Timeline objectives, which include when the different phases of the project should be completed.
- Performance objectives, especially by network application. These usually include throughput and response time and often availability and reliability.
- Maintenance objectives, which include maintenance costs and repair time.
- Training objectives, which include a description of which staff members need what sort of training. An RFP process is a good vehicle for becoming more knowledgeable about a technology.
- Implementation objectives, which include how the new network will be phased in.
- Expected deliverables, which include what the carriers should provide during the RFP process. (A sample outline for a proposal is given in a later section.)

Evaluation Criteria

Evaluating carriers and their proposals is an art rather than a science. Nonetheless, it is usually a great help to specify the criteria by which a carrier will be judged. Many analysts suggest numerically weighting the criteria along with assigning numerical ratings to each carrier for each criterion. Then spreadsheet software can give composite numerical scores that can strengthen the gut feel about a carrier or point out where perception needs to be sharpened.

Third-party consulting organizations such as the Gartner Group and the Meta Group can be useful for getting unbiased information that evaluates potential vendors.

There are several categories of evaluation criteria:

- Quality of the carrier's response, not only in the proposal itself but also in meetings and discussions with carrier staff. Quality can include the completeness and accuracy of the carrier's design of the customer's network.

- Equipment options, such as new CPE or upgrades to existing CPE, if desired.

- Circuit options, such as types of access circuit available.

- Service options, such as
  - International service availability (see Chapter 9, Frame Relay Service Pricing)
  - Protocol interworking (see Chapter 13, Internetworking with Frame Relay)
  - Integrated access (see Chapter 4, Connecting to the Network)
  - Internet access
  - Network-to-Network Interface availability (see Chapter 3, Frame Relay Architecture, and Chapter 4, Connecting to the Network)
  - Quality of service (QoS) or priority classes for different types of traffic (see Chapter 7, Engineering of Frame Relay Networks)
  - Billing and reporting alternatives

- Service level agreements and performance criteria, such as
  - Frame delivery commitments
  - Network availability
  - Network transit delay
  - Mean time to repair (MTTR)
  - Service installation lead times
  - Change order lead times
  - Escalation procedures and problem resolution

  (See Chapter 8, Network Management, for more details about SLAs.)

- Network management and operations, such as options for network management by the customer, proactive network monitoring by the carrier, and options for managed network services (see Chapter 8).

- Disaster recovery, including carrier rerouting of failed virtual circuits, PVC rehoming, and recovery options for failed access circuits. (See Chapter 4, Connecting to the Network; Chapter 5, Frame Relay Virtual Circuits; and Chapter 11, Design of Frame Relay Networks.)

- Price, including flexible pricing schemes and flexible contract terms. Both monthly recurring charges and one-time (installation and change) charges should be included. (See Chapter 9, Frame Relay Service Pricing, and a later subsection in this chapter.)

- Support, such as customer service, implementation support, and field support.

- Carrier's reputation in the industry. This may include checking contact references and finding out why each contact switched from his or her *previous* carrier.

- Internal network engineering, including:
  - Design of the carrier's backbone network, including hardware, topology, and architecture
  - Number and location of frame relay switches
  - Internal network management facilities and expertise
  - Ability to recover from failures
  - Capability for upgrading and for migrating to new technologies

The RFP

More than likely, the RFP outline will need to be modified to fit a particular company's needs.

I. Introduction

This section provides an overview and the conditions of the project.

- Project overview, which can include the key objectives for the RFP.
- Timeline for the RFP process itself and then for implementation.
- Ground rules, such as whether carriers will be able to rebid their price after the initial proposal or whether proposals that do not meet the format will be accepted.
- Summary of the customer's network organization, including staffing and network management tools. The purpose of this subsection is to give the carrier an idea of who will be supporting the new network when it is completed. Some network managers maintain that this should be only an internal process with the purpose of making sure that the customer is adequately staffed to handle the new network.

II. Current Network

This section describes the current network, so that carriers can know how the company has solved its networking problems to date. Generally, the more information a company supplies about its current network, the better the carriers can design an appropriate alternative.

- Overview of the current network.
- Description of the physical topology, with diagrams. Each circuit should have a description of the applications supported, the access type, the CPE in use, disaster recovery provisions, circuit backup, and performance information, such as utilization. However, if all the CPE selection and management will be done in house, the need for application and protocol descriptions becomes less important because the carrier will not be providing the routers or FRADs.

- Site information, including location, applications in use, number of users, CPE, disaster recovery requirements, and traffic patterns.
- Applications, including hardware, software, and protocols in use; traffic patterns; availability requirements; and performance information, such as size and frequency of transactions.
- Near-term plans.
- Limitations of the current network.

Much of this information can be presented as tables in an appendix. For some information, such as traffic patterns, the customer may want to present the data in a site view, in an application view, or in both.

III. Proposed Network

This section describes the results of the customer's design efforts. (See Chapter 11, Design of Frame Relay Networks.) The customer's design can be very minimal, but the danger is that it will be very hard to make an apples-to-apples comparison of the carriers' designs. A better approach is to give the carriers a detailed and careful customer-designed configuration that meets all of the customer's objectives and then let the carrier price it out. In the next section, give the carrier an opportunity to describe an alternative improved design.

- Overview of the customer's network design.
- Detailed objectives, as developed earlier in the RFP process, including all of the requirements for each site and application, and desired SLAs.
- Details of the customer's design, to the extent available.
- Contract conditions, which include both requirements and provisions that will be considered. An example might be a service satisfaction warranty or credit provisions for nonperformance by the carrier.

IV. Alternative Network Designs

This section is an invitation for the carrier to propose an alternative design (or designs) that better meets the customer's objectives and that more cost-effectively utilizes the carrier's products and services.

V. Additional Questions

This optional section gives the customer an opportunity to ask specific questions about the carrier's background, technical approaches, or other issues.

VI. Response Document

Specifying the format of the carrier's response to the RFP makes it much easier to compare what each carrier is offering. Here is a suggested outline:

Cover Document. Identifies respondent, contact personnel, and references.

Section I. Executive Overview

Section II. Background on Carrier

Section III. Proposed Network

Part 1. Proposed Network Design. The proposed design will include diagrams and descriptions of the proposed solution, using the customer's design as a basis. The proposed solution should offer greater detail and insight as to the specific implementation proposed by the carrier.

Part 2. Pricing. The pricing information should include total one-time and ongoing costs of the proposed network. This should be followed by a breakdown by site and by service component (equipment, access, ports and virtual circuits, maintenance, management, and ancillary services).

Part 3. Service Level Agreements Offered.

Part 4. Network Management. This describes the network management reports available, their frequency, and how close to real time the reports are.

Part 5. Disaster Recovery.

Part 6. Implementation Plan.

Part 7. Carrier's Experience. This might include descriptions of the carrier's experience with similar networks or with the customer's CPE.

Section IV. Alternative Designs.   In this section the carrier can propose alternative network designs that better utilize the carrier's strengths or better meet the customer's objectives.

Section V. Responses to Additional Questions.   Here the carrier should respond to the additional questions of the customer.

Section VI. Attachments.   The carrier can include additional carrier background, positioning, and collateral material.

VII. Attachments

This is where the customer can include any other material that might help the carrier create an improved design. Examples might be simulation studies, customer design worksheets, or additional traffic data.

VIII. Glossary

A glossary is particularly helpful for those terms that have an idiosyncratic use within the customer's organization. (And there are often many such unique terms!)

Contract Negotiations

Because of the difficulties in a point-to-point comparison of frame relay services, a comparison of contract bottom lines for a specific network may be necessary. Even this may be complicated if each carrier designs its own solution for the customer's network and the solutions have different performance goals or topologies. In addition, the usual nonmonetary factors, such as the carrier's reputation, "chemistry" with the customer, network management provided, reroute capabilities, architecture, and the like, all play a part in a contract decision.

The frame relay marketplace is very dynamic, and competition among service providers is keen. Even though tariffed rates may increase, overall prices of package contracts may well decrease, leading some market observers to recommend that prospective frame relay customers consider the following points:

- Seek bids from all service providers in order to maximize competitive forces.
- Whenever possible, compare specific prices for ports, PVCs, and CIR (if applicable).
- Ask for volume discounts, waivers of minimum usage commitments, free installation, and service credits for other use of the carrier's non-frame-relay services.
- Ask for free service for a month or more, while the frame relay service is on trial or in a side-by-side comparison with another carrier's service.
- Use growth in the customer's data traffic to renegotiate contracts for more favorable rates and terms.
- Bundle voice with frame relay traffic to obtain better rates for both.
- Keep contract terms short to take advantage of possible declines in overall market prices. Or demand a mid-contract fresh-look clause that allows renegotiation if market prices decline.
- Ask for reduced termination liability in case the customer wants out of the contract later.
- Include a business downsizing clause that allows the customer organization to reduce its volume commitment if its business takes a turn for the worse or if part of the organization is sold off.
- Never sign an exclusivity clause.
- Ask for a technology migration clause that doesn't limit the customer to frame relay if a better technology comes along.

- Demand that carriers' service quality standards are true performance guarantees, with penalties, and not just "service objectives."
- In service level agreements, distinguish between performance guarantees that involve traffic *offered* to the network and traffic *accepted* by the network. Guarantees about offered traffic are typically more useful because they correspond more closely to the performance needed by the end user.
- Seek flexibility in service substitutions, especially if service levels are not being met.
- Seek outage credits and damages in the case of service outages.
- Recognize that negotiating leverage increases with the size of the network.
- Use contracts or procurement departments, if available, because the staff are often professional negotiators familiar with the intricacies of contract terms.
- Consider separating the financial information from the technical information so that the technical recommendations can be based on technology without pricing biases.

Monitoring the Contract

The following are some tips for monitoring the contract:

- Meet regularly with both sales and technical carrier staff to stay on top of the network performance and contract provisions.
- Use the carrier's network management reports to verify, as much as possible, that the SLAs are being met. It is best to have independent data to compare against the carrier's reports.
- In many cases, the carrier's management reports are not adequate for verifying SLA provisions, especially transit delay guarantees. In such cases, consider installing WAN SLA monitoring tools if it seems worth the expense. (See Chapter 8, Network Management, for more details.)

Chapter 11

Design of Frame Relay Networks

In this chapter we discuss the design of user networks. We begin with an overview of the three scopes of network design. We follow this with a discussion of the issues in physical network and virtual circuit network design. The physical design issues include both backbone and access networks.

We outline the process of designing a customer's frame relay access network. This process can be carried out by the customer or by the service provider working with customer input. It includes setting objectives, collecting data, and choosing CIR and port speeds.

Frame relay networks typically match the underlying traffic patterns more closely than private line networks do. This usually results in a "flatter" network, with fewer concentration hubs and a less hierarchical structure. The frame relay network often has more mesh connectivity than traditional private line networks.

Next we discuss a simple example of a private line network. We redesign this network as star shaped and examine the new design's advantages and disadvantages.

We also redesign the private line network as a hybrid frame relay network, which combines both frame relay transport and a private line. We discuss the advantages and disadvantages of this hybrid design as well.

Finally, we change the traffic flow assumptions for the private line network so that the flows are more distributed rather than strictly centralized. This leads to a partial mesh frame relay redesign, which we also discuss.

We close by mentioning other design issues—namely, designing for performance, for switched virtual circuits, and for disaster recovery.

Overview

Frame relay network design can mean different things to different people. For example,

- Design of a public service provider's cloud
- Design of a customer's physical and virtual circuits for access to a public frame relay service
- Design of an enterprise's end-to-end private frame relay network

Design of a public service provider's cloud includes selecting a frame relay switch vendor, laying out the backbone trunks between switches, and sizing the network. These are all physical design issues, usually dealt with by a team from within the service provider's organization, who are often experienced at designing other types of networks and have the resources of a carrier to apply to the design problem.

Design of a customer's access network for connection to a public frame relay service includes both physical design and virtual circuit, or logical, design issues. The physical issues encompass number and size of local loops and types of customer premises equipment (CPE). The virtual circuit design issues encompass layout of virtual circuits, choice of CIR, performance, and generally the handling of traffic flows. Note that the physical access design focuses geographically on the area between the CPE and the port on the provider's switch. The virtual circuit access design focuses on virtual circuits that go from local CPE all the way "through the network" to remote CPE.

Various groups can perform access design; a customer design team might at least begin it. As discussed in Chapter 10, Procurement of Frame Relay Services, the customer will be in a better position for comparing proposals if it has done a complete network design in the RFP. However, service providers can also typically perform network design "from scratch," although they may bias the solution toward the features of their service or products. Consultants can always be hired to perform a relatively neutral design.

Design of a private frame relay network is the combination of cloud and access design, with the end-to-end network built and managed by a single enterprise for its own use. Thus, private network design shares much in common with public provider design. However, the designers of private frame relay networks may have less experience, although they typically have more control over the type and amount of traffic the network will have to carry. Private network designers also usually turn to enterprise class hardware, such as smaller frame relay switches, for their clouds rather than the more powerful and expensive carrier-class hardware found in public provider networks. Note that in spite of the word "private," designers of private networks typically lease the underlying physical circuits, both access circuits and backbone trunks, from a public carrier. "Private" indicates only that the resulting network is for the private use of the company that built it.

Public frame relay services are so mature that designing a private frame relay network involves more risk. A private solution involves a larger investment in skills and equipment, while it may not provide as many features or as much performance as a public frame relay service. Their investment includes the design, deployment, and management of the frame relay infrastructure.

Physical Network Design

Physical network design has two parts: design of the backbone network (the cloud) and design of the access network (the local loops). As stated in the previous section, physical design issues encompass number and size of circuits and selection of hardware, such as switches and CPE.

Backbone Network Design

Design of frame relay backbone networks, or clouds, is similar to backbone design for many other technologies, such as ATM or X.25 packet-switched networks. For public service providers the overriding design constraint is the amount of money they are willing to invest at a given point in time. A business decision is made to implement a certain amount of capacity at a given set of locations. If customer demand exceeds this capacity, the carrier will simply have to forgo the business until the next infrastructure expansion cycle, or else risk straining the network beyond its design limits.

The basic "hard," or quantitative, issues are

- Location of the switches
- Layout, or topology, of the backbone trunks
- Capacity of the trunks

The "softer," but still important, issues for backbone design are

- Handling growth of the network
- Developing a nondisruptive migration strategy for future services, applications, and technologies
- Handling traffic congestion
- Selecting a switch vendor and appropriate switch features

Carriers will have network design tools, often proprietary, to help them with the quantitative issues. Private network designers may turn to commercial network design tools or consultants to obtain them. These design tools typically rely on techniques such as queueing theory or computer simulation from the fields of operations research and mathematical optimization.

For these tools to work well, they need explicit input in the form of how much traffic on the average will be sent from each ingress switch to each egress switch, and how much various speed circuits will cost between each pair of switches. Unfortunately, network designers, especially those who design public networks, often do not know average traffic flows in advance, even if they might know where the switches will be located. Thus, backbone network designers are typically faced with many uncertainties and need to make crucial guesses about the traffic that the network must carry.

One alternative to the "rational," tool-based approach we have been describing is to simply throw together some switches and backbone circuits, see how much customer demand materializes for the resulting network, and plan on upgrading the network quickly if it runs out of capacity. The disadvantage with this approach is that the backbone network can be wastefully underutilized in some regions while it is simultaneously overutilized, and hence congested, in other regions. Backbone design in a dynamic environment is not easy, as Internet service providers already know.

We also note that large public frame relay service providers do not actually use frame relay in the core of their networks, but use an ATM backbone instead. This does not change the fundamental frame relay backbone design problem. Rather, the trunks between frame relay switches become ATM circuits, and all the frame relay switches become edge devices on the ATM cloud. Then the ATM backbone must provide the reliability and capacity needed by the frame relay "backbone." (See Chapter 14, Frame Relay and ATM, for more details about frame relay and ATM interworking.)

Now we look briefly at each of the design issues mentioned before.

Switch Location

Location of frame relay switches is constrained by several factors:

- How much money the carrier is willing to spend to roll out frame relay switches.
- How expensive it is to backhaul a circuit from a carrier's point of presence (POP) to the nearest frame relay switch. Note that a carrier may have many more POPs than frame relay switches.
- Where the carrier, or enterprise, can physically locate switches. In particular, whether the carrier can colocate at a LEC's premises if it does not have its own physical facilities.

Commercial network design tools usually have modules for finding optimal switch locations. However, as discussed earlier, because of the lack of input data, designers may have to wing it and make ad hoc decisions about placement.

When possible, requirements for the location of switches should have input from the marketing and sales divisions. Pricing, promotion, and sales strategies will affect the deployment of new infrastructure.

Backbone Trunk Layout

Layout of the backbone trunks means which switches will be directly connected to which other switches by backbone circuits. This is also commonly known as topology design or sometimes meshing or alternate pathing. Layout is one factor in the cost of the network. It is also important because it determines the connectedness of the network, which means its robustness in the face of trunk or switch failures. Highly connected backbone networks are more reliable and have higher availability, but are also more expensive to build.

Note, though, that a highly connected network is an advantage only if the carrier can reroute virtual circuits in the event of failure. If a carrier has no reroute capability, then, when a trunk breaks, all the virtual circuits that travel across it will remain down until the trunk is fixed, even if alternate physical paths are available.

Again, network design tools can help with the topology design problem and decrease network costs. However, to use a design tool well may require some knowledge of graph theory and a time investment to become familiar with the tool. To avoid the use of such tools, some network designers simply use rules of thumb, such as connect each switch to at least two other switches. These rules of thumb are also often used for design of a customer's router networks.

Trunk Capacity

The last piece of quantitative network design is sizing, or determining the capacity of, the backbone trunks. Sizing clearly affects costs. It also affects performance because the capacity of the trunks is one of the major determinants of average network delay across the network. As usual, capacities only come in certain increments, such as OC-3 (155 Mbps) or OC-48 (2.5 Gbps).

Network Growth

Carriers, or private network designers, need to plan for growth in the network. Growth can occur in traffic volumes, in numbers of virtual circuits, and in new services. Here are some questions to ponder. If traffic volumes double, can the backbone design be incrementally scaled, or must it be completely redesigned? How can new switches and trunks be rolled out with minimal impact on existing customers? How can new services, such as SVCs or priority classes of service, be implemented with minimal disruption of the existing network? Since these are soft issues rather than quantitative ones, commercial network design tools will have only a minor role, which is to answer "what if" questions.

Traffic Congestion

As discussed in Chapter 6, Traffic Management, congestion can be a serious problem for networks of all types. Carriers need provisions for avoiding congestion in the first place and for controlling it if it does occur. However, the particular switch type chosen by the carrier will determine many of the mechanics of congestion control. As discussed in Chapter 7, Engineering of Frame Relay Networks, once a carrier chooses a switch type, it may then be locked in to supporting and marketing its particular congestion mechanisms.

Switch Vendor Selection

Once a design team has identified the required and desirable features of their frame relay network, they can sort through the available vendors' switches to determine which one is the best compromise for their needs. As usual, this is a complex process, where technical, political, sales, and economic factors all play a role.

Access Network Design

Like backbone design, physical access network design includes determining circuit capacity and vendor hardware. However, unlike backbone design, the issues of equipment location and circuit layout are usually obvious, and handling network growth and congestion is usually left to the service provider. Thus, the physical access designer must decide the following:

- Number, type, and service provider for local loops between customer premise equipment and the service provider's cloud
- Capacity of each local loop, which in turn determines the port speed for the carrier's end of the local loop
- Backup, if any, for each local loop
- Type and features of customer premise equipment

As with backbone design, rational access design depends on reasonably accurate cost and traffic estimates. In this case, the traffic forecasts are for the total number of bits per second that need to be transmitted in each direction for each customer site over some predefined time interval, such as "the busy hour." Network designers often obtain these totals from the virtual circuit network design, described later. Unlike backbone design, a spreadsheet is usually sufficient for access design rather than more sophisticated design tools.

The network designer may also want to consider voice requirements of each site. By using integrated access for the voice and frame relay traffic, he or she may by able to lower costs without sacrificing performance.

Since the inputs to physical access design often depend on the results of the virtual circuit network design stage, described next, a later section will give more detail about the customer's entire network design process.

Virtual Circuit Network Design

Now that we have introduced physical network design, which focuses on the physical components of a frame relay network, we turn to virtual circuit design, which focuses on the end-to-end traffic flows through the network. The specific issues are

- Layout of the virtual circuits to handle the traffic flows
- Choice of CIR for each virtual circuit
- Performance expectations

Connection-oriented packet-switched networks, such as frame relay networks, have an important advantage over older leased line/multiplexer networks. With leased line networks, if a designer wants to support a traffic flow between two locations, he has to provision a leased line between the two locations or else send the traffic through one or more intermediate hub locations, typically routers. An individual leased line is expensive and, if its utilization is low, also inefficient. Sending the traffic through an intermediate router increases the number of router hops and can increase the delay time.

With a virtual circuit network, the designer may be able to cost-justify a virtual circuit between the two locations, which will typically be less expensive than a physical circuit. Such a virtual circuit will also decrease the number of intermediate router hops, and, if the utilization of the virtual circuit is low, the unused bandwidth will be allocated to other users. Thus, virtual circuits offer design alternatives that are not economical or feasible with physical circuits.

The usefulness and simplicity of virtual circuits for supporting traffic flows is illustrated in a simple case study later in this chapter. Choosing CIR and managing performance expectations are discussed later as well.

The Access Network Design Process

Now that we have surveyed network design issues, we look at the process of designing a customer's frame relay access network, which is the most common design activity a customer will be involved with. The customer may initiate this design process or may ask the service provider to do it. In either case, our "roadmap" gives guidance on the steps to follow. Note that even if the service provider's design team comes up with the final design, they will still need substantial information from the customer, in the form of requirements and traffic data. The following steps in the design process are discussed next:

1. Set objectives
2. Inventory the sites
3. Collect traffic statistics
4. Sketch the PVC map
5. Consider asymmetric PVCs
6. Determine CIR
7. Determine port connection speed

8. Determine access circuit speed
9. Decide on backup options
10. Plan for implementation
11. Implement and fine-tune

Set Objectives

The basic measurable objectives are response time or network delay (for interactive applications), throughput (for batch applications), and availability or reliability of the network. Less measurable, but still important, might be to have consistent response times throughout the network or to minimize human network management. (Network objectives were discussed in Chapter 10, Procurement of Frame Relay Services.)

The more the network objectives can be quantified, the better. When asked about network objectives, the typical response from a senior executive is, "Give me the fastest, most reliable network at the lowest price." This is a good qualitative goal, but it is almost useless for analyzing the quantitative trade-offs that show up in actual design. Numbers like a maximum 1-second response time for SNA, a maximum 60-millisecond response time for interactive character-based applications, and availability of 99.996%—all for $500,000—are *much* more useful for rational network design. Sometimes, prototype systems that executives can play with are helpful for giving them the "feel" of various performance objectives.

Although some network managers only pay lip service to this step, setting objectives in some fashion is vital for the later steps of making decisions about connectivity, CIR, costs, and so forth.

Inventory the Sites

The network designer needs to know what sites are, or need to be, on the network. She must be aware of which sites are backup data centers for disaster recovery and what their capabilities are. In addition, the designer needs to understand what hardware, software, applications, protocols, and network access are available at each site. It is also helpful when designing backup to know how critical each site is. In some cases, the designer may also be interested in non-frame-relay traffic that might be migrated to frame relay or that might contribute to a volume discount in the contract.

When faced with the problem of simply identifying all of a company's sites, one new designer had the clever idea of dumping the human resources database to find where everyone's offices were located and then calculating a head count for each location.

Collect Traffic Statistics

Along with the site inventory, the designer needs to know what the traffic patterns are between sites. The traffic patterns depend on which applications are used at each site. Traffic patterns can include averages for messages per second, total bytes per port, and daily and monthly utilization patterns. Expected traffic growth is also important. Some designers estimate that the inventory and data collection steps can take over half of the entire design effort. If voice will be sent over frame relay, or if two different networks will be consolidated, appropriate traffic statistics will also need to be collected.

Traffic statistics are valuable for network sizing. However if they cannot be collected, it is still possible to make guesstimates and refine the network design after examining several weeks of performance reports. One helpful guesstimate is to assume that the total of bits per second generated at a site is proportional to the head count at that site, regardless of the site's actual mix of applications.

Since frame relay projects are often precipitated by packaged business applications, such as SAP and PeopleSoft, business owners cannot always anticipate the traffic that will traverse the network. However, the vendors of these packaged applications can often provide models to estimate traffic volumes and even CIRs. In this case, network designers would do well to speak to the application vendors to obtain these modeling tools or at least the rules of thumb to use.

Sketch the PVC Map

The network designer plots all of the company's sites on a map and then sketches in the direct frame relay connections. The direct connections—the PVCs—are determined from the traffic statistics. If two sites need to communicate and the volume of data is large enough, a PVC between them is cost justifiable. Note that the PVC map does *not* need to reflect the existing private line network, as seen in the case study later in this chapter. Another trap to avoid is assuming that every branch office needs to communicate only with its regional office. In some cases the branch office may have enough traffic to cost-justify a PVC to headquarters.

Still another trap is to provision too many PVCs on a single router WAN port. The designer may want to speak to the router vendor's technical staff to ensure that the equipment can handle the desired number of PVCs on a single serial port. As a point of reference, a Data Network Associates study estimates that the average number of PVCs per 56/64-Kbps frame relay switch port is about 2 and that the average number of PVCs per T1/E1 port is about 12 but that a few ports have more than 256 [DNA-99].

Since the PVC map has a big effect on the subsequent design steps, the designer may want to try several "what if" scenarios at this step and see which one leads to a better design.

Consider Asymmetric PVCs

If the amount of traffic in one direction is much greater than in the other direction, the designer may want to consider the use of asymmetric PVCs, sometimes also called simplex PVCs. This allows the CIR sizing to be different in each direction. (See Chapter 6, Traffic Management, for more details.) However, not all carriers offer asymmetric PVCs. In addition, the extra design effort might not be worth the cost savings, especially since the cost of CIR is relatively low compared to that of port capacity and local loops. If asymmetric virtual circuits are used, a systematic way to handle them is to consider only the *outbound* traffic requirements from each site. The inbound traffic across a virtual circuit to a site will then be the outbound traffic across "the other end" of the virtual circuit from some other site. Also note that even if the designer does not want to use asymmetric connections, it may still be worthwhile to estimate the CIR in each direction of the connection and then use the greater of the two values as "the" CIR for the bidirectional connection.

Determine CIR

Taking into account the previously collected traffic statistics, or the best available guesses, decide the committed information rate (CIR) for each PVC. The CIR should support the expected average traffic rate across the PVC over relatively long periods of time, say, the busy hour.[1] Generally, the burst capability of the PVC should not be counted on for routine transmission, but should be viewed as bonus capacity for handling large file transfers, for busy periods, and for generally smoothing out performance. Even for zero CIR PVCs, the designer needs an estimate of average traffic rate to determine the port speed.

---

[1]Defining the busy hour exactly can be a controversial process. Different industries seem to take different approaches. One question that always arises is whether the busy hour will be defined by the high-water mark of traffic volume or some percentage of it or some kind of average maximum.

Another method for estimating CIR is to rely on equipment vendor suggestions. For instance, a voice FRAD vendor will likely suggest a specific CIR for optimal operation of the FRAD. Also, a company may have developed rules of thumb from its own experience with how much throughput is needed to support certain applications.

If the carrier allows the maximum burst rate (excess information rate, or EIR) to be set, it should be set to support momentary traffic peaks. More often, though, the carrier automatically sets the maximum burst rate at the speed of the local loop, which is the same as the port speed.

There is an alternative approach for setting the CIR. Some designers set it as low as possible without compromising the frame discard percentage and the network transit time on the PVC. This is a risky strategy because network congestion will have a stronger effect on these "narrow" PVCs than on PVCs with an adequate CIR. On the other hand, for an over-engineered carrier's network, and especially when the local loop carries only one PVC, this can be an effective cost-saving strategy. To defeat this approach, some carriers place limits on how small the CIR can be compared to the port speed. Other carriers may allow, for instance, a single PVC with a 4-Kbps CIR on a 64-Kbps port, but maintain that it will hurt the application.

Determine Port Connection Speed

Once the PVC layout and the CIR of each PVC have been decided, determine the port connection speed for each access circuit into the frame relay network. Start with the *total* of all CIRs coming *in* to the customer's router or other CPE. (Inbound PVCs are not buffered at the routers the way outbound PVCs are, so their port connection speeds are more critical.) Adjust for the oversubscription level (see Chapter 6, Traffic Management), typically between 100% to 200%, which will depend on how intermittent and mutually exclusive the applications are. For instance, if the sum of all the inbound CIRs is 300 Kbps and the port subscription amount is 200%, consider a port speed of at least 150 Kbps (300 ÷ 2 = 150), and then check this tentative port speed for being able to handle the aggregate *outbound* PVCs from the customer's location. The result is the appropriate port connection speed. Note that the port speed applies separately to the inbound and outbound traffic. For instance, a port speed of 64 Kbps means that the port hardware will handle 64 Kbps inbound and also 64 Kbps outbound at the same time, without interference between the two data streams. Also note that a PVC that is inbound to the customer is outbound from the carrier's perspective.

When a port carries only one PVC, the method described above, which uses the sum of the CIRs coming in to a port, does not apply. Instead, some designers use the rule of thumb that the port speed should be about double the CIR of that lone PVC to give some headroom for bursting above the CIR. Hence, one might see a 32-Kbps CIR PVC on a 56-Kbps port.

Determine Access Circuit Speed

Sizing the access loop is relatively easy. It needs to be at least as fast as the port connection to which it is attached. The private line options are relatively limited: 56/64 Kbps (DS-0), fractional T1 ($n \times 64$), and T1, possibly higher. (See Chapter 4, Connecting to the Network, for more discussion about access options.)

Decide on Backup Options

As discussed in Chapter 4, the designer has four major options for backup of the access circuit:

- Dial backup, which can be used to dial around a failed access circuit or, more commonly, to bypass the entire frame relay network and go straight to the remote site
- Physically diverse SONET rings for access
- Alternate networks, such as a data-oriented VPN
- Waiting for repair by the local loop service provider

More on application backup in the later section, Designing for Disaster Recovery.

Plan for Implementation

The network designer may want to consider a pilot network to test out the design assumptions. The pilot network can be the first phase of a phased roll-out of frame relay. The designer can run the pilot in parallel with the existing network and benchmark the two. Make sure there is enough time at the beginning of the implementation plan for shaking out the inevitable problems. As one wag says, "Implementation is not a benign process!"

Implement and Fine-Tune

One of the advantages of frame relay is that it is relatively easy to reconfigure PVC paths, CIRs, and port speeds. Once the designer has developed a historical base of performance reports, this fine-tuning can begin. Changing access circuits is not quite as easy because it usually involves reprovisioning from the local telco. However, the original access circuits may have enough extra capacity to support some growth in PVC traffic.

Case Study: Redesigning a Private Line Network

Suppose a customer wants to redesign a traditional hierarchical private line data network as a frame relay network. Furthermore, suppose the private line network has a particularly simple *centralized* traffic pattern. All the regional offices and branch offices need to communicate only with headquarters, not with each other. Thus, the network has a physical star topology (or compound star, or hub and spoke). It is also a logical star (in terms of traffic patterns). A simple example of such a network is shown in Figure 11.1.

Solution 1: Star Topology Frame Relay Network

Figure 11.2 shows the result of redesigning the private line network as a frame relay network. Here we consider a frame relay network with PVCs rather than SVCs, because PVCs are much more common in the market-

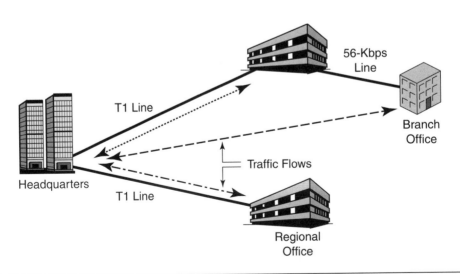

FIGURE 11.1 Private Line Network with Centralized Traffic. *A star-shaped private line network can be easily redesigned as a frame relay network.*

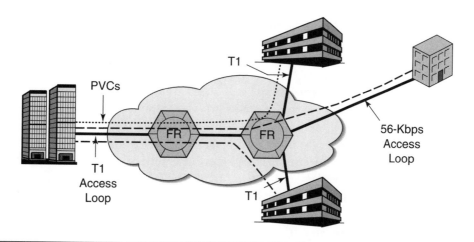

FIGURE 11.2 Star Frame Relay Network. *The results of redesigning a star-shaped private line network as a frame relay network.*

place. Like the traffic flow of the private line network, the PVC configuration in the frame relay network is star shaped. Later in this chapter we consider the selection of CIR and port speeds for this example.

Advantages

Note several general advantages of the frame relay network in this example:

- The headquarters site needs only half as many access circuits, DSU/CSUs, and router ports (assuming routers are being used). This means lower local loop and equipment costs at the headquarters site.
- The headquarters site may still be able to make do with a single T1 access loop because of the benefits of oversubscribing the port connection in the nearby frame relay switch. This of course depends on the traffic characteristics, but a subscription rate of 200% is not unreasonable for intermittent traffic. Oversubscription would translate into lower access line costs and lower port connection charges at headquarters.
- Replacing the long-distance T1 lines into headquarters with PVCs will likely reduce costs. This is because frame relay access circuits are typically at least 10% to 30% cheaper than end-to-end long-distance circuits.

- The carrier will typically provide automatic reroute capability within the frame relay cloud in the event of failure. Even though the access circuits do not have backup in this example, the frame relay network is still likely to have higher availability than the private line network. This is because the private line network has no built-in redundancy.
- From the customer's point of view, the topology of the frame relay network is simpler than the private line network. The frame relay topology has only one level, and each site is connected directly to the frame relay cloud. The private line network has two hierarchical levels, and the regional sites are traffic hubs for the branch sites. Hence, the frame relay network will likely have reduced administrative and management costs.
- The overall performance may benefit because of the frame relay network's ability to handle bursts of traffic across the network. As discussed in Chapter 6, Traffic Management, if the network has extra capacity, a PVC can transmit more traffic than its agreed-upon CIR. Depending on how the virtual circuit is provisioned, the service provider's policies, and the amount of congestion, a PVC may be able to burst up to the speed of its access loop.

Disadvantages

The frame relay network also has some disadvantages:

- The customer will need either frame-relay-capable equipment at all of the sites or FRADs located within the carrier's network that can convert the customer's legacy protocols to frame relay. Upgrading modern routers with frame relay cards is easy. Upgrading front-end processors and cluster controllers may not be so easy.
- Frame relay network response time is not as consistent or predictable as that for the private line network. However, at roughly 30–100 milliseconds for one-way transit delay through the carrier's network, frame relay response time is likely to be adequate. In addition, as discussed in Chapter 8, Network Management, service level agreements (SLAs) can increase the customer's comfort level about network delay.
- Network management staff need to become familiar with new network management tools, a new service offering, a new protocol, and possibly a new service provider.
- Depending on distance and tariffs, giving the branch office its own PVC into headquarters may not be cost effective. If not, a possible hybrid solution should be considered.

The Branch's View

We look at the example of the star frame relay network yet again, this time from the point of view of the branch office.

- The branch office *may* experience less delay and better performance because its PVC now goes directly to headquarters (through the frame relay network). In the private line network the branch office had two hops into headquarters. However, performance depended on how much delay the regional hub introduced and on how much delay the frame relay network had. A multilevel hierarchical private line network with many hubs in tandem could have a relatively large amount of delay, especially round trip delay. Typical public frame relay networks usually have less than five switches in a PVC path or have a fast ATM backbone between edge frame relay switches. Private frame relay networks usually have only one or two switches to cross.

- In the frame relay network the regional office sees less congestion because it is not acting as a hub for the branch office. However, this might also cause some political fallout because the regional office might no longer be able to justify the larger budget that supported the branch office.

- Replacing the private line from the branch into the regional office with an access circuit into the frame relay network *may* reduce costs. However, this depends on distance and tariffs. Because frame relay is distance insensitive, its intraLATA connections of more than a few miles are often less expensive than private lines.

  As a rule of thumb, the mileage crossover points are a few miles for intraLATA connections, roughly 100 miles for connections from regional providers, and roughly 400 miles for connections from national IXCs. Beyond these distances a frame relay connection is likely to be less expensive than a private line.

- The branch office will likely see higher network availability because it is not held hostage by failures in the regional office equipment or in the links in and out of the regional office.

- The frame relay solution may be attractive if the customer operates the network using a full cost recovery model. The customer's network operations staff can more easily calculate and justify the frame relay chargeback to the branch office. The chargeback calculations for a shared leased line network can be quite complex.

- As the private line network grows more complex, the vulnerability of the branch office to upstream failure becomes worse geometrically. As a frame relay network grows more complex, its vulnerability to failure increases much more slowly.

Solution 2: Hybrid Frame Relay Network

Suppose that, in the example of a star topology frame relay network, giving the branch office its own PVC cannot be cost justified. Then we might want to keep the tail circuit from the regional office to the branch, as shown in Figure 11.3. This has some advantages:

- The hybrid solution keeps costs down without sacrificing connectivity.
- The tail circuit part of the private line network can be preserved. Sometimes it is simplest to maintain the status quo at small branch offices and minimize the introduction of new networking equipment.

Hybrid solutions such as this one may be especially appealing if

- The remote site has low traffic volume.
- The remote site is close to a customer's regional site, or other hub, but far from the frame relay carrier's nearest POP. Note that it usually doesn't matter how distant the carrier's frame relay switch is, because the carrier will backhaul from its POP to the switch, if necessary, at

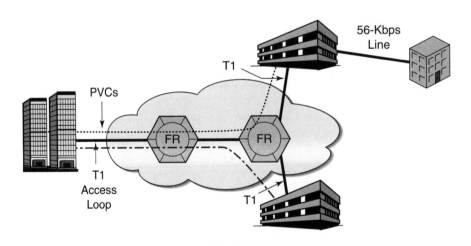

FIGURE 11.3 Hybrid Frame Relay Network.   *A star-shaped private line network can also be redesigned as a hybrid frame relay network.*

no charge. However, also note that some local exchange carriers (LECs) do charge for backhauling.

For a hybrid solution such as the one pictured, the customer may want to consider the use of FRADs at the regional office. FRADs are especially designed to concentrate traffic from various non-frame-relay sources and convert it to frame relay format for transmission to a carrier's switch. Of course, a frame-relay-capable router can also be placed just in front of the hop to the carrier's switch.

The idea of hybrid private line and frame relay networks is also useful in other situations:

- Suppose two data centers are connected by an existing private line network, and the company wants to maintain tight control of its intra-center link but also wants to expand frame relay connections to its remote sites. The company could use a router at each data center that would decide whether a particular packet should be routed across the private net or through the frame relay network. The frame relay network could even be used as a backup for the private net.
- Suppose a company uses two separate local frame relay networks that do not have a Network-to-Network (NNI) interface between them. The company could use a leased line to connect the two frame relay networks, possibly with a private NNI implementation. Alternatively, the two frame relay networks could meet at a common router that is operated as a frame relay gateway by the customer.

Solution 3: Partial Mesh Topology Frame Relay Network

Now suppose the traffic pattern in Figure 11.1 is not completely centralized but more distributed. In particular, suppose the two regional offices also need to communicate with each other, as shown in Figure 11.4. In the private line network, the inter-regional traffic must go through headquarters because of the star topology of the network.

In the redesign of the private line network as a frame relay network, the logical connection between the two regional offices can be handled by a PVC between them, as shown in Figure 11.5. This illustrates one of the major advantages of frame relay. A mesh network of PVCs can handle the actual traffic flows, or put another way, a frame relay network can capture the underlying traffic pattern more cost effectively than a private line network can. The logical traffic pattern does not have to be force-fitted onto the physical network.

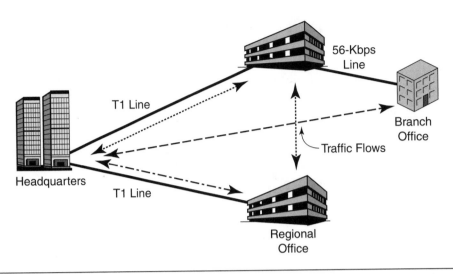

FIGURE 11.4 Private Line Network with Distributed Traffic.   *A private line network similar to that in Figure 1.1, but with traffic added directly between the two regional offices.*

Thus, we have these advantages of the partial mesh frame relay solution:

- Adding another PVC to handle a logical traffic flow is relatively inexpensive. Since PVC charges are generally low compared to port connection charges, the marginal cost of adding another PVC out of a port is relatively low. Furthermore, if the PVC is simply handling traffic that otherwise would have gone a more roundabout path, the port speed does not need to be increased when the PVC is added.
- Provisioning another PVC for an existing frame relay network is easy for carriers. The maximum time should be several days, often much less.
- As noted earlier, adding a PVC between the two regional offices eliminates an extra hop through headquarters. This not only improves delay between the regional offices, but also decreases "pass-through" congestion at headquarters.

We also note these disadvantages:

- PVCs cost money. The network costs for a partial mesh network are usually higher than for a star network. This may be offset, though, by less need for large port connection speeds, routers, and equipment at the central site.

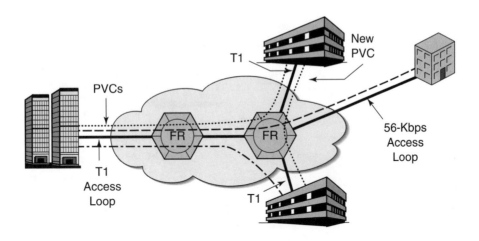

FIGURE 11.5 Partial Mesh Frame Relay Network. *A private line network with distributed traffic can be redesigned as a partial mesh frame relay network.*

- The customer may need to be somewhat more careful about PVC CIR sizing, since multiple PVCs are sharing an access circuit. However, this is not as serious as it sounds, because performance reports can indicate when the initial CIR estimates need to be changed.

Note that two locations not connected by a PVC can still communicate through a third site. For instance, the branch office can communicate with the other regional office through headquarters, but it will need *two* hops through the frame relay network.

The extreme case of a partial mesh network is to put a PVC between *each* pair of customer locations—this is a *fully meshed* network. It is probably unnecessarily expensive for most companies' connectivity requirements.

Finally, for the partial mesh frame relay network of Figure 11.5, we show in Figure 11.6 the results of choosing CIR and port speed. Note that, according to the design process steps listed earlier, we would first decide CIRs, then port speeds, then finally local loop speeds, to get the resulting network in Figure 11.6.

Other Design Issues

Designing for Performance

From the customer's point of view, the following are several design possibilities for improving the performance of a frame relay network.

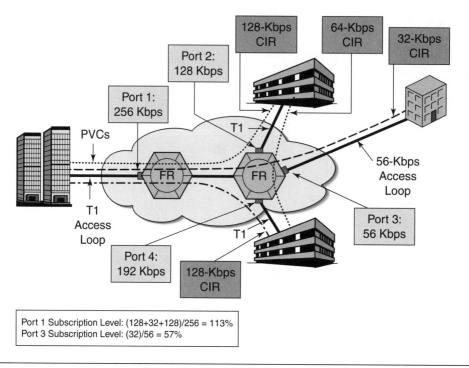

Port 1 Subscription Level: (128+32+128)/256 = 113%
Port 3 Subscription Level: (32)/56 = 57%

FIGURE 11.6 Sample Frame Relay Network Design.   *CIRs and port speeds can be added to the partial mesh design shown in Figure 11.5.*

- Adjust CIR or port speed. Changing CIR for a PVC will affect the performance of that PVC relative to another PVC on the same access circuit. Increasing CIR will likely decrease the PVC's frame discard percentage if the percentage is high (above a few percent). It will likely increase throughput of that PVC, but may not improve transit time by much. Increasing port speed will have a more dramatic effect, because it will allow the customer to send more total traffic into the frame relay network per unit of time, thus likely improving both throughput and transit time.
- Use one of the new bandwidth managers, or traffic shapers, to better allocate bandwidth on the local loop to high-priority applications.
- Use class of service (CoS) features from the carrier, if the carrier supports them, to give priority to selected applications, such as SNA or voice.

- Enable traffic priority features on the CPE. Chapter 13, Internet-working with Frame Relay, says more about this.
- Segregate traffic so that each traffic type has its own PVC, its own CIR, and possibly also its own relative priority.
- Convince the carrier to decrease the number of hops within its cloud. This might not be easy.

From the carrier's point of view, the major design possibilities for improving performance are

- Increasing trunk capacity, which will likely have the greatest impact
- Decreasing the average number of hops within the cloud
- Improving the congestion control mechanism to reduce transit delay due to congestion
- Implementing class of service mechanisms to allow customers to select appropriate priorities for their applications

Designing for Switched Virtual Circuits

The major reason for an enterprise network manager to use SVCs in a frame relay network is to cut costs. Given that SVC pricing is usage based, an infrequently used SVC may be less expensive than a PVC.

However, SVCs have notable disadvantages. Perhaps the most serious is that routers sending layer 3 packets over a frame relay network must do a route recalculation each time an SVC is turned up or brought down. That is, the routers must collectively share the information about the change in the network topology. (See Chapter 13.) For a large IP network, a route recalculation might take 10 minutes. SVCs that come and go every few minutes would put an intolerable strain on such a network. Looked at another way, "Since routers are switching traffic and supporting connections at Layer 3 (via IP), dynamic establishment of connections at Layer 2 is redundant" [Passmore97].

SVCs also have the disadvantage of being more complex to set up than PVCs from the customer's point of view. And since they are not well accepted in the marketplace, field experience with them is scarce.

Designing for Disaster Recovery

Disaster recovery is backup for applications running at data centers rather than backup for physical or virtual circuits. Thus, a backup site needs to be available if the primary data center has a disaster. The following are the methods for disaster recovery:

- Rehoming PVCs, also known as repointing or network reconfiguration. The carrier will take all PVCs that converge on the primary data center and redirect them to the backup data center. Usually this is done under manual or semiautomated control by the carrier at the customer's request. Part of the service level agreement with the carrier may state the maximum amount of time this process can take.
- Adding secondary PVCs, also known as shadow, backup, or alternate PVCs, or sometimes as dual homing. The customer establishes *two* PVCs from each remote site. The primary PVC goes to the primary data center; the secondary PVC goes to the backup data center. If the primary data center fails, the remote-site CPE can be programmed to automatically switch over to the secondary PVC. Or the switchover can be done manually. Although this option may seem expensive, it provides a high level of system reliability, the shadow PVCs are always in place for testing, and many carriers offer discounted prices for it. Some carriers offer usage-based PVCs for this purpose.
- Adding network-level dial backup. The customer can dial directly from a remote site into the backup data center. This method appears to be less common, partly because of expense and administrative issues.
- Adding access: level dial backup is another method of disaster recovery, especially for failure of the access network, is to have the remote-site router dial directly into the frame relay cloud. Some service providers offer dial-up ports in the frame relay network designed specifically for this purpose.

Exercise

For the sample frame relay network design of Figure 11.6, what is the subscription level for

1. Port 2?

2. Port 4?

Chapter 12

Voice over Frame Relay

This chapter discusses how voice can be carried over frame relay networks. First, we describe the advantages and then the challenges of voice over frame relay, mentioning how voice quality is typically measured. Then we discuss several common techniques for improving voice over frame relay performance.

Having looked at voice, we turn our attention to fax over frame relay and then video over frame relay. Many of the issues are similar to those of carrying voice.

Next we consider a number of issues related to voice over frame relay—namely, performance, quality, technology, administration, and perception. We close with a brief review of the two Frame Relay Forum specifications that relate to voice over frame relay.

Advantages

Many network managers are interested in the economic benefits of sending voice traffic over frame relay networks. Combining voice and data networks has the potential for 30% to 50% savings in total network costs, part of which is due to network consolidation, also called network convergence or network integration. It is easier to manage and pay for a single network that handles both voice and data traffic than to have two separate networks. Another part of the savings is that the per-minute cost of sending a voice call over a frame relay network is usually less than the cost of using a traditional voice public carrier. Some vendors of voice over frame relay equipment claim payback periods of six months to a year for customers who convert.

Although a network manager can use a frame relay network exclusively for voice, it is much more common and more cost effective to combine voice with data and even fax traffic. As we will discuss later, most **voice frame relay access devices** (VFRADs) handle data and fax along with voice. Thus, frame relay can become an integrated WAN access method.

Voice over frame relay (VoFR) is especially strong in certain circumstances:

- When there is extra capacity in the customer's frame relay network. In this case the marginal cost of carrying voice will be low.
- For international voice calls, which tend to be quite expensive compared to U.S. domestic calls.
- For the small office/home office (SOHO) segment, where the cost savings of voice on the frame relay network justifies a leased rather than a dial-up line for the data traffic.

Challenges

The basic technical challenge in sending voice over a frame relay network is that the frame relay technology was originally designed only for data traffic. Adding voice capability is a somewhat clumsy retrofit to the original design.

Data traffic is typically bursty and delay tolerant, and can be high volume. Standard (PCM-encoded) voice traffic is continuous (sometimes referred to as **constant bit rate**, CBR), delay sensitive, and relatively low volume (64 Kbps per call). Frame relay was designed to be efficient in the data environment, but it is not a natural fit for the voice environment. In particular, it does not necessarily deliver traffic at a steady rate, but may have gaps in the traffic flow at some times and bursts of frames at other times. Frame relay services also do not necessarily deliver frames quickly, that is, with low delay (latency) across the network, unless the network is engineered with special care. Contrast this situation with ATM, which was designed from the ground up to work well in both the data and voice environments.

A number of historical factors have also contributed to the challenges that face a network manager who wants to use voice over frame relay. However, a growing market awareness of its advantages and increasing work by standards groups is ameliorating many of these factors.

- Lack of standards for VoFR CPE and interoperability problems between the CPE of different vendors. The Frame Relay Forum's FRF.11 and FRF.12 partially remedy this problem, as discussed later.
- Poor voice quality due to poor compression algorithms. Within the last few years considerable progress has been made in this area, as discussed later.
- Lack of standards for defining acceptable quality of the delivered voice. The Perceptual Speech Quality Measurement (PSQM) group of the ITU-T is working on this issue. However, the most familiar measurement of voice quality is the subjective **Mean Opinion Score** (MOS), also discussed later.
- Carrier problems with VoFR. At present, frame relay networks have no standards-based quality of service (QoS). Hence, carriers can only use proprietary methods to give priority to voice traffic, and many carriers do not even do that. Moreover, setting service level agreements for voice is problematic. In addition, some carriers have over-subscribed their internal networks, causing congestion that can destroy voice quality. With all of these problems, it is not surprising that voice over frame relay is handled *outside* of the carrier's network, in customer premise equipment such as VFRADs.
- Conflict between voice and data traffic. Since the voice traffic must be given a higher priority than the data traffic, improperly sized frame relay access circuits can adversely affect the data traffic during times of heavy voice use. Many network managers have noted this type of degradation. Some analysts believe that this prioritization conflicts with the primary purpose of the frame relay network, which is to support data traffic.

Measuring Voice Quality

The most widely quoted measure of voice quality is the Mean Opinion Score. It is a subjective rather than objective score that is averaged over a large number of speakers, phrases, and listeners. MOS is often used to measure voice quality because *quantitative* technical measurements of received voice signals do not always reflect the listener's subjective impression. Table 12.1 gives the value scale of MOS.

TABLE 12.1 Mean Opinion Score

Score	Quality
4.0–5.0	Excellent (toll quality)
3.0–4.0	Good (communication quality, "near toll quality")
2.0–3.0	Fair (synthetic quality)
< 2.0	Poor

Improving Voice Performance

The key device for handling voice over a frame relay network is a voice over frame relay access device (VFRAD), which is a type of FRAD that multiplexes voice, fax, and data traffic onto frame relay virtual circuits. A VFRAD may be stand-alone, or it may be integrated into other CPE. Thus, a router may have an integrated VFRAD function so that users can connect analog or digital PBXs, standard telephones, and fax machines directly to it.

VFRADs have a number of features for meeting the special requirements of voice. We discuss these features in the following subsections.

Voice Compression

The standard digital encoding for voice in the public telephone networks is **pulse code modulation** (PCM) at 64 Kbps. This technique, which has been widely used for about 35 years, gives excellent voice quality (a toll-quality MOS of 4.4) and is quite adequate for handling fax and modem analog signals. However, PCM is over-engineered for handling voice, because lower speed bit streams can still deliver toll-quality.[1] For instance, **adaptive differential pulse code modulation** (ADPCM) can deliver an MOS of 4.1 at 32 Kbps. Thus, analog signals generated by true human voices can be digitized into a bit stream of much less than 64 Kbps.

---

[1]Note, however, that PCM is *required* for high-speed modems (≥ 9600 bps) and for fax machines (Group-3 fax). ADPCM and lower speed encoding algorithms do not have a large enough bit stream to adequately recreate the analog signal that is needed by the receiving modem or fax. This is a major reason why public carriers pack only one "voice" call into a 64-Kbps DS-0. The voice call may very well be modulated data or fax, which requires the 64-Kbps data rate.

Research in **very low bit rate voice** (VLBRV) compression algorithms has recently reached new milestones. One popular technique is **conjugate structure–algebraic code excited linear predictive** coding, (CS-ACELP or just ACELP), which has been standardized by the ITU-T in G.729 and in G.729 Annex A for a reduced-complexity version. An ACELP **vocoder** (voice codec) produces a bit stream of 8000 bps from the analog voice signal and produces *toll-quality* voice at the receiving vocoder (an MOS of about 4.2).[2] Some proprietary compression algorithms can run as low as 4.8 Kbps and still achieve near toll quality.

In principle, a frame relay network could transmit PCM-encoded voice at 64 Kbps. In practice, though, voice compression, such as ACELP, is necessary to keep the voice bandwidth requirements within reasonable bounds. Thus, a 56-Kbps frame relay port could handle five to seven compressed voice conversations but not even one standard PCM-encoded conversation. Note that voice is compressed for transmission over frame relay networks for the same reason, and via the same techniques, as transmission over IP networks (**VoIP**).

Silence Suppression

A person on a telephone call is actually generating speech only about 40% of the time.[3] Most of the inactivity happens when the person is listening, but there are also pauses between sentences and some words. Given this, removing the pauses from speech can *significantly* reduce the bandwidth required to digitally transmit the call. For instance, a G.729 ACELP vocoder will produce a continuous stream of 8 Kbps, but with silence suppression added, the *average* data rate drops to about 3.5 Kbps. Note that the resulting bit stream is composed of variable-length talk spurts at 8 Kbps, interleaved with variable-length periods of silence that require no bandwidth. However, the sending vocoder must include some overhead (**silence insertion descriptor**) about how long the period of silence is, so that the receiving vocoder can accurately reconstruct the pauses in the voice. Usually the silence insertion descriptor also contains parameters about how to

---

[2]Two reasons why ACELP produces such good quality at a low bit rate is that it uses advanced digital signal processors (DSPs) and sophisticated modeling of the human vocal tract. The downside of vocal tract modeling is that speakers of different languages use their vocal tracts in different ways. Thus, a pair of vocoders that are "tuned" to English may not produce good quality for people speaking Chinese, which is a tonal language, or French, which is a nasal language.

[3]According to some studies [FRF96], 56% of normal speech is made up of pauses, and 22% is repetitive sound patterns. Only 22% is essential speech components that need to be transmitted for complete voice clarity.

regenerate background, or "comfort" noise, so that the listener does not think the line has gone dead.

Silence suppression is also called **digital speech interpolation** (DSI). It is the digital version of the old **time assignment speech interpolation** (TASI) technique that was used to improve utilization on transoceanic analog telephone cables.

Voice-Engineering Techniques

VFRADs typically contain several technical features for improving voice quality.

Jitter Buffers

Jitter buffers, also called playout buffers, help smooth out the variable delays introduced by the frame relay network. Jitter is the variation in the time differences between each arriving frame. At the receiving VFRAD, the jitter buffer collects the irregularly spaced voice frames and then plays them out continuously to the listener. This technique is similar to anti-skip techniques on portable audio CD players.

There is a trade-off between the size of the jitter buffer and the amount of delay that it introduces. One VFRAD vendor uses a jitter buffer that stores 72 milliseconds of voice; some other jitter buffers are configurable.

Echo Cancellation

Echo occurs when the transmitted voice is reflected back to the source. In traditional voice networks, echo cancellation devices are used within the carrier's network when the propagation delay increases to the point where echo is noticeable to the speaker—about 15 to 20 milliseconds round trip. Since frame relay carriers do not use echo cancellation equipment within their frame relay networks, it is up to the VFRAD vendor to address echo problems.

Dynamic Congestion Control

Most VFRADs can respond to FECN and BECN bits sent by the frame relay network. As discussed in Chapter 6, Traffic Management, these bits indicate that congestion is occurring within the network. Depending on the vendor's design, the VFRAD's responses can include

- Throttling back data or voice traffic from the end-user devices attached to the VFRAD

- Queueing traffic within the VFRAD to reduce the load on the network
- Varying the voice frame size or digitization rate, which may degrade voice quality but decrease congestion

Small Voice Frames

Frames that contain voice need to be small so that they can be filled up quickly and sent on their way. This helps to minimize the end-to-end delay in the frame relay network. Typical frame sizes are 40 to 83 bytes, depending on the vendor. Standards for packaging compressed voice into frame relay payloads are called "transfer syntaxes" and are described in FRF.11, discussed later.

Fragmentation of Data Frames

Fragmentation of data frames into smaller cells is important so that voice frames won't be delayed behind large data frames. (ATM uses the same general technique with its small cell size.) A standards-based method for fragmentation is described in FRF.12, discussed later.

Priority of Voice Frames

VFRADs give priority to voice (and fax) frames over ordinary data frames on the outbound access circuits into the frame relay network. This is important for minimizing voice delay. Note, however, that the VFRAD has no control over priority once the frames are inside the frame relay network. VFRADs often have some type of "fair share queueing" on the priority queues so that low-priority queues do not suffer starvation.

QoS in the Frame Relay Network

Network quality of service, in the form of low and constant delay and low frame discard rate, is important for maintaining adequate voice quality. However, at present there are only proprietary approaches to providing QoS. Furthermore, the approaches typically give only *relative* QoS (sometimes called class of service, CoS) rather than quantitative ("hard") QoS.

Fragmentation of *all* data frames, as in FRF.12, helps with QoS. As we discussed above, when all frames in the network are small, voice frames will not get stuck behind large data frames. This is sometimes referred to as reducing the convoy effect.

Prioritizing voice frames at all the frame relay switches is a good approach, but is currently vendor specific.

For public frame relay networks, an ATM core helps QoS by providing low and constant delay across the backbone trunks between the edge frame relay switches. This is discussed more fully in Chapter 14, Frame Relay and ATM.

For private frame relay networks, good network design can help QoS—in particular, by minimizing the number of hops within the frame relay network itself and managing traffic flows by good PVC routing. (See Chapter 11, Design of Frame Relay Networks.)

Fax over Frame Relay

Just as some network managers are saving money by sending voice over frame relay networks, some are doing so by sending fax traffic that way. There is a problem, however, for the VFRADs. A sending fax machine produces an analog fax signal that is normally sent over a telephone line to the receiving fax machine. The sending VFRAD cannot use low-bit-rate compression of the analog fax signal because the decompression stage at the receiving VFRAD cannot adequately recreate the sensitive analog fax signal. The sending VFRAD could theoretically use 64-Kbps PCM-encoding of the analog fax signal, but this would require too much bandwidth for a typical branch office access circuit.

The solution is for the sending VFRAD to demodulate the analog fax signal back into the digital bit stream originally produced by the scanner portion of the fax machine.[4] This digital bit stream is packaged into frames for transmission across the frame relay network. The receiving VFRAD then remodulates it into an analog signal for transmission to the receiving fax machine. Cumbersome, but it works.

Note that a 14.4-Kbps fax will generate up to 14,400 bps to be packaged into frame relay frames. Compare this to the 64,000 bps that would need to be packaged into frames for PCM-encoded analog fax signals. See *FRF.11 Voice over Frame Relay Implementation Agreement, Annex D—Fax Relay Transfer Syntax*, for detailed information about how to package fax bit streams in frame relay payloads.

---

[4]The digital bit stream produced by the scanner portion of a G3 (ITU Group-3) fax machine is actually a compressed version (using Modified Huffman–Modified Read compression, MH/MR) of the raw 0s and 1s generated when the charge coupled device (CCD) hardware scans the image. MH/MR compression reduces the amount of digital information down to 1/20th [FRFN4Q98].

Two technical issues for fax over frame relay are as follows:

- The VFRAD must be able to recognize the initial fax handshaking tones so that it can begin demodulating the incoming fax data. The tones must also be transmitted to the receiving fax. (See FRF.11 Annex D for more details [FRF.11-97].)
- Some vendors maintain that fax frames should have higher priority than voice frames because fax is actually more sensitive to delays than voice [ACT95]. Fax transmission does have automatic error detection and retransmission, however, so the faxes should be able to get through eventually even in the face of congestion and delay. Note that this situation is not true for voice, where there is no automatic retransmission and where congestion and delay lead to poor, even unintelligible, voice quality.

Voice-Band Modem Data over Frame Relay

Transmission of analog modem signals has problems similar to transmission of analog fax signals. The low-bit-rate compression algorithms cannot recreate the analog signals generated by high-bit-rate modems. For instance, a 16-Kbps compression algorithm called LD CELP limits modem speed to only 2400 bps.

The VFRAD could demodulate the analog signal and package the digital bit stream into frames. However it is easier simply to send the unmodulated bit stream directly into the frame relay cloud without any use of modems.

At present, FRF.12 does not include any transfer syntax for voice band modems. Many VFRADs do not support analog signals from voice band modems.

Video over Frame Relay

Video over frame relay has issues similar to those with voice over frame relay, because it is also delay sensitive. However, because video requires so much more bandwidth than voice, it needs a much larger CIR and is correspondingly more expensive. Nonetheless, video over frame relay has potential cost savings compared to the alternatives of long-distance ISDN or leased lines for video transmission.

Three major applications for video are videoconferencing, distance learning, and surveillance. However, even as it continues to gain momentum, video over frame relay is still new. Customers have relatively little experience with it, and there are relatively few CPE products to support it.

As with voice over frame relay, video over frame relay has a trade-off between CIR and quality. Poor quality for video can take the form of

- Less than the industry standard of 30 fps (video frames per second) for full-motion video
- Poor picture resolution, including tiling faults and frame drops
- Problems with audio lip-sync

Nonetheless, for some applications, such as video surveillance, low-quality video may still be adequate.

Good-quality videoconferencing needs

- Unfailing end-to-end QoS. The single most important factor in the delivery of acceptable videoconferencing over frame relay is protection of the video stream from frame drops [Brown98].
- Adequate bandwidth of the video system, which depends on the system type. Room-based systems need 384 Kbps or more, desktop systems need 128 to 256 Kbps, and surveillance systems need up to 56 Kbps. However, camera controls and collaborative traffic will increase the system bandwidth requirements. For instance, a room-based system may need 496 Kbps—the same bandwidth required for systems that use circuit-switched connections, such as ISDN.
- Adequate CIR. One rule of thumb is to set the CIR 1% to 3 % higher than the system's bandwidth. The extra capacity is needed for the frame relay frame overhead.
- Adequate port speed. Since the video FRAD will likely be multiplexing other data traffic onto the same frame relay access circuit, the port speed (and access circuit speed) must be adequate to support all the traffic. For instance, a room-based collaborative videoconferencing system that requires 496 Kbps might need a CIR of 512 Kbps but a port speed of 768 Kbps.

The components of a video over frame relay system are as follows. The camera, monitor, and microphone(s) feed an analog signal to an H.320 video codec. The video codec feeds the resulting digital bit stream to a framer, which packages the bit stream into the payload of frame relay frames. The framer then feeds the frame relay frames to a video FRAD, which multiplexes the video traffic along with other traffic onto the frame relay access circuit. Video traffic receives the highest priority in the video

FRAD. In some cases the framer may be integrated into the video FRAD; in others it is stand-alone.

At present, the Frame Relay Forum has not issued any specifications governing video over frame relay. Hence, all current video FRAD implementations are proprietary.

Considerations

Performance and Quality Issues

For CIR sizing, a rule of thumb is to use 12 Kbps of CIR for every 8-Kbps compressed voice channel. Thus, a 56/64-Kbps port can support about 6 to 7 ACELP voice conversations, with a small amount of port oversubscription. As long as the VFRAD uses silence suppression, the port oversubscription can be justified by the fact that voice conversations are inherently half duplex.

For zero CIR virtual circuits, the advice is to try it first.

Some VFRAD vendors recommend carrying all voice traffic in a separate virtual circuit from data traffic. Many vendors allow multiplexing of all traffic on a single virtual circuit.

If the carrier will support it, mark the voice traffic as delay sensitive, which will give it higher priority than non-delay-sensitive traffic within the network. Also, network performance will be better over a robust backbone, such as ATM or T3.

In spite of the claims that G.729 ACELP compression is toll quality, most actual VFRADs in real-life tests appear to produce a lower, near-toll quality. For instance, one study found that across all products the average score on a MOS-like rating scale was 2.9, with ranges from 1.8 to 3.4 [Newman96]. This quality is probably sufficient for routine intracompany calls but not for CEOs, sales reps, and employees who must interact with the general public.

One major factor in the observed poorer quality of voice over frame relay is the variable and unpredictable delay of public frame relay networks. Thus, voice quality may vary in unpredictable ways from moment to moment. The problem is compounded by the fact that customers who are not even associated with a company can cause congestion for many people in a public network.

End-to-end delay, including VFRADs, for voice over frame relay varies from roughly 70 to 250 milliseconds or more. Generally, VFRADs with lower delays have higher voice quality scores [Newman96]. Compare these delays to typical public switched telephone network (PSTN) delays of 50 to 70 milliseconds and satellite delays of 250 to 300 milliseconds. The threshold at which delay becomes annoying is roughly 200 milliseconds, but a delay as short as 30 milliseconds is perceived by the human ear as a drop in quality. These statistics back up the claim that most VFRADs produce near-toll quality rather than toll quality.

VFRADs give higher priority to voice than to data, so initiating a voice call across a frame relay network can greatly slow down the delivery of the data traffic. Many customers have noticed this effect. Some situations are particularly troublesome. Non-SNA synchronous data traffic does not mix well with voice traffic. In particular, time division multiplexed (TDM) synchronous channels cause problems because they never release bandwidth. Also, time-sensitive non-SNA synchronous traffic, such as IBM's Bisynch, causes problems because the voice traffic overwhelms it.

Lastly, tandem compression—that is, compressing, then decompressing, then recompressing—will seriously affect voice quality. This can occur if voice traffic is carried through an intermediate PBX and all the tie lines between the PBXes are actually frame relay links.

Technical Issues

Off-net calling (across the private network and then out to the public telephone network) can be a challenge, for the following reasons:

- Voice signal levels in the PSTN are usually lower, which may cause difficulty in hearing.
- The PSTN may produce undesirable echoes.
- It may be difficult to bill the caller correctly.
- Off-net calling is illegal in some countries.

Management and Administrative Issues

For customers who are used to a familiar telephone billing system, changing to voice over frame relay can be a shock. Customers may find major changes in

- Consolidated voice billing and invoice itemization
- End-user chargeback capabilities
- Use of ID and accounting codes

Although such changes may seem trivial, some industry observers argue that they can turn a smoothly running administrative function into a nightmare. Some observers have also suggested that this issue is one of the obstacles to wider acceptance of voice over IP.

Perception Issues

Some network manager surveys indicate that users will not shift from conventional voice to voice over frame relay unless they see a significant cost saving, on the order of 30%. The main obstacle is fear of poor voice quality. This fear does not extend to fax over frame relay, which means that fax over frame relay may see earlier widespread acceptance.

VoIP and ATM are often seen as competitors of frame relay for carrying legacy voice traffic. Some network managers want the dust to settle before committing themselves to a capital-intensive change in their well-functioning voice networks.

Standards

The Frame Relay Forum developed two Implementation Agreements (IAs) to help with interoperability of voice over frame relay products. These two specifications in turn refer to a number of other standards, especially ITU-T standards. See the IAs for the references.

FRF.11 Voice over Frame Relay Implementation Agreement

The primary purpose of FRF.11 is to specify how to carry compressed voice within frame relay frames. Secondary purposes are to support a diverse set of voice compression algorithms and to make efficient use of frame relay virtual circuits.

A simplified reference model for voice over frame relay is given in Figure 12.1. The VFRADs allow CPE to exchange voice and signaling information. The CPE can be

- A switching system, such as PBX (shown)
- An end-system device, such as a PC with telephony software (shown) or a standard analog telephone (shown) or a fax machine (not shown)
- A transparent multiplexing device, such as a channel bank (not shown)

Any CPE device can communicate with any other CPE device through the VFRADs and appropriate virtual circuits. A VFRAD could be stand-alone (shown), integrated into a router, integrated into CPE, such as a PC, or, rarely, integrated into a frame relay switch.

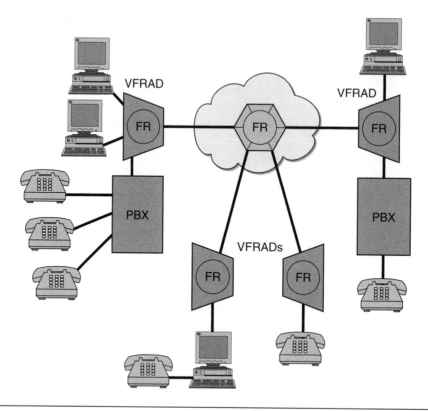

FIGURE 12.1 Simplified Reference Model for Voice over Frame Relay.   *Voice FRADs allow a frame relay network to carry both voice and data traffic.*

For FRF.11, frame relay frames have two types of payload—primary and signaled. The following are the primary payloads.

- Encoded voice, packaged according to the rules of a voice transfer syntax. Transfer syntaxes are described in the annexes of the IA.
- Encoded fax, which is actually demodulated fax data in "baseband" format, as discussed in the section Fax over Frame Relay. The encoded fax transfer syntax is described in Annex D of the IA.
- Data payloads, which are supplied by the end user. The payloads are packaged according to the rules of Annex C. They do not need to be related to the voice traffic, but could be IP datagrams or X.25 packets. One voice-related application allows transparent tunneling of common channel signaling messages between two PBXes.

Signaled payloads are used to carry signaling information from one CPE device across the virtual circuit to another device. They include dialed digits, **channel associated signaling** (CAS) signaling bits, fault indications, and silence information descriptors.

FRF.11 allows a flexible form of multiplexing primary and signaling payloads within frame relay frames. Each payload is packaged as a subframe within a frame's information field, and subframes may be combined within a single frame to increase processing and transport efficiencies. Each subframe contains a header and a payload. The header identifies the voice/data subchannel associated with the payload; when required, it also identifies the payload type and length. Thus, for instance, a single virtual circuit could support 3 voice subchannels and 2 data subchannels. The maximum subchannel ID is 255, so a virtual circuit could support up to 255 voice or 255 data subchannels.

FRF.11 has two classes of compliance. Class 1 is for higher speed links that require what is commonly referred to as carrier-class voice compression such as PCM and ADPCM. The default algorithm for Class 1 is ADPCM G.727 at 32 Kbps. Class 2 is for devices that utilize lower speed links such as 64 Kbps, which use low-bit-rate voice compression algorithms. The default algorithm is CS-ACELP G.729/G.729 Annex A at 8 Kbps [FRFN2Q97].

Some issues as yet unresolved in FRF.11 are MIBs, negotiation of parameters, SVC support, and voice-band modem support.

FRF.12 Frame Relay Fragmentation Implementation Agreement

The purpose of FRF.12 is to specify how frame relay equipment can fragment long frames into a sequence of shorter ones, which is then reassembled into the original frame by the receiving equipment. Frame fragmentation is necessary to control delay and delay variation (jitter) when real-time traffic such as voice is carried across the same interfaces as data. It allows the interleaving of delay-sensitive traffic on one virtual circuit with fragments of a long frame on another virtual circuit utilizing the same interface.

FRF.12 supports three applications of fragmentation:

- Locally across a frame relay access circuit (UNI interface) between a frame relay DTE and the frame relay switch. UNI fragmentation is provisioned on an interface-by-interface basis. When it is used on an interface, all frames on all DLCIs, including DLCI 0, PVCs, and SVCs, are preceded by a fragmentation header.

- Locally across a frame relay NNI interface between two frame relay switches. NNI fragmentation is also provisioned on an interface-by-interface basis similar to UNI fragmentation.
- End to end between two frame relay DTEs interconnected by one or more frame relay networks. When used end to end, fragmentation is transparent to the frame relay network(s) between the two DTEs. End-to-end fragmentation is restricted to selected PVCs.

See FRF.12 for details about the fragmentation formats [FRF.12-97]. Appendix A to FRF.12 contains comments about selecting the end-to-end fragmentation size.

Chapter 13

Internetworking with Frame Relay

This chapter examines several issues related to internetworking with frame relay. We begin with a discussion of the two major families of routing algorithms: distance vector and link state. This leads into a discussion of the routing protocols based on these algorithms, such as RIP and OSPF.

Since routers are such a typical part of internetworks, we explain some of the ways they affect internetworking with frame relay, as follows:

- Configuration of frame relay interfaces on routers
- TCP and congestion control
- Routers and congestion control
- How routers prioritize traffic, including fair queueing
- Effects of frame relay on router interconnectivity
- Solving the "split horizon" problem for routers in frame relay networks

We describe how RFC 1490/2427 multiprotocol encapsulation allows different protocols to travel over the same frame relay connection. We include a discussion of address resolution over frame relay networks and some common misunderstandings about RFC 1490.

Next, additional issues that come up when routers send routable protocols over a frame relay network are discussed. We focus on TCP/IP and IPX.

The installed base of IBM SNA networks is large, and many network managers are interested in the economies of frame relay. After giving some background about SNA, we outline a number of approaches to the problem of sending nonroutable SNA over frame relay, as follows:

- IBM hardware/software support for sending SNA traffic directly over a frame relay network. These techniques include **Boundary Network Node** (BNN), **Boundary Access Node** (BAN), **Advanced Peer-to-Peer Networking** (APPN), and APPN with **High Performance Routing** (HPR).
- SNA gateways, which encapsulate SNA within TCP/IP at the SNA end-user device.
- RFC 1490 multiprotocol encapsulation, which allows routers and FRADs to send SNA over a frame relay network.
- IBM's **Data Link Switching** (DLSw), which is a specific method of encapsulating SNA in TCP/IP packets.

Lastly, we discuss how to send other nonroutable protocols over frame relay. We focus on IBM's NETBIOS and DEC's LAT.

Routing over Frame Relay Networks

The router is the jumping-off point into the wide area network. As routers are very common devices in networks, especially with the popularity of TCP/IP and other Internet protocols, we should discuss them from the point of view of frame relay networks.

Routing Protocols

Routing protocols control how routers forward packets through an internet. They are not directly visible to end users, but they can have a major influence on the performance of the overall network. In particular, the choice of a routing protocol can affect the throughput and delay in a frame relay network. Moreover, not all network and transport layer protocols work with all routing protocols.

A loose analogy for a routing protocol is two people at lunch in Los Angeles exchanging information about the L.A. freeways. Later, each person can use the information to make better on-the-spot decisions about which freeway to take.

There are two major families of routing algorithms: distance vector and link state (Figure 13.1). Any given router will implement a routing protocol based on one of these. However, because routing is so complex, there

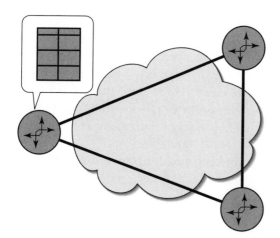

**Distance Vector
Routing Protocols**

- All routers maintain own routing tables
- Periodic updates: "chatty"
- Slow to converge
- Can have routing loops
- Simple routing, based on hop count only
- No load balancing
- OK for small networks

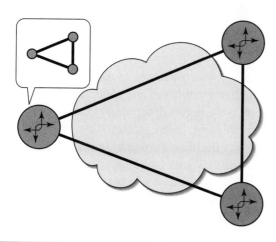

**Link State Routing
Protocols**

- All routers know entire network topology
- Update-only: only send changes, as needed
- Faster convergence
- Avoid routing loops
- Sophisticated optimal routing
- Support load balancing
- Scale well to large networks

FIGURE 13.1 Routing Protocols.   *The two major families of routing protocols differ in several ways.*

are many different protocol implementations in use, some proprietary but many based on published standards, such as the IETF RFCs.

Distance Vector Algorithms

Each router maintains a table (vector) giving the best known "distance" to each destination router and the line to use to get there. The metric for distance is usually just hop count. The routing tables are updated by exchanging information packets with neighboring routers.

The basic distance vector algorithm is sometimes also known as the distributed Bellman-Ford or Ford-Fulkerson algorithm. It was the original ARPANET routing algorithm and is also used in the Internet under the name **Routing Information Protocol** (RIP)–formerly RFC 1058. AppleTalk and Cisco routers use improved distance vector algorithms. Cisco's flagship (proprietary) routing protocol, in particular, is the **Enhanced Interior Gateway Routing Protocol** (EIGRP),[1] but it is so much improved over the basic RIP that it behaves more like a link state algorithm.

Distance vector algorithms do not keep a real-time comprehensive view of the entire network topology. Instead, each router keeps a table of where to send each incoming data packet. In addition, in most implementations each router periodically sends routing update packets (also known as route advertisement packets) to each of its neighboring routers. These updates are important for distributing information about changes in the network (new DCLIs, broken access lines, etc.), but they consume network bandwidth. For each update, the router broadcasts a copy of its complete routing table over each DLCI. It may broadcast every 30 seconds.

RIP, as an example of a distance vector protocol, is easy to implement and works well in a relatively small and stable environment. However, it is slow to converge, meaning that when the network topology changes, it takes a long time for distant routers to find out. Even worse, while the routing updates are slowly propagating through the network, the routing tables may be inconsistent (this is sometimes known as the count-to-infinity problem), which can lead to routing loops that waste network bandwidth.

A partial solution to the routing loop problem is to enable **split horizon** in the router[2] (although, as we will see, this used to cause problems for partial mesh frame relay networks). The split horizon scheme omits routes learned from one neighboring router in updates to that neighbor. Thus, it eliminates many, but not all, routing loops for distance vector protocols. Tanenbaum [Tanenbaum96] gives an example to show that the split horizon rule does not eliminate all routing loops.

For this reason, RIP does not scale well to large networks. In addition, it does not support load sharing, nor does it allow optimal routing based on link capacity, congestion, or cost.

---

[1]"Gateway" is the old (ARPANET) term for a router. "Interior" indicates that all routers interior to a "domain" run the same routing protocol.

[2]There is some controversy over the use of the phrase "enable split horizon." *Newton's Telecom Dictionary* [Newton98] calls this "*disabling* split horizon."

Link State Algorithms

Because of the limitations of distance vector protocols like RIP, many routers now implement routing protocols based on **link state algorithms**. Some of these implementations, such as **Open Shortest Path First** (OSPF) (RFC 1247, updated in RFC 1583), are widely used in the Internet and in router-based enterprise internets.

In the basic link state algorithm, each router maintains a real-time comprehensive view of the entire network topology. This view is embodied in the topology table, also known as the link state table. The router uses this information (the state of all the links) to compute the shortest path to each destination and then caches the results in a separate routing table for later use.

In addition, each router sends only *changes* in the link states to its neighbors rather than full status messages, as in RIP. These update packets are also sent *only* when a change occurs, not, as in RIP, every 30 seconds. This process is called "update-only," or "flash update," and it significantly reduces the amount of broadcast traffic on the network, compared to RIP's periodic update strategy. A rule of thumb for broadcasts is to keep the amount of router update traffic to 20% or less of the access circuit speed.

As an aside, these update-only protocols typically send a keep-alive signal (heartbeat) between the routers every 10 seconds. In addition, every 30 minutes each router broadcasts a full status report to its neighbors.

Examples of link state or enhanced routing protocols, together with the network-level protocols they commonly route, are given in Table 13.1.

TABLE 13.1 Improved Routing Protocols

Network Protocol	Commonly Used Routing Protocols*
IP	OSPF, IS-IS, EIGRP
Novell IPX	NLSP, EIGRP
AppleTalk	AURP, EIGRP
DECnet	IS-IS
ISO CLNP (rare)	IS-IS

*OSPF (Open Shortest Path First)—widely used. IS-IS (Intermediate System–Intermediate System)—designed for DECnet, adopted by ISO; used in many backbone nets. EIGRP (Enhanced Interior Gateway Routing Protocol)—proprietary routing protocol developed by Cisco; evolved from distance vector algorithms; routes many network layer protocols. NLSP (NetWare Link Services Protocol)—Novell's IS-IS variant. AURP (Apple Update Routing Protocol). CLNP (Connectionless Network Protocol)—ISO version of IP.

Advantages of link state protocols, compared to distance vector protocols, are that they

- Send less inter-router update traffic; that is, they are less "chatty."
- Converge quickly (information about network changes propagates more quickly)
- Avoid routing loops completely
- Allow computation of optimal routes based on combinations of metrics (hop count, delay, queue length, load, link capacity, cost of link, reliability, etc.)
- Support load sharing (the ability to balance traffic across multiple links to the same destination)
- Scale well to large, multiprotocol internetworks

The main disadvantages of link state protocols are complexity, high processing requirements at the router, and the existence of many different implementations.

Conclusion.   Unless a network is small and static, link state routing protocols, such as OSPF, are preferable to distance vector protocols, such as RIP.

Frame Relay Interfaces for Routers

A router needs to be configured before it can handle frame relay traffic. In router terminology, configuring the router interface means telling the router the essential information so that it can properly route packets over the frame relay network. In this context, "interface" means the software that manages a hardware port on the router.

Static Router Configuration

To configure a router interface for frame relay, a network technician must first specify what type of data link layer protocol will be used at the router interface (router port). For our purposes, we assume the link layer (layer 2) protocol is frame relay, but Point-to-Point Protocol (PPP), Synchronous Data Link Control (SDLC) or X.25 are possibilities for other types of wide area networks.

The network tech must then configure the virtual circuits on the router port. In router terminology, this is often called configuring the subinterfaces on the frame relay interface. The network tech typically specifies the following values for each subinterface:

- Data link connection identifier (DLCI), which is the numeric "baggage tag" for the virtual circuit on that subinterface.
- Committed Information Rate (CIR), so that the router can throttle back burst traffic to the specified rate when it notices that the frame relay network is becoming congested. Frames coming in to the router with the BECN bit set indicate network congestion. This feature is proprietary and is not always enabled even if it is available.
- Source IP address (IP address of the subinterface), so that the subinterface will be visible and addressable by other routers. For instance, if the subinterface has an IP address, it can be pinged (for diagnostic purposes) from the other end of the virtual circuit.
- Target IP address (IP address of the remote subinterface, at the other end of the virtual circuit), so that the router can "see" the remote subinterface. This helps the router keep track of the fact that this virtual circuit can furnish a path to the target IP address. The source and target IP addresses are not strictly necessary for frame relay operation, but are desirable for configuration and diagnostics.
- Type of layer 3 protocol carried by this frame relay virtual circuit, in the case of multiprotocol routers. Uniprotocol routers just assume that the virtual circuit is carrying IP datagrams. Multiprotocol routers can handle not only IP but also other layer 3 protocols, such as IPX, Apple-Talk, and DECnet. When RFC 1490 multiprotocol encapsulation is being used (see later discussion), the network tech must also inform the router that multiprotocol encapsulation is enabled on the subinterface.

Thus, when the router calculates its routing table at a later time, it will have the information that a particular virtual circuit, with a particular DLCI, can be used to forward datagrams to a particular IP address.

When a network tech configures a router in advance, giving it all the necessary information, it is known as static configuration. Unfortunately, static configuration is tedious, requires a detailed knowledge of router features, and is error prone. We now look at some techniques to help with this problem.

Dynamic Router Configuration

The idea behind dynamic router configuration, sometimes also called auto-configuration, is to automate as much of the configuration process as possible. One helpful technique is to make use of the Local Management Interface (LMI) information that is passed from the frame relay switch to the router across the access circuit. As we discussed in Chapter 8, Network Management, the LMI periodically sends a status message from the switch that contains the DLCI, the Active/Inactive status, and the New/Old status for every virtual circuit on the access link. The router can use this information, particularly when triggered by the New status bit, to dynamically configure the subinterface that corresponds to the new virtual circuit on the frame relay interface.

An additional helpful technique is to make use of the **Inverse Address Resolution Protocol** (InARP) (RFC 2390, previously RFC 1293) on the router. InARP is an extension to the familiar ARP protocol. Given the DLCI of the virtual circuit, InARP allows the router to discover the IP address of the machine at the other end of the virtual circuit. (Actually, InARP is even more general and allows the discovery of any protocol address at the remote end, not just an IP address.) InARP is more efficient than sending ARP messages on every virtual circuit for every address the router wants to resolve, and it is more flexible than static configuration.

Frame Relay Interfaces Are Serial

The virtual circuits from a single router port cannot transmit simultaneously. If a router receives several LAN frames at once, it will send them into the frame relay network on a first-come, first-served basis, unless prioritization guidelines have been programmed into it (more on prioritization later). Because the router's output interface is serial, the virtual connections across the access line are not active all at the same time. Hence, although we sometimes think of a port's virtual circuits as being simultaneously active, they are not. Rather, they are only "virtually simultaneous" in the same way that processes are "virtually simultaneous" on a timesharing computer because they are all sharing the computer's CPU.

TCP and Congestion Control

The Transmission Control Protocol (TCP) is a sophisticated protocol. Although software implementations vary in terms of support for advanced features, the common features of TCP include

- Flow control, so that the sending host cannot drown a slower receiving host. The flow control technique uses a variable-size sliding window that tells the sender how many bytes the receiver is willing to accept.

- Congestion control, so that the sending host will throttle back the flow of segments into a congested network.[3] The congestion control technique uses a congestion window, which is the maximum number of bytes the sender thinks is safe to send into the network. The actual number of bytes sent is the smaller of the flow control window and the congestion control window.
- A **slow start algorithm**, an enhancement to congestion control. With slow start, the congestion window starts at a small value but doubles in size as long as acknowledgments keep being returned before their timeout timers expire. A timer expiring indicates that a segment was lost and the network is therefore suffering congestion. If a timer does expire, TCP will precipitously lower the congestion window down to its initial size. Slow start is actually not slow at all but exponential. In practice, it is combined with the other TCP congestion techniques, such as dynamic adjustment of timeout timers. The effect is that TCP will quickly ramp up its output data stream until it reaches a maximum steady state determined by the smaller of the receiver's flow control window and the congestion window. However, if the receiver's window changes or if network congestion changes, TCP will quickly adapt its effective transmission rate, albeit with a hiccup along the way.[4]

Thus, for frame relay networks several factors can cause TCP to (temporarily) lower its effective transmission rate. These factors are packet discards due to congestion in the IP networks, frame discards due to congestion in the frame relay network, or **Internet Control Message Protocol (ICMP)** Source Quench messages passed to TCP after receipt by IP. Source Quench messages, which are rarely used now because they tend to make congestion worse, tell a host that it should throttle back the flow of packets into a network.

However, note that clever people are continuing to work on improving TCP, and its behavior depends heavily on the particular implementation.

---

[3]In keeping with Internet terminology, we call the unit of information passed from TCP to IP a **segment**. It is also sometimes called a **TCP PDU** or a **Transport Protocol Data Unit** (TPDU), which harks back to OSI vocabulary. As always, we call the unit of information passed from IP to the frame relay interface an **IP datagram**, a **datagram**, or **IP packet**.

[4]This adaptive behavior of TCP explains one of the reasons why Web browsers sometimes appear to freeze. TCP may simply be slowing the data stream to a trickle because it believes there is congestion in the network, as evidenced by timeouts due to packet discards. Of course, the Web server could also be overloaded.

Routers and Congestion

Routers typically have several characteristics that affect how they behave in a frame relay network (see Figure 13.2), as described in the following paragraphs.

A router has a serial interface into the frame relay network. Hence, when it sends a frame out onto the access line, it sends it a bit at a time at the speed of the access line (which is the same as the port connection speed on the receiving switch). This port speed is often higher than the CIR, even much higher, which is an advantage in that the frame makes it to the switch more quickly over the access line. However, it is then relatively

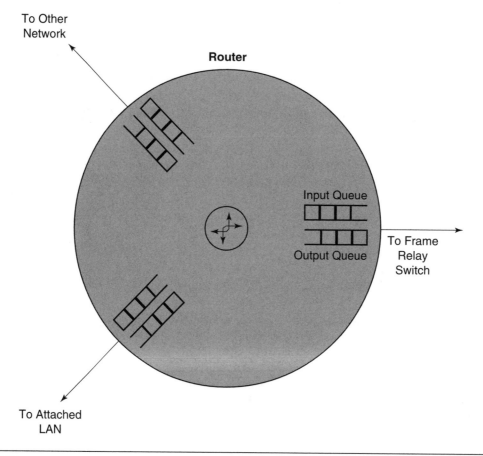

FIGURE 13.2 Router Queues.   *Most routers are limited in their ability to control congestion in a frame relay network.*

easy for a router to flood a frame relay switch with one frame after another, even on the same virtual connection. Or the router may flood the remote end system unless that system has some type of higher layer flow-control mechanism, such as TCP. For instance, if the local frame relay access circuit is 256 Kbps but the remote access circuit is only 128 Kbps, the egress frame relay switch might get flooded with frames to send over its slow outbound 128-Kbps link.

Some router vendors use **traffic shaping** to help with the flooding problem (and to help with network congestion). One major router vendor offers a proprietary traffic-shaping mechanism that can set an upper bound on the burst bit rate over a virtual circuit. Optionally, traffic shaping can also set a lower bound on the bit rate to which traffic will be shaped when BECNs are received over the virtual circuit. Thus, the actual bit rate will be between the upper and lower bounds when this proprietary traffic shaping is applied.[5]

Most routers do not recognize the frame relay CIR. A router simply pumps the frames into the frame relay network as fast as it receives them ("hot potato"). From the point of view of the frame relay network, most routers do not attempt to throttle back the flow of frames coming into the frame relay switch. Instead, they simply burst all available frames into the network as fast as they can. However, some routers do have proprietary methods for regulating the flow of frames into the network (see the preceding traffic shaping discussion).

Many routers do not recognize the DE, FECN, or BECN bits in incoming frames, although some do heed the BECN bit. (See Chapter 6, Traffic Management, for more discussion of DE, FECN, and BECN.) Because they do not pay attention to the congestion notification bits, they cannot take any action when the network attempts to tell them that it is suffering congestion.

Routers are not particularly effective at direct flow control. Suppose a router *does* attempt flow control toward the frame relay switch in order to alleviate existing congestion. For instance, it may receive frames from the switch with the BECN bit set and attempt to throttle back the flow of frames into the switch. The router can buffer up frames destined for the switch, but it has only a finite amount of memory and so may eventually

---

[5]Interestingly, this proprietary traffic-shaping mechanism claims to "reflect" FECN bits received by the remote router by converting them to BECN bits sent back to the source router, so that the source router can slow down its flow. Thus, traffic from the local end can be throttled back even if the flow is primarily away from the local end and toward the remote end. The exact details of how this operates are vendor proprietary, however.

have to start discarding frames at the router itself. Furthermore, since LANs do not have any flow control built into them, the router also cannot stem the tide of incoming frames from its attached LANs. Note that TCP, at layer 4, rides above the routers and LANs, and hence its sophisticated flow control is not directly available to the router.

Some routers use a clever technique called **random early detection** or **random early drop** (RED) to trick TCP into performing flow control in order to avoid congestion.[6] When RED is enabled on a virtual circuit, the router will randomly discard IP packets when it notices its outbound queue filling up for that virtual circuit but before serious congestion sets in. As discussed in an earlier subsection, a packet discard will cause a timeout for the appropriate acknowledgment timer within TCP. Hence, TCP will close the congestion window down to the minimum size, begin the slow start algorithm, and then quickly ramp its transmission back up to a rate the router can sustain.

By increasing the probability of discarding packets, the router can force TCP to lower its average transmission rate. RED also has benefits for non-adaptive traffic flows, such as User Datagram Protocol (UDP) flows. The voice over Real-Time Protocol (RTP) over UDP over IP is an example of a nonadaptive UDP flow. In this case RED would cause the loss of many small random portions of the voice conversation as opposed to losing fewer but larger chunks.

Note that RED directly benefits the router by reducing congestion within it, and indirectly benefits the network by reducing the amount of traffic sent into it. As always, RED has many proprietary variations, which are usually given related names, such as **weighted random early detection** (WRED).

The overall conclusion is that routers vary from poor to mediocre at helping to control congestion within a frame relay network.

Prioritizing Traffic within Routers

A router will often have a queue, or buffer, of frames waiting to be sent out over a frame relay interface. How it decides which frame to send next is determined by the queueing protocol (also known as the scheduling discipline) configured into it (see Figure 13.3). When traffic is light, and hence there is no congestion at the outbound interface, frames are transmitted out

---

[6]Rumor has it that RED was originally called "random early *discard*" in the research literature, but that name didn't appeal to corporate marketeers, so it was changed to "random early *detection*."

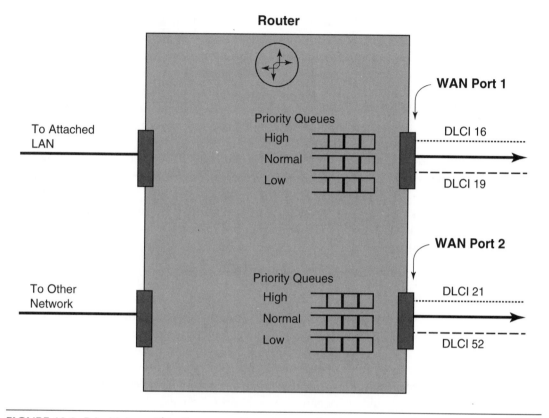

FIGURE 13.3 Prioritizing within Routers.   *Routers can prioritize output traffic based on various criteria.*

the interface as soon as they arrive. But when traffic is heavy and there is congestion at the outbound interface, frames are transmitted according to their assigned priority and the queueing mechanism configured for the router. The queueing protocol can have a significant impact on the virtual circuit's QoS and can help control congestion, especially within the router.

The simplest type of queueing protocol is **first-come first-served** (FCFS), also known as **first-in first-out** (FIFO). FCFS does not use priority or classes of traffic. Instead, transmission of frames out the interface occurs in the order of their arrival. FCFS is simple to implement and is perfectly adequate when access circuit congestion is minimal, but it has several potential disadvantages, as follows:

- Ill-behaved sources can unfairly consume available capacity.
- Bursty sources can cause delays in time-sensitive or important traffic. This is sometimes called the convoy effect, drawing an analogy with how military convoys slow down passenger car traffic.
- Important traffic may be dropped because less important traffic fills the queue.

The main alternative to FCFS is a queueing protocol based on traffic prioritization or classes of traffic. Depending on the router, different priority levels can be assigned based on protocol, TCP or UDP port number, packet size, or DLCI. The router may be able to assign priority across DLCIs within a router's WAN port or across traffic types within a DLCI (see the later discussion of RFC 1490), or combinations. This can be helpful in several ways:

- PVCs can be segregated to carry different traffic types such as SNA and TCP/IP. Each traffic type can run over its own virtual circuit, and the mission-critical SNA transaction traffic can have priority over the TCP/IP traffic. This solution has higher costs because more virtual circuits are required. Having more virtual circuits also increases the amount of routing protocol traffic (chatter) because the routing update packets are broadcast over *each* PVC.
- Digitized voice can also be handled on a segregated, higher priority PVC. However, as noted earlier, this technique is most effective if the frame relay switches also can assign priority by PVC, which only some can.
- Multiprotocol encapsulation can be used to keep costs down by allowing different traffic types to traverse the *same* PVC (see later in this chapter). Some routers can prioritize traffic on a single PVC by protocol type.
- Personal computers on the network might support high-priority Telnet sessions and lower priority file transfers, both over TCP/IP. The router may be able to give the Telnet sessions higher priority by their TCP port number.

One important issue is how the priority queues are served. A simple, but potentially troublesome, method is strict priority service, in which the router will empty the highest priority queue completely before moving on to the next-highest-priority queue. The lower priority queues may starve with this queueing discipline.

Some routers allow each queue to have a guaranteed level of throughput, which keeps the low-priority queues from starving. This is also known as queue reservation or guaranteed sampling, and there are many variations.

A related queueing technique is called **fair queueing**. At the outbound interface the router has a queue for each source of traffic. When the access line attached to the interface becomes idle, the router scans the queues round robin, taking the first frame on the next queue. In this way, with n hosts competing for a given output line, each host gets to send one out of every n frames. Sending more frames will not improve this fraction. Fair queueing is helpful for low-speed WAN links.

Various improvements are possible for the fair queueing algorithm. Cisco has a variation called **weighted fair queueing** (WFQ), which dynamically schedules interactive traffic to the front of the queue to reduce response time and fairly shares the remaining bandwidth among the high-bandwidth flows. The fair sharing can be weighted by priority. The WFQ weights are affected by the DE, FECN, and BECN bits. Once congestion is indicated by the congestion bits, the WFQ weights are altered so that the connection encountering the congestion transmits less frequently. In summary, WFQ gives low-volume traffic, such as Telnet sessions, priority over high-volume traffic, such as FTP file transfers, but concurrent file transfers get balanced use of the remaining link capacity. WFQ, especially based on traffic classes, is better suited for high-speed backbones where fair queueing is not as important as achieving good quality of service.[7]

Effects of Frame Relay on Router Interconnectivity

Frame relay virtual circuits allow some possibilities and raise some challenges that are not encountered with leased line connections between routers.

More Meshing Options

Since virtual circuits are relatively inexpensive compared to frame relay port and access costs, network managers can cost-effectively provision more (virtual) links between routers than can be done with traditional leased lines. This can lead to fewer hops between routers, which in turn

---

[7]For more information on fair queueing and weighted fair queueing, see Prakash's white paper at *www.cisco.com/warp/public/cc/cisco/mkt/ios/qos/tech/qos72_wp.htm/*

can lead to lower transfer delay across the network. Frame relay networks, which typically have a transfer delay well under 100 milliseconds, are often faster than router-based networks, especially router networks with many hops and low-speed inter-router links.

A higher degree of meshing between routers can also simplify the router topology. For a fully meshed router network, all routers are just edge routers feeding into a common frame relay cloud. This avoids issues for a packet that must transit intermediate routers on the way to its destination, such as delay and the intermediate router's capacity. Thus, the edge routers can be cheaper because they do not have to handle transiting traffic.

SVC Issues

Frame relay switched virtual circuits (SVCs) have many potential advantages, as discussed in Chapter 5, Frame Relay Virtual Circuits. Some of these advantages are easier administration, backup for access circuit failure, rerouting flexibility, spillover for overflow traffic, and the possibility of making a direct connection between two sites whenever they need it (cut-through switching). Nonetheless, SVCs add little or no value to a router-based network, which helps explain why public frame relay SVCs have not been very popular in the marketplace. The main limitations of SVCs are as follows [Passmore97]:

- The dynamic establishment of connections at layer 2 is redundant, since routers already switch traffic at layer 3 (via IP). Thus, PVCs are perfectly adequate for network trunking between routers. If a failure occurs in a router network, rerouting occurs automatically at layer 3. There is little value in having the frame relay network establish a new virtual circuit when routers can handle the problem.
- SVCs can put an intolerable burden on the routing protocol update process by coming and going quickly. When a new SVC link is established, the routing protocol must propagate the information about the new link. Very large router-based networks, such as ISPs, can take as long as 10 minutes to rebuild the topology tables on all of their routers.
- Staff that run the enterprise data networks (Netheads) see little need for SVCs because of their background in TCP/IP. On the other hand, traditional carrier and telecom staff (Bellheads) are familiar with switched circuits because of their work with the public switched telephone network (PSTN), a connection-oriented service.

Solving the Split Horizon Problem

As discussed earlier, many routers originally implemented the split horizon rule, which stated that a router would not advertise a route out of the
same port on which the routing update packet came in. However, such a
rule meant that a partial mesh frame relay topology could not be supported because a router would not be able to forward traffic back into the
frame relay network when both virtual circuits were on the same physical
access circuit.

The solution adopted by router vendors is the virtual WAN connection.
Each virtual connection (with its associated DLCI) is treated independently, as if it were a leased line with its own port. Here the modified split
horizon rule is "Don't advertise a route out the same *DLCI* that the advertisement came in on." This modification allows partial mesh frame relay
networks, but still decreases the chances of a routing loop occurring.

In practice, this modified split horizon rule is widely adopted in "modern" routers. Only some old routers struggling to handle frame relay do
not include this solution to the original split horizon problem.

RFC 1490/2427 Multiprotocol Encapsulation

Network managers may want different protocols to travel over the *same*
frame relay virtual circuit. For instance, a manager might want SNA and
TCP/IP packets to use the same PVC (or SVC) to cut costs, and RFC 1490
multiprotocol encapsulation allows this. Without a standard such as this
one, the router would have to be configured to expect only *one* type of
higher layer protocol over a virtual circuit. With RFC 1490, the router can
use the RFC 1490 header (see below) to decide which higher layer protocol
is actually being carried over the virtual circuit.

The advantages of RFC 1490 encapsulation are these:

- A virtual circuit can be shared among different types of traffic. This
  may make more cost-effective use of virtual circuits and can help
  with load balancing.
- Frame relay CPE vendors can use an "open" standard encapsulation
  method rather than a proprietary method.
- SNA (and other nonroutable protocols) can be carried directly in a
  frame relay frame. With this standard, frame relay becomes a serial
  (connection-oriented) layer 2 protocol for SNA, which means that for
  SNA traffic, frame relay becomes an alternative to SDLC.

This multiprotocol encapsulation was originally described in RFC 1294, which was updated in RFC 1490 and again in RFC 2427, upwardly compatibly. The term "RFC 1490" has become deeply embedded in the literature, so we use it instead of the more correct "*RFC 2427 Multiprotocol Interconnect over Frame Relay*." The Frame Relay Forum published *FRF.3.1 Multiprotocol Encapsulation Implementation Agreement* [FRF3.1], which is an IBM-authored extension to RFC 1490, which describes how SNA traffic should be encapsulated. When vendors and analysts encourage users to evaluate "an RFC 1490 solution," they usually mean the combination of RFC 1490 (updated by RFC 2427) and FRF.3.1, even if they don't quite say that.

Terminal equipment that supports an encapsulation method must know which virtual connections will carry the method. Encapsulation procedures must be used only over PVCs that have been explicitly configured to carry encapsulation or over SVCs that are established indicating encapsulation during call setup.

RFC 1490 Encapsulation Formats

RFC 1490 encapsulation operates by using a "secondary" or encapsulation header at the beginning of the frame relay payload. This is somewhat similar to the frame format of LMI messages. The RFC 1490 header contains an **Network Layer Protocol Identifier** (NLPID) field, which identifies which protocol is being encapsulated. NLPID values are defined in ISO/IEC TR 9577 [TR9577] and include several common layer 3 protocols, such as IP (value CC in hex) and ISO CLNP (value 81 in hex). The header can contain extensions to indicate other layer 3 protocols and also layer 2 protocols, such as 802.3 (Ethernet) and 802.5 (Token Ring). The extensions can indicate proprietary protocols, such as SNA subarea and NETBIOS.

LAN-to-LAN traffic can be routed (by routers at layer 3) or bridged (by bridges or LAN switches at layer 2). Hence, **routed** and **bridged** are the two basic types of data packet that travel within a frame relay network. The RFC 1490 header and optional extensions mentioned before indicate which type of packet a frame contains.

Routed packets are typically layer 3 packets and are handled by the layer 3 processing software in the router. Bridged packets are typically layer 3 packets that are encapsulated within a MAC header and possibly also a MAC trailer (which contains the checksum).[8] The RFC 1490 encap-

---

[8]MAC stands for medium access control (some say media access control) and generically refers to IEEE 802.3 (Ethernet), 802.5 (Token Ring), etc.

sulation header indicates the type of MAC frame contained in the frame relay frame.

Since the complete bridged-format encapsulation method contains a MAC header with a 6-byte destination MAC address and a 6-byte source address, it is longer than the routed-format encapsulation header.

To refine this discussion of the encapsulation header and extensions, we include the three basic types of multiprotocol header formats:

Direct NLPID (the "short format"). The direct NLPID format requires only 2 bytes for the multiprotocol encapsulation header. It identifies the protocol carried inside the frame. This format is used for routed packets and is available only for protocols, such as IP, that have an NLPID defined in ISO TR 9577.

SNAP encapsulation (the "long format"). The **Subnetwork Access Protocol** (SNAP) uses an NLPID value of 80 in hex and contains two additional fields (the SNAP header) to specify the protocol carried in the frame. These fields are the **Organizationally Unique Identifier** (OUI) and the **Protocol ID** (PID), which together identify a distinct protocol. Multiprotocol encapsulation using SNAP takes 8 bytes. This format can be used for routed packets that do not have an NLPID assigned to them. It can also be used for bridged packets, which then need to contain a MAC header after the SNAP header.

NLPID "escape" format. This format uses an NLPID value of 08 in hex (which indicates ITU-T Q.933 and is an "escape" value). The 4 bytes following the NLPID include both layer 2 and layer 3 protocol identifiers. The NLPID escape format is used for some connection-oriented protocols and other protocols that cannot be supported by the other two formats. In general, it is used for routed packets because it does not contain MAC addresses. This format is particularly important for SNA traffic because it is often used to carry SNA over frame relay, as we will see. It takes a minimum of 6 bytes, although the SNA version takes 10 bytes because it also includes an LLC2 (IEEE 802.2 Logical Link Control Type 2, also called ISO 8802/2) header of 4 bytes.

Figure 13.4 shows the format of an IP datagram encapsulated within an RFC 1490 frame. This is the direct NLPID short format described above. The first 2 octets after the flag are the standard frame relay header, as defined in ITU-T Q.922 Annex A or ANSI T1.618. The next octet (03 in hex, the first octet of the RFC 1490 header) is for compatibility with other

Encapsulation with RFC 1490

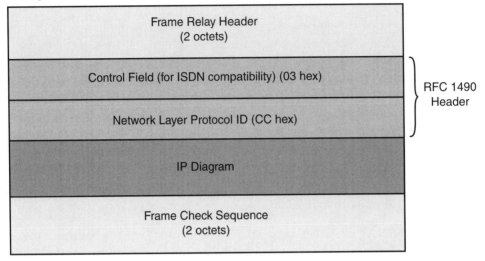

Normal Encapsulation

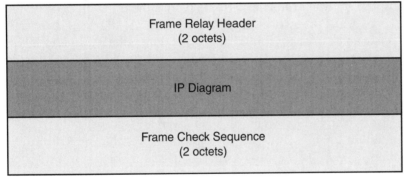

FIGURE 13.4 RFC 1490 Multiprotocol Encapsulation.   *An IP datagram can be encapsulated using RFC 1490. An IP datagram can also be carried "normally" within a frame relay frame.*

sections of ITU-T Q.922, which specify ISDN-related data link control issues.[9] The next octet (value CC in hex) is the NLPID for IP. The entire IP datagram follows, closed by the standard frame relay trailer, which contains the checksum.

---

[9]Hex 03 indicates that the field is the Unnumbered Information (UI) control field for the HDLC/LAPF protocol. This field is used in a similar way for LMI messages and SVC call control messages.

Address Resolution with RFC 1490

RFC 1490 provides a method for dynamically resolving a protocol address over a PVC. For instance, a router might know the IP address of a host but want to learn the associated DLCI so that it can send an IP datagram to that host over a PVC. The RFC 1490 method is to encapsulate a standard Address Resolution Protocol (ARP) message within a SNAP-encoded frame relay frame (the second type of multiprotocol encapsulation described above). **Reverse ARP** (RARP) works in a similar way.

Address resolution with ARP is best handled by multicasting the ARP request to all end stations that might be able to resolve the address. Since multicasting is not yet common in frame relay networks, an alternative is often used: The end station simply sends a copy of the ARP request through each relevant PVC, thereby simulating a multicast.

Because of the inefficiencies of emulating broadcasting in a frame relay environment, a new address resolution variation was developed by the authors of RFC 1490 called **Inverse ARP** (InARP)—see RFC 1293, updated in RFC 2390. As mentioned earlier, InARP describes a method for resolving a protocol address, such as an IP address, when the DLCI is already known. It is useful for router autoconfiguration.

Encapsulation of X.25

In some cases a network manager may want to interconnect X.25 devices via a frame relay network. An example is X.25-based automatic teller machines that need to take advantage of the savings of frame relay compared to leased lines. RFC 1490 multiprotocol encapsulation procedures are an option, but a simpler method is single-protocol X.25 encapsulation, described in ANSI T1.617a-1994 Annex G. This is often referred to as "Annex G encapsulation," without specific mention that it is Annex G of ANSI T1.617a.

RFC 1490 Misunderstandings

RFC 1490 is sometimes misunderstood because it does not specify the "value-added" capabilities that vendors implement to boost performance, optimize bandwidth, and so forth. For instance, features such as protocol prioritization, dynamic rerouting, and local acknowledgment (discussed later) are all vendor specific. RFC 1490 and its companion FRF.3.1 merely specify encapsulation format.

Routable Protocols over Frame Relay

We explain some additional issues that occur when routers send routable protocols over a frame relay network.

TCP/IP over Frame Relay

The combination of TCP and IP was specifically intended to tie networks together over WAN links. As discussed earlier, TCP has a built-in sliding window flow control mechanism that adapts to the throughput of the underlying network. It has checksums and sequence counters so that it can provide quality assurance on the lower layers of the network. Those lower layers include the "unreliable" IP protocol at layer 3 and any other host-to-network protocols underneath IP. For all practical purposes, TCP/IP works transparently over a frame relay network. Figure 13.5 shows the format of an IP datagram as normally encapsulated within a frame relay frame (without multiprotocol encapsulation).

TCP/IP over Frame Relay    Works well!

	Small Network	Large Network
Distance Vector Routing Protocol	☺	☹
Link State Routing Protocol	☺	☺

Novell's IPX over Frame Relay   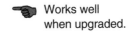 Works well when upgraded.

With Packet Burst Mode and SAP filter upgrades   ☺

FIGURE 13.5 TCP/IP and IPX over Frame Relay.

Also discussed earlier, a link state routing protocol is especially useful if the network is large (more than about 20 DLCIs per router) or complex, or if the virtual circuit rates are low (64 Kbps or less). Within the family of link state protocols we include OSPF as a common example but also Cisco's EIGRP because of its advanced features, even though EIGRP's origins are in the distance vector family.

IPX over Frame Relay

Internet Packet Exchange (IPX), a network layer protocol developed by Novell for LAN environments, is part of Novell's NetWare LAN architecture. By some estimates, 70% of large enterprise networks support at least some IPX traffic, although this figure is declining as enterprises try to standardize on just a few protocols, such as IP. Novell originally designed IPX to operate over very high-speed local connections, not over WANs. With earlier versions of NetWare, IPX performed poorly over any WAN for the following reasons:

- It required one acknowledgment for each packet transmitted (stop-and-wait). Over a WAN this greatly limits throughput.
- The Service Advertisement Protocol (SAP) required that a host offering services periodically announce its offering to all other network users. Hosts typically broadcast a SAP every 60 seconds, which generated a lot of unnecessary network traffic.
- NetWare used the RIP distance vector routing protocol (see the earlier discussion), which was not as efficient as a link state routing protocol, especially for large networks.

However, Novell now has software upgrades, called **NetWare Loadable Modules** (NLMs), that solve these problems:

- Packet burst mode, or P-Burst, which gives IPX a more typical sliding window acknowledgment method. This significantly improves network performance.
- The SAP filter, which reduces excessive SAP broadcasts and hence reduces congestion.
- The link state routing protocol **NLSP**, which replaces RIP. Like other link state protocols, NLSP improves general network performance and offers such features as load balancing and intelligent route selection.

These modules are usually included in recent releases of NetWare.

IBM's SNA over Frame Relay

Traditional SNA is unroutable—the messages from end users do not include the network layer addresses that a router needs to transfer packets between a LAN and a WAN. In addition, SNA typically has characteristics, such as low tolerance for delay, that make it not easily compatible with, say, TCP/IP traffic. For these reasons, sending SNA over frame relay networks, which are usually router based, is not completely straightforward.

However, SNA networks are common—there are over 50,000 by some estimates—so it is not surprising that some SNA traffic finds itself traveling over frame relay networks. Many network managers are integrating SNA traffic with LAN and Internet traffic, such as TCP/IP. When this consolidation is done using a frame relay infrastructure, users report total savings of up to 50% to 80%.

Before outlining the major approaches to sending SNA over frame relay, we give some background about SNA that will enhance understanding of the major approaches.

SNA Background

IBM has evolved the following three major generations of SNA:

Subarea SNA, first released in 1974, is the "traditional" form of SNA, in which the network roles are hierarchical (master-slave). A typical small network has a host node (mainframe), a front-end processor (communications controller), and several peripheral nodes (workstations/PCs or cluster controllers with attached terminals).

Advanced Peer-to-Peer Networking (APPN) supports any-to-any connectivity among SNA devices rather than the master-slave connectivity of subarea SNA. Released in 1986, APPN is IBM's foray into the distributed world of peer-to-peer and client/server networking, providing traffic routing over SNA networks with arbitrary topologies. It requires no specialized communications hardware, although front-end processors and cluster controllers are certainly still common in APPN networks. The APPN protocol is open so that non-IBM vendors can either build or purchase the code. The APPN standards organization is the APPN Implementers' Workshop (AIW), which is sponsored by IBM. In 1994 IBM added the **Dependent Logical Unit Requester** (DLUR) product, which allows traditional subarea SNA traffic to be converted to APPN and routed over an APPN network. For instance, a traditional cluster controller could interface with DLUR software in an APPN router; the router could in turn route the traffic to a mainframe. Since many of IBM's devices support both APPN/HPR and frame relay, traditional subarea SNA can be routed directly over a frame relay network with DLUR.

High Performance Routing (HPR) is an extension of APPN and improves on it in much the same way that frame relay improves on X.25. Using the existing APPN control algorithms for locating resources and selecting routes, HPR adds nondisruptive rerouting, improved routing performance, and rate-based congestion control. IBM's intent with HPR is to provide a serious alternative to TCP/IP networks for SNA traffic. FRF.3.1 describes how HPR, as well as subarea SNA and APPN, can be encapsulated with RFC 1490 techniques so it can be run in parallel with other protocols over a frame relay network.

Data Link Control Protocols

Traditionally, SNA used Synchronous Data Link Control (SDLC) as its layer 2 protocol. SDLC, a member of the High-level Data Link Control (HDLC) family of bit-oriented, "modern" protocols, is used for point-to-point and multipoint connections. It provides sliding window flow control and error detection and correction. Thus, it is a "reliable" connection-oriented layer 2 protocol. Because SDLC is typically used over leased lines, which have fixed and short delay, its timeout timers are usually set tight so that they will expire quickly. This is appropriate behavior in traditional SNA networks, but it is a liability in networks that have unpredictable delays— the Internet or router-based ones. The SDLC timeout periods can be lengthened, but SNA devices do not always make the reconfiguration easy.

After SDLC became widespread, IBM began using the newer **Logical Link Control Type 2** (LLC2) especially to support Token Ring LANs. Token Ring provided much-needed speed and flexibility compared to the older point-to-point cabling. LLC2 is described in IEEE 802.2 and is specifically designed to provide a connection-oriented service over LANs. Like SDLC, it is in the HDLC family and provides sliding window flow control and error detection and correction. However, it is able to multiplex and identify up to 127 users of its service, which is a definite advantage over SDLC. These multiplexing fields are known as **service access points** and are part of the 4-byte LLC2 header. Also, the timeout settings for LLC2 are typically more forgiving, because LLC2 must be able to function over bridged networks that can be slow.

Many of the approaches to sending SNA over frame relay include converting SNA SDLC traffic to LLC2 traffic for transmission across some intermediate network.

Sessions

SNA uses the idea of a session, which is a sequence of interactions between end users. A route, or path, through the SNA network is determined when the session is set up and, once determined, does not change for the session duration. In subarea SNA all available paths must be predefined (static routing), whereas in APPN each path is determined dynamically when the session is set up. However, for both types if any link or node along the path fails, or if a timeout timer repeatedly expires, then all sessions using that failed resource are terminated and must be restarted by the end user or application. These session drops are an annoyance. HPR is an improvement because if there is a failure along the path, it will dynamically find and switch to a new path without disrupting the session.

Spoofing

Spoofing, also known as **local acknowledgment**, is a clever technique for reducing the amount of unnecessary traffic across a WAN. Normally, polling traffic will cross the entire SNA network, which can use up a considerable amount of bandwidth on slow WAN links. However, if the devices, usually routers, at each edge of the WAN terminate the layer 2 connection, they need to pass only user data across the WAN instead of all the polling messages.

For instance, if a **front-end processor** (FEP) polls an SNA workstation, the polling message will be intercepted by the router nearest the FEP, to which the router will return a "no traffic reply." The near router will not send the polls across the WAN. At the same time, the router closest to the workstation (on the other side of the WAN) will be "artificially" generating periodic polls and sending them to the workstation. When the workstation does finally generate some user data, it will respond to an "artificial" poll from its nearby router by sending the user data to it. The router will then forward the user data across the WAN to the router near the FEP. This router in turn will forward the user data to the FEP in response to a poll by the FEP. Clever.

In addition to cutting down on unnecessary traffic, spoofing has another vital advantage. Because the layer 2 connections are *locally* acknowledged, they rarely time out. Thus, a slow WAN link will contribute to slow response time at the user's end, but will not cause annoying session timeouts.

Many vendors use spoofing as one of their SNA-over-frame-relay performance improvements. Spoofing is not mentioned in RFC 1490/FRF.3.1 documents, but it is commonly included anytime a vendor uses a multi-protocol encapsulation technique.

Problems with Direct Encapsulation of SNA

The simplest method of handling SNA traffic, especially SNA/SDLC, is to put all the SNA traffic, including polls, protocol messages, and data packets, directly into frame relay frames without any additional encapsulation or spoofing. Each remote SNA device communicates over its own PVC.

This technique is expensive, however, because of the volume of traffic and the large number of PVCs needed. In addition, it is likely to have severe performance problems, especially session timeouts, if the frame relay network is underengineered or performs poorly. We look at more practical methods of sending SNA over frame relay in the next section.

Vendor Variations

Vendors use *many* techniques for sending SNA over frame relay. Some are closely based on published specifications such as RFC 1490 or Data Link Switching (DLSw) (see later discussion). Some vendors, such as Cisco, start with the published specs and add many enhancements and options; other vendors have completely proprietary solutions.

Three general groups among vendors are FEP oriented, router oriented, and FRAD oriented, although the distinctions are not at all sharp. FEP vendors tend to favor solutions in which the FEP connects directly to the frame relay network. Router vendors prefer a router between the FEP and the frame relay network, or even replace the FEP with a router. Not surprisingly, FRAD vendors maintain that a FRAD can do the job well enough and more cheaply than a router.

The vendors' white papers in this area tend to be quite complex and often have vendor biases that are not readily apparent.

SNA over Frame Relay

We outline several approaches to the problem of sending SNA traffic over a frame relay network. Details of these approaches and the intricacies of SNA in general are beyond our scope.

IBM Hardware/Software Support for Frame Relay

IBM offers considerable support for sending SNA traffic directly over frame relay. This is an alternative to the traditional approach of sending SNA traffic over the point-to-point link layer WAN protocol SDLC. The 3745 FEP and the 3174 cluster controller have optional frame relay interfaces, as discussed in Chapter 4, Connecting to the Network, and thus become FRADs. In addition, IBM's Network Control Program (NCP), Release 6 (and later) allows the FEP to become a "frame handler," a frame relay switch.

If a company already has a large investment in SNA and needs to integrate little non-SNA traffic into the existing network, the IBM hardware/software solutions may be useful for migrating to frame relay without jeopardizing the network applications. However, some analysts estimate that only about 5% of SNA networks use these solutions, partly because TCP/IP is so commonplace.

We outline three IBM hardware/software approaches for sending SNA over frame relay. These approaches are also supported by some third-party vendors, such as Cisco.

Boundary Network Node

The technique called Boundary Network Node (BNN) is essentially the third basic type of RFC 1490/FRF.3.1 multiprotocol encapsulation discussed in the section on RFC 1490. It uses the NLPID "escape" encapsulation format. The total length of the header, including the standard Q.922 frame relay header but excluding the flag byte, is 12 bytes, which makes BNN a very-low-overhead way of transporting SNA data (**Path Information Units**, PIUs) across a frame relay network (see Figure 13.6).

IBM introduced BNN support for FEPs with the release of its Network Control Program, Version 7.1. This release enabled an FEP to connect directly to a frame relay network and to communicate directly with remote frame relay devices. Thus, a separate router is not necessary, although it may be useful for handling both SNA and TCP/IP traffic.

BNN's strengths are low frame overhead and low initial costs, and it may be a reasonable solution for stable environments. It's weaknesses are high recurring costs, low resiliency, complex configuration, and awkward multiprotocol support.

Boundary Access Node

The technique called Boundary Access Node (BAN) is essentially LAN bridging (see Figure 13.7). It uses the bridged format of the second basic

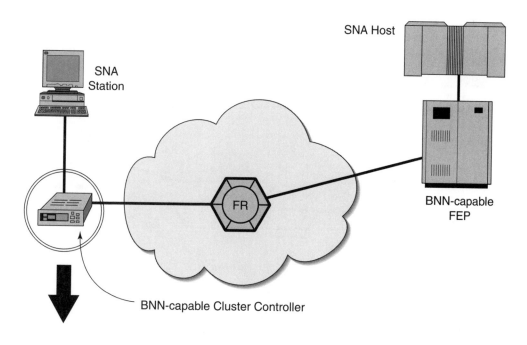

Frame Format on Station Side (SNA over SDLC)

SDLC Header	SNA PIU	SDLC Trailer

Frame Format on Frame Relay Side

FR Header	RFC 1490 Header	LLC2 Header	SNA PIU	FR Trailer

PIU = SNA Path Information Unit
SDLC = Synchronous Data Link Control
LLC2 = Logical Link Control Type 2

FIGURE 13.6 Boundary Network Node. *IBM equipment can use frame relay directly with Boundary Network Node (RFC 1490 routed format). [The rectangles indicate the header structure of the frame on each side of the cluster controller.]*

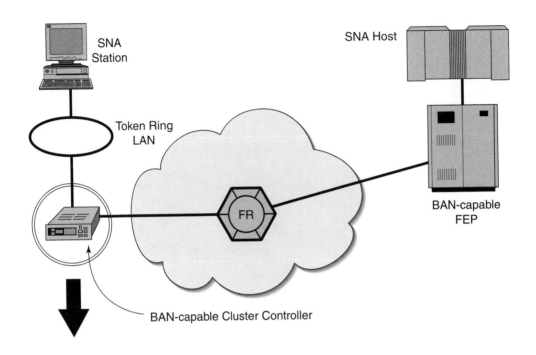

Frame Format on LAN Side (SNA over Token Ring)

Frame Format on Frame Relay Side

FR Header	RFC 1490 Header	MAC/LLC2 Header	SNA PIU	MAC Trailer	FR Trailer

FIGURE 13.7 Boundary Access Node.   *IBM equipment can also use frame relay directly with Boundary Access Node (RFC 1490 bridged format).*

type of RFC 1490/FRF.3.1 multiprotocol encapsulation discussed in the section on RFC 1490. BAN includes a MAC header as part of the RFC 1490 encapsulation header, thus making its encapsulation header longer (about 28 bytes) than that for BNN (12 bytes).

     IBM introduced BAN support for FEPs with the release of NCP, Version 7.3. Whereas BNN was designed for the serial world, the purpose of

BAN is to accommodate LAN-attached devices. BAN was designed to overcome the limitations of BNN when supporting large numbers of LAN devices. It distinguishes one SNA device from another based on the MAC header, which in many cases will be a Token Ring header.

Like BNN, BAN enables an FEP to connect directly to a frame relay network, potentially eliminating the need for an intermediate router or FRAD. Also like BNN, BAN can incorporate spoofing to reduce the likelihood of session timeouts and to decrease the amount of polling traffic flowing across the network.

BAN's strengths are easier configuration and troubleshooting, because the MAC addresses are "visible" in the frame relay frame; flexibility; and relatively low hardware costs. Its main weaknesses are somewhat greater frame overhead and the lack of support in older versions of NCP.

Advanced Peer-to-Peer Networking and High Performance Routing

As discussed in the previous section, IBM has two later versions of SNA— namely, Advanced Peer-to-Peer Networking (APPN) and High Performance Routing (HPR). These are useful for larger mainframe clusters, especially when there is little TCP/IP traffic. Both support dynamic peer-to-peer networking and directly support frame relay; HPR, in particular, provides nondisruptive rerouting around failures. However, these solutions tend to be memory and processor intensive, and they are "Big Blue" solutions, with all that that implies.

SNA Gateways

With this method, gateway software in the SNA end-user device encapsulates the SNA message within TCP/IP (or IPX) and then sends it on through the wide area network (see Figure 13.8). IP provides the network layer addressing. At the SNA host, the gateway strips away the TCP/IP encapsulation and delivers the pure SNA message to the SNA application. A variation of this method is to *translate* or *convert* the lower layers of the SNA message to TCP/IP format rather than just encapsulate it entirely.

Thus, the gateway is software residing on the SNA end-user device (usually a PC) and on the mainframe. The gateway can also be a hardware gateway server, usually attached to the mainframe.

Vendors offer many variations of this encapsulation method. A popular one is the SNA terminal emulation standard **tn3270**, which lets TCP/IP

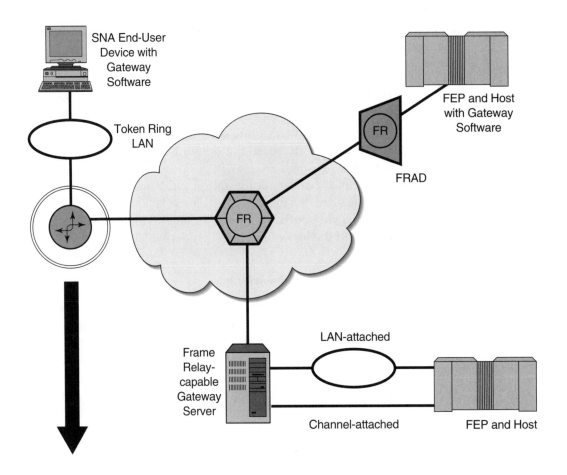

Frame Format on LAN Side

MAC/LLC2 Header	IP Header	TCP Header	SNA Path Information Unit	MAC Trailer

Frame Format on Frame Relay Side

FR Header	IP Header	TCP Header	SNA Path Information Unit	FR Trailer

FIGURE 13.8 SNA Gateways. *Gateway software in the SNA end-user device encapsulates the SNA message within TCP/IP.*

networks carry SNA application data using TCP/IP's telnet capability. Other encapsulation methods are proprietary, although many vendors may support them.

TCP/IP encapsulation methods have limitations, such as support for remote printing, SNA compatibility issues, and problems with multivendor interoperability.

Router-Based RFC 1490 Multiprotocol Encapsulation

Router (and FRAD) vendors often support some type of RFC 1490 multiprotocol encapsulation (see Figure 13.9). These are in contrast to BNN and BAN (discussed earlier), which also use RFC 1490 but are intended to be front-end processor solutions.

For SNA networks, RFC 1490 in general has the important advantages of simplicity and low overhead. Unless spoofing is used, it has the disadvantage of possible session timeouts.

RFC 1490 encapsulation is sometimes combined with **segregated PVCs** so that the SNA traffic has its own PVC. If the routers *and* the frame relay switches along the path can give the SNA traffic higher priority, session timeouts will be less likely and overall performance will improve. However, most frame relay switches and some routers cannot yet prioritize by traffic type.

RFC 1490 is available on routers and FRADs, but compliance is sometimes spotty. In particular, the header extensions for SNA may not be supported, even if the "basic" RFC 1490 header is implemented.

Data Link Switching

Data Link Switching is an IBM-originated method for encapsulating SNA (and NETBIOS) within TCP/IP. It is described in RFC 1795, although the status of this RFC is informational rather than standards track. DLSw, depicted in Figure 13.10, is a type of serial tunneling, which means that each SNA data stream has its own "tunnel" through the TCP/IP network to its destination. It is typically implemented in routers rather than in end-user devices. Many router vendors, including Cisco, offer variations on DLSw or other proprietary tunneling approaches. Many router vendors also include an RFC 1490 encapsulation header along with the DLSw and TCP/IP headers, even though the DLSw specifications do not require it. DLSw will work over any wide area network that supports TCP/IP, not just frame relay.

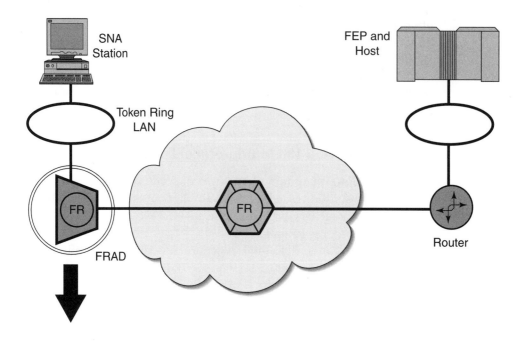

Frame Format on LAN Side (SNA over Token Ring)

MAC/LLC2 Header	SNA PIU	MAC Trailer

Frame Format on Frame Relay Side

FR Header	RFC 1490 Header	LLC2 Header	SNA PIU	FR Trailer

FIGURE 13.9 Router-Based and FRAD-Based RFC 1490 Multiprotocol Encapsulation. *Routers and FRADs can provide RFC 1490 encapsulation of SNA traffic.*

DLSw has three main features:

• In a LAN environment, a DLSw-capable router "routes" traffic according to the Medium Access Control (MAC) address. It does not need to examine any of the SNA-specific address fields. The router finds the destination MAC address by a broadcast search scheme

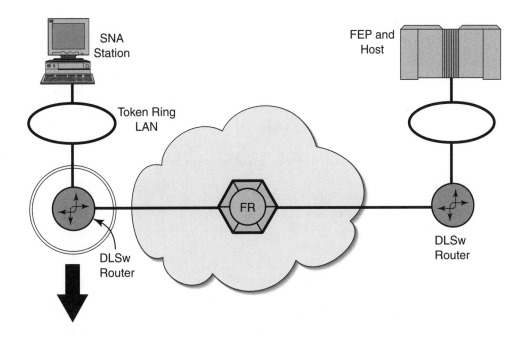

Frame Format on LAN Side (SNA over Token Ring)

MAC/LLC2 Header	SNA PIU	MAC Trailer

Frame Format on Frame Relay Side

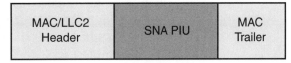

FR Header	IP Header	TCP Header	DLSw Header	SNA PIU	FR Trailer

FIGURE 13.10 Data Link Switching. *A DLSw router encapsulates the SNA message within TCP/IP and sends it across the WAN.*

similar to Token Ring's source route bridging. However, DLSw contains features such as address caching to minimize broadcast storms.

- DLSw provides spoofing. In particular, it terminates the LLC2 connections typical of SNA LANs at the nearest DLSw router. The router supplies LLC2 acknowledgments as if it were the destination FEP,

which reduces traffic across the WAN and reduces the chances of LLC2 session timeouts.
- The TCP/IP layer assumes full responsibility for delivering the packet across the WAN. If a packet is dropped by the WAN, the router, not the SNA devices, assumes responsibility for error recovery. The TCP/IP layer will also handle routing around network problems, such as failed links.

DLSw has disadvantages, especially for large networks:

- It does not scale particularly well. Large networks may need thousands of concurrent TCP/IP sessions at the host routers. In addition, very large networks can still suffer from session timeout problems or poor response time.
- When SNA traffic is encapsulated in TCP/IP, the SNA network management tools, such as IBM Netview, can lose sight of it. In addition, the management tools for TCP/IP networks are not as advanced as the SNA tools.
- It is not plug and play, even though it uses a variation of Token Ring's source route bridging. IP address administration typically requires more manual predefinition than, say, RFC 1490 encapsulation.
- Over frame relay it has about 64 bytes of overhead, counting the TCP/IP headers, the DLSw header, and the frame relay overhead. In contrast, the simplest RFC 1490 encapsulation for SNA has only 16 bytes of overhead, counting the two flag bytes and the checksum.

Sending SNA over Frame Relay

The above approaches for sending SNA over a frame relay network can be categorized three ways:

- APPN, APPN/HPR, BNN, and most other routed-format RFC 1490 solutions are **native transport** methods, because each uses frame relay simply as another layer 2 protocol.
- DLSw, BAN, and most other bridged-format RFC 1490 solutions are **tunneling** methods, because each builds a "tunnel" through the frame relay cloud based on MAC addresses.
- SNA Gateways and tn3270 are **conversion** (or **translation**) methods, because each at least partially converts SNA to another protocol, usually based on TCP/IP.

Nonroutable Protocols over Frame Relay

IBM's NETBIOS and DEC's Local Area Transport (LAT) are like SNA without APPN/HPR—they are unroutable. Thus, much of the previous discussion about handling SNA over frame relay also applies to them. The main alternatives for sending NETBIOS and LAT across a frame relay network are

Bridging.   Bridging may work well for small, especially higher speed networks. In this case the small, fast network acts more like a single LAN, which is what NETBIOS and LAT were designed for.

Proprietary TCP/IP encapsulation.   NETBIOS or LAT can be encapsulated into a TCP/IP packet before being sent over the wide area frame relay network. IBM's Data Link Switching (DLSw) can handle NETBIOS in addition to SNA. Some routers can handle DEC LAT by first **translating** it into Telnet TCP/IP messages. This translation, rather than pure encapsulation, reduces the amount of overhead.

RFC 1490 multiprotocol encapsulation.   The RFC 1490 standard provides ways to handle all layer 2 and layer 3 protocols. It has escapes for handling proprietary protocols. The FRF.3.1 Implementation Agreement associated with RFC 1490 includes specific extensions for NETBIOS.

Chapter 14

Frame Relay and ATM

This chapter contains an expanded discussion of the comparisons between frame relay and ATM technologies mentioned in Chapter 1 (see Table 14.1).

First we discuss three successively more sophisticated ways to migrate from frame relay to ATM:

- Network interworking
- Service interworking
- Frame User-Network Interface (FUNI)

Each of these possibilities has the advantage of not requiring hardware upgrades to the customer premise equipment, at least at the remote locations. Thus, users can preserve their investment in existing frame relay equipment.

We conclude with a summary of frame relay's advantages.

Comparison

Asynchronous transfer mode (ATM) is a connection-oriented "fast packet" technology. It has the following advantages:

- It provides dynamic bandwidth allocation, like X.25 and frame relay, which leads to efficient handling of bursty traffic.
- It is scalable in capacity (from 45 Mbps to gigabit speeds, but also lower speeds).

- It is scalable in topology (from LAN to CAN to WAN).
- It is specifically designed to accommodate *all* media types (voice, data, image, video).
- It supports quantifiable ("hard") QoS.
- It is based on extensive international standards.
- It allows integrated network management.
- It can be deployed in public, private, or hybrid networks.

ATM can be considered a direct outgrowth of circuit switching, packet switching, and frame relay. Like frame relay, which is also a packet-switched technology, ATM switches look for routing information in the header and do not attempt error recovery. Unlike frame relay, ATM switches do not even attempt error detection on the user data but only on the header. Thus, ATM takes frame relay's motto, "Just blast the data across the network," one step further.

However, ATM transmits only fixed-size frames, called cells, not variable-size frames, as frame relay and packet switching do. The standard for ATM cell relay is 53-byte cells (48 bytes of user data, 5 bytes of header). With only fixed-size cells to process, cell relay switches can per-

TABLE 14.1 Comparison of Frame Relay and ATM

	FR	ATM
Dynamic bandwidth allocation	☺	☺
Frame size	Variable	Fixed
Scalable to high speeds	😐	☺
Suitable for WANs, MANs	☺	☺
Suitable for LANs, Campus Area Networks	☹	☺
Carries data	☺	☺
Carries voice and/or video	😐	☺
Supports quantifiable QoS	☹	☺
Cost effective for data-only medium-speed requirements	☺	😐

form significantly faster than either frame relay or ordinary packet switching. More important, fixed-size cells allow ATM to support quantifiable QoS, which in turn allows it to handle "isochronous" traffic, like voice and videoconferencing, which is not easy for frame relay to handle.

Like frame relay, ATM allows both permanent and switched virtual circuits (PVCs and SVCs). However, ATM SVCs are more widely available from service providers and are an essential part of ATM for LAN emulation (LANE).

ATM has a more extensively developed set of standards than frame relay has. For instance, whereas frame relay has no standards to describe how switches communicate with each other *within* a frame relay network (the Network-to-Network Interface only describes how switches communicate *between* networks), ATM has specific standards to describe interswitch communication within the ATM cloud.

ATM is already quite common as the underlying cell-switching backbone for frame relay services and for the IP networks of many ISPs, as well as being available for end-to-end services. However, it is just barely a mature technology: Its standards still need to be refined, it needs to be implemented more extensively in silicon, its costs need to come down, and users need to gain experience with it.

Since ATM is typically more expensive than frame relay (although at higher speeds it may actually be cheaper per bit transmitted), why do customers migrate to it? The advantages we discussed above are factors, but the two main drivers are

- The need for greater capacity than frame relay can handle
- The need to support mixed-media traffic, especially voice and video

With the recent revision to the **ATM Adaptation Layer Type 2** (AAL2) specification, there is rekindled interest in sending compressed voice traffic over ATM, as opposed to the traditional uncompressed 64-Kbps PCM-encoded voice traffic that ATM has been able to handle for a long time. AAL2 can more efficiently support voice over IP across ATM architectures.

One sometimes hears, "Frame relay is only a transitional technology along the path to ATM." However, frame relay has the advantages of being currently available, widely supported, fairly well understood, and cost effective for a large niche of data networks. In particular, frame relay is better suited than ATM for data-only, medium-speed (56/64-Kbps, T1) requirements. For frame relay, the ratio of header size to frame size is typically much smaller than the overhead ratio for ATM, which makes frame relay more efficient.[1] In addition, frame relay will likely be used into the future as an access protocol for higher speed backbone ATM networks. Thus, frame relay and ATM are likely to be complementary rather than directly competitive technologies for quite a while to come.

Network Interworking

Network interworking between frame relay and ATM allows two frame relay devices to communicate with each other over an ATM backbone network. The two devices use the frame relay protocol between them, but a network interworking function encapsulates the frames within ATM cells for transmission across the ATM backbone, as in Figure 14.1. At the destination ATM switch, another network interworking function recombines the cells into the original frame relay frames and sends them on to the other frame relay device. Interworking may be implemented as a function of an ATM switch, as we have shown, as a function of the customer premise equipment, or even as a separate unit.

This encapsulation technique is similar to encapsulation techniques, such as IBM's Data Link Switching (DLSw), discussed in Chapter 13, Internetworking with Frame Relay. The difference is that here frame relay is being encapsulated in ATM rather than being the encapsulating protocol. Thus, one can also say that frame relay is being tunneled through the ATM cloud.

The important advantage of network interworking is that it permits a gradual and transparent conversion of the backbone network to ATM while continuing to support legacy frame relay devices. This may be especially important for companies that have just bought a lot of frame relay CPE. Many frame relay service providers built their initial frame relay networks with proprietary cell-based backbones, because of the inherent advantages of cell-based architectures. Now most of these providers have migrated to true ATM, and this conversion is quite transparent to customers.

Migration to ATM backbones is attractive for several reasons:

- ATM operates at DS-3 speeds (45 Mbps) and higher, even much higher.

---

[1]The overhead ratio for ATM is 5 bytes of overhead divided by 53 bytes of cell size, which gives about 10% overhead. This is often called the **ATM cell tax**, in humorous reference to a sales tax. Whether the cell tax is a *serious* negative feature of ATM is often a matter of debate.

- ATM networks allow for great economies of scale because they can support data, video, and voice.
- ATM networks typically travel over Synchronous Optical Network (SONET) rings, which are specifically designed for good network management and for very fast self-healing in the event of failure.
- ATM has QoS parameters, congestion control mechanisms, and network management capability beyond what is offered by frame relay.

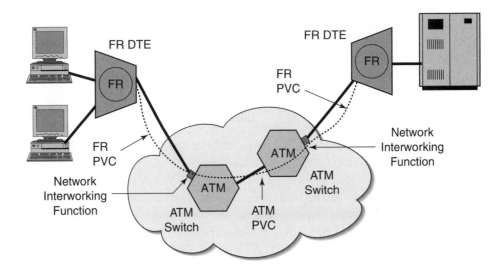

Architectural View

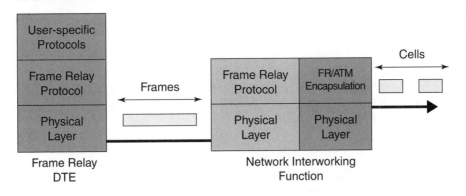

FIGURE 14.1 Network Interworking with Frame Relay and ATM. *Network interworking allows two frame relay devices to communicate over an ATM backbone.*

Network interworking with frame relay and ATM is described in *FRF.5 Frame Relay/ATM PVC Network Interworking Implementation Agreement* [FRF.5-1994], jointly developed by the Frame Relay Forum and the ATM Forum. FRF.5 describes how to encapsulate frame relay frames in ATM cells and is summarized here. (See the Glossary for brief explanations of ATM terms. For a more complete understanding of FRF.5, the reader may need a considerable familiarity with ATM.)

- Frame relay traffic is carried over a **variable bit rate–non-real-time** (VBR-nrt) ATM PVC using ATM Adaptation Layer Type 5 (AAL5). VBR-nrt is the ATM virtual circuit service category that is most appropriate for bursty, delay-tolerant traffic. AAL5 is an efficient method for chopping the frame relay frame into 48-byte blocks that can be inserted into the payload of an ATM cell.
- Frame relay virtual circuits can be multiplexed one to one onto ATM virtual circuits. Optionally, several frame relay virtual circuits can be carried by one ATM virtual circuit, which can reduce the number of circuits needed. DLCIs must be mapped appropriately to ATM **virtual path identifiers/virtual channel identifiers** (VPI/VCIs).
- The frame relay CIR is mapped to the ATM **sustainable cell rate** (SCR), which specifies the average amount of traffic the VBR-nrt virtual circuit must be able to carry.
- The frame relay maximum burst rate (which could be just the access rate) is mapped to the ATM **peak cell rate** (PCR), which specifies the maximum amount of traffic the VBR-nrt virtual circuit must carry.
- The frame relay **discard-eligible** (DE) bit is mapped to the ATM **cell loss priority** (CLP) bit, which functions in a similar way, and the frame relay forward explicit congestion notification (FECN) bit is mapped to the ATM explicit forward congestion indication (EFCI) bit. There are complexities in these mappings, which are described in FRF.5.
- The ATM encapsulation method will transparently transport frames that contain an RFC 1490 multiprotocol encapsulation header. (See Chapter 13, Internetworking with Frame Relay, for more details about RFC 1490.)

Note that FRF.5 defines network interworking only for PVCs. Support for SVCs, which involves mapping frame relay Q.933 signaling messages to ATM Q.2931 signaling messages, is a work in progress.

Network interworking is sometimes known as "inter*net*working." However, this term emphasizes that two *distinct* networks are being connected in some way—for instance, two Ethernet LANs might be joined by a point-to-point link. The term "network interworking" emphasizes that a protocol on a *single* network is being encapsulated by some other protocol for transparent transport across a backbone. For instance, as just discussed, the frames on a single frame relay network may be transported across an ATM backbone.

Service Interworking

Service interworking between frame relay and ATM allows a frame relay device to communicate with a native ATM device over an ATM network. The frame relay device uses the frame relay protocol to send and receive its data; the ATM device uses ATM protocols to do this. A service interworking function performs the protocol conversion so that neither end device knows that the other is "not what it seems."

As with network interworking, the service interworking function can be built into the ATM switch, as shown in Figure 14.2, or into the CPE, or implemented in a separate box.

Service interworking is a relatively complex function because frame relay and ATM functions cannot be mapped exactly into each other. For instance, ATM offers several service classes, including a premium class (constant bit rate, CBR) with hard QoS guarantees that is suitable for standard voice and video. At present, except for some proprietary carrier offerings, frame relay service is "one size fits all." Even the proprietary carrier service offerings have much softer QoS guarantees than ATM routinely provides. Thus, mapping frame relay service into ATM service is fairly easy, but mapping ATM service into frame relay may degrade the service quality of ATM. For that reason, service interworking between frame relay and ATM is limited to the lowest common denominator, which is usually the frame relay functionality.

Nonetheless, service interworking provides an important advantage. It allows conversion of selected customer sites to native ATM while still maintaining the ability to communicate with legacy sites that have not yet converted to ATM.

We now describe how network interworking and service interworking differ in their handling of the frame relay header. With network interworking, the 2-byte frame relay header is just encapsulated within ATM and transported across the ATM network. At the destination side of the ATM network, it is "reattached" to the reassembled frame relay payload and then passed to the destination CPE. In contrast, with service interworking the 2-byte frame relay header is torn apart and the bits are

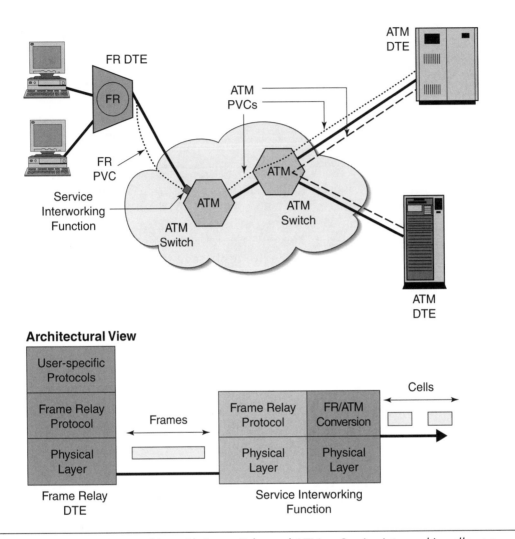

FIGURE 14.2 Service Interworking with Frame Relay and ATM.   *Service interworking allows a frame relay device to communicate with a native ATM device over an ATM network.*

converted into appropriate ATM header fields. The frame relay header is not reassembled at the destination because the destination is native ATM, not frame relay.

Service interworking with frame relay and ATM is described in *FRF.8 Frame Relay/ATM PVC Service Interworking Implementation Agreement* [FRF.8-1995], also jointly developed by the Frame Relay Forum and the

ATM Forum. This IA describes how to convert, or translate, frame relay frames to ATM cells, and vice versa. We summarize FRF.8 here and contrast it with FRF.5 network interworking.

Like FRF.5 network interworking, FRF.8 service interworking maps each frame relay PVC onto an ATM VBR-nrt PVC, using AAL5 for efficient "slicing and dicing." In the reverse direction, ATM to frame relay, the mapping is also reversed. Thus, each frame relay DLCI is associated one to one with a corresponding ATM VPI/VCI.

Also like FRF.5 network interworking, FRF.8 service interworking supports only PVCs, although work is under way to extend it to SVCs.

Unlike FRF.5 network interworking, FRF.8 network interworking allows the following:

- Translation of the PVC management procedures between frame relay and ATM. (In this book, we call the frame relay PVC management procedures the Local Management Interface, LMI.) PVC management procedures include link integrity verification (heartbeat), and PVC status information
- Optional translation between frame relay RFC 1490 multiprotocol encapsulation and ATM RFC 1483 multiprotocol encapsulation
- Optional fragmentation and reassembly of frame relay frames (See *FRF.12 Frame Relay Fragmentation Implementation Agreement* for more details.)
- Optional address resolution with ARP and InARP (See Chapter 13, Internetworking with Frame Relay, for more information on address resolution.)

As a general concept, service interworking also applies to any transparent conversion or translation of networking protocols. Thus, it provides the ability to interface a location to an intelligent network service using one protocol and to exit the network as a different protocol. This is the "Holy Grail" of network compatibility.

Service interworking is also known as just "interworking." However, as we have seen, it is not the same as the network interworking discussed earlier. Service interworking is conversion; network interworking is encapsulation.

Service interworking is related to the SNA gateway technique discussed in Chapter 13 in that a single SNA gateway converts between SNA and TCP/IP at the lower transmission layers. In fact, the term "gateway" is sometimes used generally to mean any kind of protocol converter.

Other types of service interworking are available today. For instance, a few carriers offer the ability to dial into a frame relay network via X.25 and to exit the network via frame relay.

The ATM Frame User-Network Interface

The Frame User-Network Interface (FUNI) is a modification of the standard ATM service provided by the ATM User-Network Interface (UNI). FUNI allows the customer equipment to submit variable-length frames to the ATM switch instead of just 53-byte cells. A FUNI interworking function at the ATM switch translates the FUNI frames to standard ATM cells and sends them on through the ATM network (see Figure 14.3).

The FUNI header is quite similar to the frame relay header. In essence, FUNI is a variable frame-length version of UNI for data applications. FUNI has two advantages compared to ordinary cell-based ATM:

- The overhead for transmitting variable length frames can be quite low. For long frames, the overhead can be below 1%. This is in contrast to standard ATM cells, which have an overhead of 5 out of 53 bytes—about 10%. Hence, FUNI can be as efficient as frame relay over low-speed access lines.
- Customer equipment that supports FUNI is typically less expensive than ordinary ATM interfaces. FUNI does not require CPE hardware upgrades. Instead, software can construct the FUNI frames.

FUNI also has disadvantages compared to ordinary ATM:

- It is limited to AAL5 for the ATM Adaptation Layer at the FUNI interworking function on the ATM switch. AAL5 supports ordinary delay-tolerant data traffic better than it supports voice or video traffic. Combined with the variable-length frames, use of AAL5 means that FUNI has the same problems with carrying voice and video that frame relay has.
- Because of the relatively small number of virtual circuits supported (about 1000, similar to frame relay), it is not as effective over very high-speed access circuits as ordinary ATM.

FUNI is similar to frame relay in that both allow variable-length frames across the access circuit. But FUNI supports ATM network operations and network management, which is more extensive and more standardized

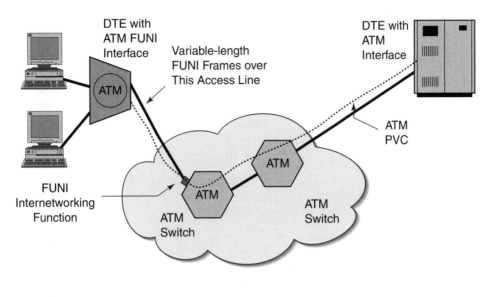

Architectural View

FIGURE 14.3 ATM Frame User-Network Interface. *FUNI is a variable frame-length version of the ATM User-Network Interface.*

than frame relay network management. This is important if the CPE and ATM networks are owned by the same organization, which would be true for private ATM networks.

FUNI offerings are still in the early stages, especially for public services. However, they may provide a useful migration path for frame relay users who need to upgrade their service levels and network management but who do not wish to upgrade their hardware. Upgrading to ordinary ATM requires a hardware change to the CPE.

TABLE 14.2 Migration Path

Stage	Branch Office	Network	HQ	Motivation
1	FR	FR	FR	Low cost
2	FR	ATM with Network Interworking	FR	Benefits to network provider
3	FR	ATM with Service Interworking	ATM	Benefits at HQ
4	FUNI	ATM with FUNI Interworking	ATM	Benefits at branch office
5	ATM	ATM	ATM	End-to-end ATM

Migration Path   We summarize a possible migration path from frame relay to ATM in Table 14.2.

Conclusion

Network managers are showing considerable interest in frame relay technology. Over 50,000 companies have converted all or part of their wide area networks to it, often with improvements in throughput and response time. Market research groups predict strong growth over at least the next two to four years, until inexpensive public wide area ATM services or data-oriented VPNs become commonplace. For managers investing in frame relay, this is a long enough time to cover the anticipated payback periods, which are often less than a year.

As noted, one of the most important drivers for frame relay is economics: Frame relay networks typically cost about 20% to 30% less than equivalent private line networks.

Network managers also see a number of other competitive advantages in frame relay. A recent survey noted these:

- Burst capability
- Consolidation of private line data networks on a single integrated facility
- Rapid reconfiguration of the network

Moreover, frame relay technology has found strong niches in the following areas:

- LAN-to-LAN interconnection, including database access and file transfers
- Access to the Internet
- Ability to carry IBM SNA traffic

Frame relay is considered by many to be one of the most successful recent networking technologies. It is certainly mature enough and valuable enough to be worthy of consideration by any manager looking to enhance his or her network.

Frame Relay Information Sources

Web Sites

http://www.frforum.com/—Frame Relay Forum; much useful information.

http://ansi.org/—ANSI.

http://www.itu.ch/—ITU-T (formerly CCITT).

http://ietf.cnri.reston.va.us/—IETF (Internet Engineering Task Force).

http://www.cis.ohio-state.edu/information/rfc.html—Internet RFCs (also available from other sites).

http://www.mot.com/networking/frame-relay/resources.html—The Motorola Web site authored by Steve Neil; many links to frame relay information.

http://www.alliancedatacom.com/frame-relay-white-papers.htm—Many good frame relay research papers.

http://www.atmforum.com/—ATM Forum.

Internet Newsgroups (Usenet)

news://comp.dcom.frame-relay—Can be valuable, but is unmoderated.

news://comp.dcom.cell-relay—The newsgroup for ATM.

Books

The Guide to Frame Relay Networking, Christine A. Heckart (Flatiron Publishing, 1994), ISBN 0-936648-63-5.   One of the best practical books on frame relay, but becoming dated.

Frame Relay Networks, 2nd ed., Uyless Black (McGraw-Hill, 1996), ISBN 0-07-005590-4.   Extensive discussion of protocols, but not business oriented.

Frame Relay Applications: Business and Technology Case Studies, James P. Cavanagh (Morgan Kaufmann, 1997), ISBN 1-55-860399-9.   Good case studies and discussion of migration to frame relay, but less emphasis on explaining the technology.

ISDN and Broadband ISDN with Frame Relay and ATM, 4th ed., William Stallings (Prentice-Hall, 1999), ISBN 0-13-973744-8.   Clear discussion of frame relay protocol in two chapters.

Frame Relay, Principles and Applications, Philip Smith (Addison-Wesley, 1993), ISBN 0-201-62400-1.   Good technical treatment of frame relay protocol, but dated.

Delivering Voice over Frame Relay and ATM, Daniel Minoli, Emma Minoli (Wiley, 1998), ISBN 0-471-25481-9.   Extensive technical treatment of voice over frame relay.

The Basics Book of Frame Relay (Motorola University Press, 1993), ISBN 0-201-56377-0, MUP-65-377.   A short and simple introduction, but dated.

Computer Networks, 3rd ed., Andrew Tanenbaum (Prentice-Hall, 1996), ISBN 0-13-349945-6.   Enlightening general coverage of networks; small section on frame relay.

Magazines (monthly)

Business Communications Review, (800) 227-1234

Data Communications, (800) 577-5356

Network Computing, (847) 647-6834

Telecommunications, (617) 356-4595

IEEE Communications Magazine, (212) 705-7018

IEEE Internet Computing, http://computer.org/internet

Periodicals (weekly)

InternetWeek, (708) 647-6834

Network World, (508) 875-6400

Communications News, (941) 966-9521

Newsletters, Mailing Lists

The Frame Relay Forum Newsletter, (510) 608-5920, or *www.frforum.com*

53 Bytes, the ATM Forum Newsletter – www.atmforum.com

Frame Relay Vendors and Carriers

The Frame Relay Forum—*http://www.frforum.com*

The Motorola Web site authored by Steve Neil—
http://www.mot.com/networking/frame-relay/resources.html

Answers to Exercises

Chapter 3

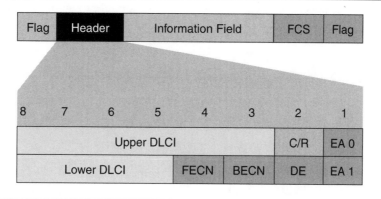

FIGURE B.1 Frame Relay Header Format *The frame relay header field contains addressing and status information.*

1a. Break this frame (in hexadecimal) into its component fields:

(beginning)	7E 04 2B 89 AB CD 12 34 7E
Opening flag field	<u>7E</u> (in hexadecimal)
Header field	<u>04 2B</u> (in hexadecimal)
Information field	<u>89 AB CD</u> (in hexadecimal)
Frame check sequence field	<u>12 34</u> (in hexadecimal)
Closing flag field	<u>7E</u> (in hexadecimal)

1b. Now break the header field into its component subfields:

Upper 6-bits of DLCI	000001	(in binary)
C/R (command/response) bit	0	(in binary)
EA 0 (extended address 0) bit	0	(in binary)
Lower 4-bits of DLCI	0010	(in binary)
FECN bit	1	(in binary)
BECN bit	0	(in binary)
DE (discard eligible) bit	1	(in binary)
EA 1 (extended address 1) bit	1	(in binary)

1c. What is the full 10-bit DLCI?

	00 0001 0010	(in binary)
	012	(in hexadecimal)
(optional)	18	(in decimal)

Notes
1. A frame-relay-capable data line monitor will also do this breakdown.
2. The binary equivalents of the hexadecimal digits are shown in Table B.1.

TABLE B.1 Hexadecimal Digits

Hex	Binary	Hex	Binary	Hex	Binary	Hex	Binary
0	0000	4	0100	8	1000	C	1100
1	0001	5	0101	9	1001	D	1101
2	0010	6	0110	A	1010	E	1110
3	0011	7	0111	B	1011	F	1111

2. Consider the network topology shown in Figure B.2 and the switch lookup tables given in Table B.2. Notice that each port is given a number, 1, 2, or 3, rather than a letter. Conventionally, switch hardware uses numbers like these.

a. Pencil in the path of the connection as it travels to its destination. *In Figure B.2, the path is the dashed line with long dashes. It goes from DTE A to Switch I to Switch II to Switch III to DTE B. The*

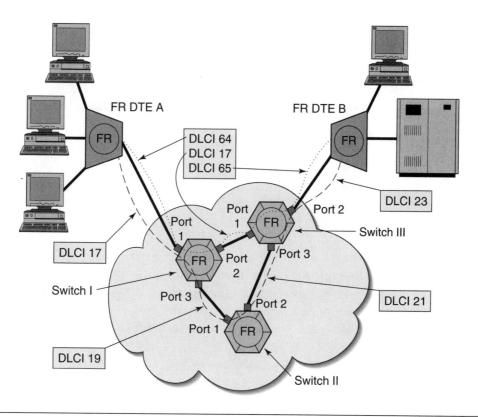

FIGURE B.2 Network Topology for Exercise 2 in Chapter 3.

TABLE B.2 Switch Lookup Tables

Switch I Lookup Table				Switch II Lookup Table				Switch III Lookup Table			
Incoming		Outgoing		Incoming		Outgoing		Incoming		Outgoing	
Port	DLCI	Port	DLCI	Port	DLCI	Port	DLCI	Port	DLCI	Port	DLCI
1	17	3	19	1	19	2	21	3	21	2	23
1	64	2	17	—	—	—	—	1	17	2	65

    DLCI values are 17, 19, 21, 23. The path is also highlighted in the
    switch tables shown in Table B.2.

b. Where is the other end of this connection?   *DTE B*

c. What is the DLCI at the other end of this connection?   *DLCI 23*

d. Is there any other virtual connection that starts at DTE A?
_Yes_____

If so, what are the DLCI values along its path? *The other virtual connection is the dashed line with short dashes in Figure B.1. It goes from DTE A to Switch I to Switch III to DTE B. Its DLCI values along its path are 64, 17, 65.*

e. Is the DLCI value "17" used more than once in the network?
_Yes_____

If so, where is it used? *It is used twice. It is part of both virtual connections (see diagram). The two DLCI 17 values are associated with different ports, so there is no danger of confusion.*

Note that for this problem we are assuming that the network is composed of frame relay switches that implement the frame relay standards between each switch. If the frame relay network is implemented internally as, say, ATM switches, the DLCI values *between* each switch will not apply.

Chapter 11

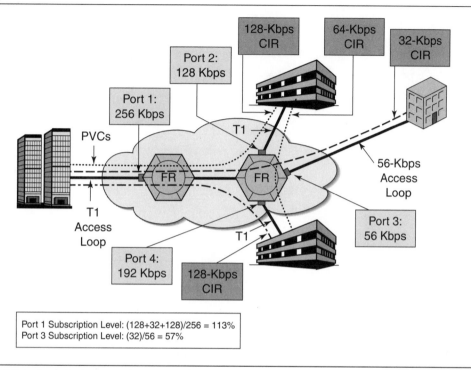

Port 1 Subscription Level: (128+32+128)/256 = 113%
Port 3 Subscription Level: (32)/56 = 57%

FIGURE B.3 Sample Frame Relay Network for Exercise in Chapter 11.

For the sample frame relay network design of Figure 11.6 (repeated in Figure B.3), what is the subscription level for

1. Port 2?

   Port 2 subscription level: (128 + 64)/128 = 150%

2. Port 4?

   Port 4 subscription level: (128 + 64)/192 = 100%

Glossary

10Base-T   Another name for IEEE 802.3 specifications (CSMA/CD) for hub-based Ethernet LAN on UTP wiring (10 = 10 Mbps, Base = baseband signaling, T = twisted-pair wiring).

100Base-T   Another name for IEEE 802.3u specifications for hub-based Ethernet LAN on UTP wiring (100 = 100 Mbps, Base = baseband signaling, T = twisted-pair wiring). (See also *Fast Ethernet*.)

1000Base-T   Specifications (IEEE 802.3z) for a 1000-Mbps Ethernet LAN operating over twisted-pair wiring. (See also *1G Ethernet*.)

1000Base-X   Specifications (IEEE 802.3z) for a 1000-Mbps Ethernet LAN over multimode fiber optics. (See also *1G Ethernet*.)

1G Ethernet   Popular name for the IEEE 802.3z specifications for Ethernet at 1000 Mbps. (See also *1000Base-T*, *1000Base-X*.)

802   See *IEEE 802.1p* through *IEEE 802.12*.

AAL (*ATM Adaptation Layer*)   A collection of standardized protocols that adapt user traffic to and from ATM 48-octet payload traffic streams. There are four types of AALs: AAL1, AAL2, AAL3/4, and AAL 5, which support a wide variety of user traffic types. (See *ATM Layers*.)

AAL0 (*AAL Type 0*)   Name given to any proprietary AAL type or to a null AAL implementation.

AAL1 (*AAL Type 1*)   AAL protocol standard for the payload encapsulation of delay-sensitive, constant-bit-rate connection-oriented traffic (e.g., audio and video) and TDM-based circuit traffic (e.g., DS-1 and E-1). AAL1 does

---

Note: This glossary is courtesy of the Frame Relay Forum and Alan Schaevitz of AYS Associates. Used with permission.

not support any multiplexing functions. Timing information is required to be exchanged between the source and the destination.

AAL2 *(AAL Type 2)*   AAL protocol standard for the payload encapsulation of delay-sensitive, low-volume, bursty, connection-oriented traffic (e.g., audio and compressed audio). AAL2 supports the multiplexing of multiple such traffic streams into one virtual connection. Timing information is required to be exchanged between the source and the destination.

AAL3/4 *(AAL Types 3 and 4)*   Originally there were two AAL protocol standards for payload encapsulation of delay-tolerant, bursty, connectionless traffic and connection-oriented traffic (data), respectively. They are now combined into one type. AAL3/4 also performs resequencing and cell identification operations in support of multiplexing several such traffic streams into one virtual connection.

AAL5 *(AAL Type 5)*   AAL protocol standard for the payload encapsulation of delay-tolerant, bursty, connection-oriented traffic (data). No timing relationship is required between source and destination. AAL5 does not support any multiplexing functions.

AAL Types   AAL1, AAL2, AAL3/4, and AAL5.

ABR *(Available Bit Rate)*   One of the five ATM service categories defined by the ATM Forum. ABR guarantees a minimum bit rate for user transmission and allows a higher bit rate, up to PCR, if there is available capacity in the network. An effort is also made to keep cell loss as low as possible. ABR provides a flow control mechanism to regulate the source's traffic rate to match network resources. Traffic parameters are PCR and MCR. (See also *CBR, UBR, VBR, flow control.*)

access rate   The bit per second (bps) rate at which a user can transmit over the lines that access the network.

ACK *(Acknowledgment)*   A message that acknowledges that a transmitted frame was received without errors. ACKs can be separate frames or piggybacked on reverse traffic frames.

adapter card   See *NIC.*

addressing   A network function for identifying various network components (e.g., hosts and nodes) by assigning to them (usually on a hierarchical basis) unique numbers (network addresses).

ADPCM *(adaptive differential pulse code modulation)*   Sometimes also *adaptive delta pulse code modulation.* A technique for converting an analog voice signal to digital format. It requires sampling the analog signal 8000 times/second and converting the sample to a 4-bit value. Hence, ADPCM requires a 32-Kbps digital channel to carry one voice connection. Used frequently between PBXs in a private network. (See also *PCM, DS-0.*)

ADSL *(Asymmetrical Digital Subscriber Line)*   An emerging ANSI standard that provides a voice connection plus a data connection on existing customer local loops that currently support only one analog voice connection. The data connection supports from 64 Kbps to 640 Kbps upstream (customer to network) and 1.5 Mbps to 8 Mbps downstream (to the customer). (See *DSL*.)

analog signal A way of representing information as a continuous set of values (waveform) within a certain range. Examples are the human voice (up to 4 kHz), raw audio, and video (e.g., TV broadcast). Analog signals are also called modulated signals. (See also *digital signal*.)

ANI (*Automatic Number Identification*) The capability of a voice network switch to provide to the called party the calling party's telephone number. Used extensively in call centers and in computer telephony integration (CTI) applications.

ANSI (*American National Standards Institute*) A U.S. standards organization. (See also *Frame Relay Forum, ATM Forum, ISO, ITU-T, IETF*)

API (*Application Programming Interface*) A set of software functions used by an application program as a means for providing access to a (communications, operating) system's capabilities.

appl (*application*) Computer program, system, or end user.

applet A Web-related term to describe a small Java program that is downloaded and executed locally at the client's system. It is also possible for an applet to use a remote server.

application layer Layer 7 (top layer) in the OSIRM. It is responsible for handling user-specific applications and services such as file transfer, email, and remote host access (Telnet).

APPN (*Advanced Peer-to-Peer Networking*) IBM architecture for supporting dynamic routing across arbitrary network topologies. Intended as a replacement for hierarchical-based SNA.

ARP (*Address Resolution Protocol*) Used in routing, a TCP/IP-based protocol for resolving local addresses in a network by mapping a physical address (i.e., a MAC address) to an IP address.

ARQ (*Automatic Repeat Request*) A generic term for any error recovery technique in which the receiver, upon receiving a damaged frame, automatically requests that the sender repeat (resend) the frame that was damaged.

ARPANET (*Advanced Research Project Agency Network*) This predecessor of the Internet was the first data communication (wide area) network. It was originally funded by ARPA (a DoD agency to promote research and future directions in various technological areas) with the goal of providing connectivity—nationwide—among military, educational, and research sites.

ASIC (*Application-Specific Integrated Circuit*) A hardware technology in which integrated circuits are manufactured for customized applications in order to reduce space and for speed and security reasons. (See also *IC*.)

asynchronous transmission   An approach for acquiring synchronization (between the sender and the receiver) on a per-octet basis. Start and stop bits are used as delimiters.

asynchronous transfer   An approach for the efficient transmission of information, where time slots are used on a demand basis (e.g., STDM, ATM) rather than on a periodic basis (e.g., TDM, STM).

ATM (*asynchronous transfer mode*)   A broadband switching and multiplexing, connection-oriented, high-performance, and cost-effective integrated technology for supporting B-ISDN services (e.g., multimedia) under specified QoS guarantees. Since capacity is allocated on demand with no clocking control between users, it is called asynchronous. Information is transmitted at very high rates (up to hundreds of Mbps) in fixed-length frames called cells. Traffic streams can be distinguished according to different QoS classes. The ATM reference model describes the various functions, services, and protocols and standards encompassed by the ATM technology.

ATM Forum   A consortium of organizations representing vendors, manufacturers, carriers, service providers, universities, research groups, consultants, and users. The ATM Forum recommends and defines specifications for ATM standards, promotes industry cooperation in the implementation of ATM technologies, and interacts with other standards and specifications bodies (e.g., Frame Relay Forum, IETF, ITU-T, ISO, and ANSI).

ATM layer   Also known as the cell layer, the second layer of the ATM protocol stack model (see *ATM layers*), responsible for constructing and processing the ATM cells. Its functions also include usage parameter control (UPC) and support of different QoS classes.

ATM layers   The ATM protocol stack consists of four layers: in bottom-up order, the physical, the ATM, the AAL, and the higher layers. The layers communicate with each other through the SAPs (software ports) where encapsulation of information units (PDUs) takes place (at the transmitting node) when they are passed from a higher to a lower layer, while decapsulation (of the PDUs) occurs (at the receiving node) when they are passed back from a lower to a higher layer. (See also cell, *OSI, SDU.*)

backbone network   The core communications system that provides connectivity between communities of users. It may span a campus or business park (campus backbone) or a larger geographic area such as a city or country, or international boundaries (WAN backbone).

bandwidth   Originally defining the frequency range supported by an analog circuit, now commonly used to define the transmission capacity of any communications medium. For analog circuits, it is measured in hertz (Hz or cycles per second); for digital circuits, it is measured in bits per second (bps).

baud A measure of the signaling speed, defined as the number of changes of the signal voltage per second. The link transmission rate (in bps) is a multiple of (though usually equal to) the line's baud rate.

B-channel (*Bearer Services Channel*) A component of an ISDN physical interface that operates at 64 Kbps (DS-0 rate). It is used for supporting user traffic (such as digital data, audio, video, and voice). (See also *ISDN, D-channel.*)

B$_c$ (also Bc) (*Committed Burst Size*) The maximum amount of data (in bits) that the network agrees to transfer, under normal conditions, during a time interval T_c. (See also B_e.)

B$_e$ (also Be) (*Excess Burst Size*) The maximum amount of uncommitted data (in bits) in excess of B_c that a frame relay network can attempt to deliver during a time interval T_c. This data (B_e) generally is delivered with a lower probability than B_c. The network treats B_e data as discard eligible. (See also B_c.)

bearer class of service Set of service characteristics and parameters, such as transfer rate, connection mode (circuit or packet), and other information transfer attributes, to describe an end-to-end ISDN connection. In ATM there exist five transport services classes: 0–4. (See *QoS classes.*)

bearer services ISDN services for supporting information transport functions at the lower layers (network, link, and physical) in the OSI model.

BECN (*backward explicit congestion notification*) A 1-bit field in a frame relay header set by the receiver (destination) or by the network (management) to indicate to the sender the presence of congestion in the network (in the source-to-destination direction). BECN is used in feedback (rate-based) flow control (i.e., it is set on any traffic flowing from the destination back to the source that passes through the congested part of the network). (See also *EFCI, FECN.*)

BER (*Bit Error Rate*) A communication quality measure, defined as the fraction of the total number of bits received by a network device that are in error (corrupted).

best effort A QoS class in which no specific traffic parameters and no absolute guarantees are made. Frame relay is normally a best-effort service. For ATM, UBR is a best-effort service. (See also *service types.*)

BGP (*Border Gateway Protocol*) A routing protocol run by gateways that connects separate (autonomous) networks. (See also *EGP, RIP, OSPF.*)

B-ISDN (*Broadband Integrated Services Digital Network*) A protocol platform, introduced by ITU-T, to support the integrated, high-speed transmission of data, audio, and video in a seamless fashion. B-ISDN is intended to support transmissions systems and services at capacities well above those defined for the ISDN standards. ATM emerged as a suitable transport standard. The B-ISDN architecture model has been adopted by ATM and is referred to as the ATM reference model.

B-ISUP (*Broadband–Integrated Services User Part*)   An extended SS7 (ISDN) protocol that provides the signaling to control B-ISDN related functions and services.

blocking   Refers to situations where a packet, message, or circuit (i.e., a call in telephony) is blocked (denied access to the network) because of the unavailability of sufficient network resources (bandwidth, buffer capacity).

bps (*bits per second*)   Transmission speed or rate defining the transmission capacity of a circuit in terms of the number of bits per second it can sustain.

BRI (*Basic Rate Interface*)   An ISDN service specification that provides two 64-Kbps B-channels and one 16-Kbps D-channel, all sharing the same physical medium (link). BRI is intended for carrying (compressed) video, voice, and data over a voice-grade wire pair. (See also *PRI*.)

bridge   A networking device that connects two homogeneous broadcasting networks (e.g., LANs). It stores and forwards frames without modifying them and operates at the data link layer. (See also *hub, concentrator, gateway, router, switching*.)

broadband   Defined by ITU-T as a service or system requiring transmission channels capable of supporting rates greater that the primary rate in ISDN (1.5 Mbps/2 Mbps). (See also *B-ISDN, N-ISDN*.)

broadcasting   A method for transmitting a signal or data to all other stations or nodes in a network. (See also *multicasting, unicasting*.)

burst   A short flow (train) of frames. Bursts are followed by idle periods where there is no transmission activity. In the context of frame relay, a burst is the amount of data transmitted into a frame relay network in excess of the CIR.

burstiness   In the context of a frame relay network, data that uses bandwidth only sporadically; that is, information that does not use the total bandwidth of a circuit 100 percent of the time. During pauses, channels are idle, and no traffic flows across them in either direction. Interactive and LAN-to-LAN data is bursty because it is sent intermittently. In between data transmissions the channel experiences idle time waiting for the user to send more data.

bus   A LAN technology where the attached stations (computers) access and share a common transmission (physical) medium and use broadcasting to transmit.

byte   A common term used to identify a group of 8 bits. However, since "byte" has been used to identify other groupings of bits (e.g., 6 or 7), a less ambiguous and more internationally acceptable term for a group of 8 bits is "octet."

CAN (*Campus Area Network*)   A network that covers a campus-wide area, which can consist of smaller LANs. FDDI is an example of a network that might be implemented in a CAN. (See also *LAN, MAN, WAN.*)

CAS (*channel associated signaling*)   Inband call signaling techniques (sometimes called ABCD; bit-robbed signaling; or RBS, for robbed-bit signaling) used by conventional PBXes. It may be used between two PBXes connected by dedicated circuits (called tie lines), or it may be used on trunks between a PBX and a public network switch. (See also *ISDN, DSS1, PSS1, Q-Sig.*)

CAT-3 (*Category-3 Unshielded Twisted Pair*)   A type of UTP, commonly used for transmission at low speeds (up to 10 Mbps) and at distances up to 100 meters.

CAT-5 (*Category-5 Unshielded Twisted Pair*)   A type of UTP commonly used for higher speed transmission (more than 10 Mbps) and at distances up to 100 meters.

CATV (*cable, or community antenna, TV*)   A wired (coaxial-based) network used for TV broadcasting.

CBR (*constant, or continuous, bit rate*)   One of the five ATM service types in which a virtual circuit is configured to support a constant (fixed) amount of end-system traffic for the duration of the connection. This amount is characterized by the peak cell rate (PCR). All QoS parameters are specified. CBR supports circuit emulation as well as the transmission of any continuous bit stream of delay-sensitive information (i.e., real-time, isochronous traffic), such as voice and video. (See also *QoS classes.*)

CCITT (*Consultative Committee on International Telegraphy and Telephony*)   The former name for the ITU-T before it changed in the early 1990s.

cell   A fixed-size frame. In ATM networks, it is the basic transport unit: a 53-octet frame comprising a 5-octet header and a 48-octet payload. User traffic is fragmented into cells at the source and reassembled at the destination. Cells facilitate high-speed transfer through the ATM switches. Formally, a cell is the PDU constructed at the ATM physical layer.

cell header   The 5-octet ATM cell header that contains control information regarding the destination path and flow control.

cell layer   Same as *ATM layer.*

cell loss   An unfavorable network situation where cells are discarded (dropped) from the network because of insufficient resources (e.g., buffer space inside a switch) or violation of the traffic service requirements and parameters (nonconformance with the traffic contract). (See also *leaky bucket, congestion control.*)

cell relay   A method of fast packet switching for high-performance communications. The basic transport unit is called a cell and is a constant-length PDU. ATM is an example of cell relay. (See also *frame relay.*)

CEPT1 (*Conference European des Administration des Postes et des Telecommunications-1*)   The same as E1, the European standard for digital transmission at the rate of 2.048 Mbps. It is the analogy of—but not compatible with—T1. It can simultaneously support 30 DS-0 circuits.

channel   Generically, the user access channel across which frame relay data travels. Within a given T1 or E1 physical line, a channel can be one of the following, depending on how the line is configured.

unchannelized T1/E1   The entire T1/E1 line is considered a channel, where

- The T1 line operates at a speed of 1.536 Mbps and is a single channel consisting of 24 T1 time slots
- The E1 line operates at a speed of 1.920 Mbps and is a single channel consisting of 30 E1 time slots

channelized T1/E1   The channel is any one of n time slots within a given line, where

- The T1 line consists of any one or more channels, each of which is any one of 24 time slots. The channelized T1 line operates at a speed, which is a multiple of 56/64 Kbps, with an aggregate speed not exceeding 1.536 Mbps.
- The E1 line consists of one or more channels, each of which is any one of 30 time slots. It operates at speeds in multiples of 64 Kbps to 1.920 Mbps, with aggregate speed not exceeding 1.920 Mbps.

fractional T1/E1   The T1/E1 channel is one of the following groupings of consecutively or nonconsecutively assigned time slots:

- n T1 time slots ($n \times 56/64$ Kbps where n = 1 to 23 T1 time slots per FT1 channel)
- n E1 time slots ($n \times 64$ Kbps, where n = 1 to 30 time slots per E1 channel)

CIR (*committed information rate*)   A term used in frame relay that defines the information rate or capacity the network is committed to provide to the user on a given virtual circuit. It is similar to the sustainable cell rate parameter in ATM.

circuit emulation   A virtual circuit (VC) service offered to end users where the characteristics of an actual digital bit-stream (e.g., video traffic) line are emulated (e.g., a 2-Mbps or 45-Mbps signal).

circuit switching   A networking method for carrying information over a dedicated path, connecting the source and the destination through several network nodes. The connection is established over a series of physical links, on each of which a logical channel for the connection is reserved. Circuit switching is suitable for continuous flows of information such as voice in telephony. (See also *connectionless networks*, *message switching*, *packet switching*.)

class of service See *QoS classes*.

CLNP (*Connectionless Network Protocol*) A network layer protocol, developed by the ISO, to support connectionless services.

CLP (*Cell Loss Priority*) A 1-bit field in the ATM cell header that corresponds to the loss priority of a cell. Lower priority (CLP = 1) cells can be discarded under a congestion situation.

CLR (*Cell Loss Ratio*) A QoS parameter that gives the ratio of the lost cells to the total number of transmitted cells on a given VCC.

CMIP (*Common Management Information Protocol*) An ITU-T-defined management interface standard that can support administration, maintenance, and operation functions for public networks. (See also *MIB, OAM&P*.)

CO (*central office*) Premises of a carrier service provider where customer lines (i.e., telephone lines) are multiplexed and switched to other COs.

codec (*coder/decoder*) Communications device to convert analog signals into bit-oriented digital streams and vice versa. It is widely used to provide the conversion between analog and digital signals over the local access circuit.

committed burst size See B_c.

concentrator A local networking device where multiple input streams are merged into a single output stream. The difference between concentration and multiplexing is that in the former there are no preassigned slots during which the input links can transmit; thus, the output link capacity can be less than the sum of the input traffic links. Concentration is usually referred to as STDM. (See also *bridge, hub, gateway, multiplexer, router, switching*.)

congestion Network situation where there are no available network resources (bandwidth, buffer space) to satisfy additional users' needs. In packet-switched networks, a user can cause congestion by offering excess load to the network. (See also *flow control*.)

congestion control A resource and traffic management mechanism to correct, avoid, and/or prevent excessive situations (buffer overflow, insufficient bandwidth) that can cause the network to collapse. Various congestion control methods exist. (See also *flow control, traffic control*.)

connection (for ATM) A path (permanent during the life of the connection) established between two ATM hosts that runs across an ATM network (e.g., through switches) for the purpose of transferring information. The connection can be initiated and released by an end system (SVC) or be established by management procedures (PVC). An ATM connection is bidirectional but not necessarily symmetric.

connectionless networks Communications service where packets are transferred from a source to a destination without the need of a preestablished connection. IP and SMDS are examples of connectionless networks. (See also *datagram*.)

connection-oriented Communications service where an initial connection between the end points (source and destination) must be set up prior to the data transmission. ATM and frame relay are examples of connection-oriented networks. (See also *VC*.)

CoS (*class of service*) See *QoS classes*.

CPE (*customer premises*, or *provided*, *equipment*) Computer and communications equipment (hardware and software) located at the customer's site. (See also *DTE*.)

C-Plane (*Control Plane*) The higher part of the B-ISDN model (ATM reference model) responsible for establishing, monitoring, maintaining, and releasing a virtual connection (VC). In particular, it is used in managing (addressing, signaling, and routing) SVCs and is not required for PVCs. (See also *M-Plane, U-Plane*.)

CRC (*cyclic redundancy check*) A bit-error detection technique that employs a mathematical algorithm to append redundancy bits to the frame, based on the transmitted bits. The receiver, using the same algorithm, recalculates the redundancy bits and compares them to the ones it received. If the two bit sequences do not agree, the transmitted frame is then considered to be in error and corrective procedures such as retransmission can be initiated if necessary.

CRS (*Cell Relay Service*) A bearer service offered by an ATM network to the end users that directly delivers (transports and routes) ATM cells and supports ATM services.

CSMA/CD (*Carrier-Sense Multiple-Access with Collision Detection*) Known as the IEEE 802.3 standard, a medium access control technique used in LANs that allows multiple users to access a shared transmission medium. A station that wants to transmit first senses (listens to) the medium and, if it is idle, starts transmitting. If it detects a collision (with another station concurrently transmitting), it ceases transmission. Ethernet emerged as the main CSMA/CD LAN protocol implementation.

CSU (*channel service unit*) Equipment at the user end that provides an interface between the user and the communications network (i.e., T1 lines). The CSU can be combined with the DSU in the same device. (See also *DCE*.)

CSU/DSUs (*channel service unit/data service unit*) The combination of a CSU and a DSU, used as an interface between a digital line and a communication device.

datagram A data transport mode where packets are routed independently and can follow different paths. Thus, there is no guarantee of sequence delivery. (See also *connectionless network*.)

Data Link Layer Layer 2 in the OSIRM, responsible for error-free communication between two adjacent network nodes.

DCE (*Data Circuit-terminating Equipment* or *Data Communications Equipment*) A device at the user end, typically a modem or other communications device, which acts as an access point to the transmission medium. Also refers to switching equipment, such as a frame relay switch, as distinguished from the device (DTE) that attaches to the network.

D-channel (*data channel*) A component of an ISDN interface used to carry network management and control (signaling) messages over the ISDN interface. It may also carry user (packet) data. There are two standards: BRI (at 16 Kbps) and PRI (at 64 Kbps). (See also *DSS1, PSS1, B-channel.*)

DCS (*digital crossconnect system*) A device that provides an electronic patch panel for the configuration of circuit connections and channel connections within circuits. Also known as a DACS (digital access and crossconnect system).

DE (*discard eligible*) A 1-bit field in a frame relay header that indicates that a frame may be discarded in preference to other frames if congestion occurs in the network. Frames with the DE bit set are considered B_e (excess burst) data.

delay A system performance metric that refers to the actual transmission time (of the data), the waiting (queuing) time in a buffer (queuing delay— QD), the time it takes for the data to travel between any two (or end-to-end) network nodes (propagation—PD), the processing time (e.g., packetization, depacketization, protocol processing, coding), or the time for data to be switched through a switch or router (switching delay). Sometimes also called transit delay, or latency.

demultiplexing A method where multiple traffic streams grouped together into a single stream (of frames) are separated by a demultiplexer into individual streams. (See also *multiplexing.*)

digital signal A way of representing information as a set of discrete values (i.e., voltage pulses) within a certain range. Binary signals are digital signals that assume the values of 0 and 1 (bit-oriented streams). Digital signals are also called unmodulated signals. (See also *analog signal.*)

DLCI (*data link connection identifier*) A field in the frame relay header that identifies the virtual circuit over which the frame is to be transmitted. Similar to the VPI/VCI in ATM.

DNS (*Domain Name Service,* or *System*) Server-based service to provide the translation between TCP/IP domain names and TCP/IP addresses.

DQDB (*Distributed-Queue Dual-Bus*) Known as the IEEE 802.6 standard, a MAN-suitable protocol based on 53-octet frames (but not the same as ATM cells). It can support both connectionless and connection-oriented, isochronous integrated services. It is implemented as two unidirectional buses, configured in a physical ring topology, which operate in opposite directions. It is primarily defined for an SMDS access circuit where it operates in a connectionless, non-isochronous mode.

DS-0 (*Digital Signal–Level 0*)   Specifications for a 64-Kbps channel. Originally defined to digitally transport a single voice connection, it can be used to transport any 64-Kbps digital traffic. No physical specifications were ever standardized for the transport of a single DS-0 channel. (See also *DS-1, T1*.)

DS-1 (*Digital Signal–Level 1*)   Electrical interface for digital transmission at the rate of 1.544 Mbps containing 24 64-Kbps DS-0 circuits. The physical interface first defined to carry a DS-1 electrical signal is known as T1 and operates over a pair of unshielded twisted (UTP) wires. DS-1 has subsequently been specified to operate over a wide variety of media such as microwave and fiber optics. The terms "DS-1" and "T1" are often (somewhat incorrectly) used interchangeably.

DS-3 (*Digital Signal–Level 3*)   Electrical interface for digital transmission at the rate of 44.736 Mbps. It can simultaneously support 672 DS-0 circuits (28 DS-1 signals). Originally specified to operate over coaxial cable, it is now frequently implemented on digital microwave and fiber optics.

DSL (*digital subscriber line*)   General name for several specifications supporting digital customer local loops. (See *ADSL, HDSL, SDSL, IDSL, RADSL, VDSL*.)

DSP (*digital signal processing*)   A series of processes and transformations performed at the physical layer and which involve the digital modulation, demodulation, noise filtering, sampling, encoding, decoding, and frequency conversion of a signal.

DSS1 (*digital subscriber signaling 1*)   Specifications for ISDN D-channel signaling between a private ISDN PBX and the public ISDN network. (See also *PSS1, Q-sig, CAS*.)

DSU (*data service unit*)   Equipment at the user end that converts between different formats of digital signals. (See also *CSU*.)

DSU/CSU   Combination of a DSU and a CSU. Same as CSU/DSU.

DTE (*data terminal equipment*)   The host computer (PC or workstation) that provides the end user with access to a communications network. The DTE is connected to a DCE, which performs the signaling operation. (See also *CPE*.)

DWDM (*Dense Wave Division Multiplexing*)   A popular name for WDM when the number of simultaneous traffic streams is large, say 32 or more. Thirty-two light wavelengths, each carrying 2.5 Gbps (STS-48, STM-16), would result in a single optical fiber, operating at 2.5 Gbps for one light wavelength, supporting 80 Gbps total.

E1 (*European Digital Signal–Level 1*)   European standard for a 2.048-Mbps digital circuit. It is similar to, but not compatible with, DS-1 and can support 30 64-Kbps DS-0 channels. (See also *CEPT1*.)

E3 (*European Digital Signal–Level 3*)   European standard for a 34.368-Mbps digital circuit. It can simultaneously support 16 E1 circuits.

E4 (*European Digital Signal–Level 4*)   European standard for a 139.264-Mbps digital circuit.

E.164   An ITU-T–defined 8-octet (16 digits in packed decimal—4 bits per digit) international address format (comprising a 2- to 3-digit country code, optional 1- to 3-digit city code, and up to 10-digit national numbering plan). In frame relay and ATM it is typically used in public networks and is provided by the telecommunication carriers. The E.164 numbers can be used to identify the calling and called parties in a connection.

EDI (*Electronic Data Interchange*)   Standards and procedures for electronically exchanging formal documents such as purchase orders, funds transfers, and letters of credit while providing reliable and secure transmission.

EFCI (*explicit forward congestion indication*)   A 1-bit field in the ATM header of a data cell (as opposed to an OAM cell) that identifies whether congestion at an intermediate node has been experienced. The EFCI bit is set to 1 when a threshold (e.g., for buffer space) has been exceeded.

EGP (*Exterior* (or *Edge*) *Gateway Protocol*)   A routing protocol that allows gateways attached to different (possibly nonhomogeneous) networks to exchange routing information such as link status, route delays, and neighbor reachability. (See also *BGP, RIP, OSPF*.)

egress   Movement of frame relay frames leaving a frame relay network in the direction of the destination device. (Contrast with *ingress*.)

EIA (*Electronic Industries Association*)   A publishing and standards-making body of the electronics industry.

encapsulation (**for frame relay**)   A process by which an interface device places an end device's protocol-specific frames inside a frame relay frame. The network accepts only frames formatted specifically for frame relay; hence, interface devices acting as interfaces to a frame relay network must perform encapsulation. (See also *interface device, frame-relay-capable interface device*.)

end device   The ultimate source or destination of data flowing through a frame relay network; also referred to as data terminal equipment (DTE). As a source device, it sends data to an interface device for encapsulation in a frame relay frame. As a destination device, it receives de-encapsulated data (i.e., the user's data from which the frame relay header and trailer have been stripped) from the interface device. An end device can be an application program or some operator-controlled device (e.g., workstation). In a LAN environment, the end device can be a file server or host.

Ethernet   A bus-based LAN protocol using CSMA/CD, officially known as the IEEE 802.3 standard, originally designed to operate up to 10 Mbps on shared broadcast media. New approaches have emerged that enhance the operational characteristics and speed of Ethernet-based LANs. Any station may transmit a data frame so long as the bus is idle. If two stations attempt to transmit simultaneously, they must be able to detect the foreign signal (i.e., not their signal) and "back off" for a retry later. Digital, Intel, and Xerox also published a variation, which is sometimes called DIX Ethernet. (See also *10Base-T, 100Base-T, 1000Base-T, 1000Base-X, Fast Ethernet, 1G Ethernet, Switched Ethernet, Token Ring, Token Bus, FDDI*.)

Fast Ethernet   Recently evolved from Ethernet, a high-performance LAN technology that enables data transmission at 100 (and up) Mbps. It is also intended to support multimedia services. (See also *100Base-T, 1G Ethernet*.)

FCC (*Federal Communications Commission*)   A government body that deals with various communications issues and regulates and oversees the operation of the broadcasting and telecommunication companies (carriers).

FCS (*frame check sequence*)   Any implementation of a formula-based error check sequence using the bit pattern of the transmitted block of information. CRC is an example.

FDDI (*Fiber Distributed Data Interface*)   An ANSI-defined standard for implementing a high-speed (100-Mbps) LAN/MAN, based on a dual fiber optic Token Ring topology. (See also *Ethernet, Token Ring, Token Bus*.)

FDM (*frequency division multiplexing*)   A technique that allows for the channel bandwidth of a circuit to be subdivided into many channels (of smaller bandwidth) to accommodate multiple traffic streams. (See also *TDM, WDM*.)

FEC (*Forward Error Correction*)   An error correction technique where no retransmissions are made; therefore, the receiver is responsible for correcting any errors in the frames by making use of the redundancy bits. (See also *CRC*.)

FECN (*forward explicit congestion notification*)   A 1-bit field in a frame relay header set by the network in a frame traveling in the direction of the receiver (source-to-destination) to indicate the presence of congestion in the network. FECN is used in feedback (rate-based) flow control. (See also *BECN, EFCI, flow control*.)

FIFO (*first-in, first-out*)   The absolute order in which queued packets are served in a queue; those that join the queue early are served first. Also known as *first-come, first-served*. (See also *LIFO*.)

firewall   A way of protecting a private network by restricting access from a public or unprotected network. Firewalls typically reside between a company's intranet and the public Internet.

flow control   A method used in networking for traffic regulation and congestion avoidance. There are three principal techniques: *window-based* control, where a sliding window is used to determine how many packets, cells, or frames can be transmitted during a predefined period; *rate-based* control, where the rate at which the source can transmit is monitored and controlled (using forward and backward RM-cells or by setting the EFCI bit); and *credit-based* control, where a source can transmit if there is a credit available. (See also *congestion control, traffic control*.)

FQ *(fair queuing)*   A scheduling policy where a router or switch maintains separate queues for each traffic flow so as to allow for a fair resource allocation. An improved algorithm has been proposed, known as weighted fair queuing (WFQ).

FR *(frame relay)*   See *frame relay*.

FRAD *(frame relay access device)*   A device that provides an interface between a non-frame-relay CPE and a frame relay network.

frame   A variable-length PDU used to describe the unit of information passed from OSI layer 2 to layer 1.

frame relay   A medium-speed, connection-oriented packet-switching technology that provides efficient frame delivery over virtual circuits (VCs). It supports access speeds up to 1.544 Mbps (T1) or beyond, or 2.048 Mbps (E1) in Europe. The basic transport unit, which is called a frame, can be up to 4096 octets and carries both routing and user information. Much of the network layer functionality as defined in the OSIRM is handled by the frame relay link layer, including signaling, acquiring network services, and interface management.

frame-relay-capable interface device   A communications device that performs frame relay encapsulation. Frame-relay-capable routers and bridges are examples of interface devices used to interface the customer's equipment to a frame relay network. (See also *interface device, encapsulation*.)

Frame Relay Forum   A consortium of organizations representing vendors, manufacturers, carriers, service providers, universities, research groups, consultants, and users. The Frame Relay Forum defines frame relay implementation agreements, provides marketing and educational information, and interacts with other standards and specifications bodies (e.g., *ATM Forum, IETF, ITU-T, ISO, ANSI*).

frame relay frame   A variable-length unit of data, in frame-relay format, that is transmitted through a frame relay network. Contrast with *packet*. (See also *Q.922A*.)

FRF.x *(Frame Relay Forum Implementation Agreement x)*   Format for specifications produced by the Frame Relay Forum. FRF.5 is the Frame Relay/ATM Network Interworking specification, and FRF.8 is the Frame Relay/ATM Service Interworking specification.

FRS *(Frame Relay Service)*   See *frame relay*.

FTP *(File Transfer Protocol)*   A protocol developed by the IETF used for transferring files over a TCP/IP network.

FUNI (*Frame User-Network Interface*)   A standardized User-Network Interface (UNI) based on variable-length frames instead of fixed-length cells. FUNI is a native ATM interface that supports ATM capabilities and services such as signaling, ILMI, and QoS classes. This is in contrast to FRF.5 or FRF.8 (the Frame Relay/ATM Interworking specifications) that can support only frame-relay–level functionality.

gateway   A networking device that allows stations that may belong to non-homogeneous networks to communicate with each other. It forwards packets and can also perform address and format translation. Typically used in WANs, gateways operate at the transport layer and higher. *Gateway* is also an older term for a router, from the ARPANET days.

GB (*gigabyte*)   One billion bytes (or 1000 KB).

Gbps (*gigabits per second*)   Transmission speed or rate of 1 billion bits per second.

GHz (*gigahertz*)   One billion hertz (Hz).

Gigabit Ethernet   A popular name for the emerging standards for Ethernet operating at 1 Gbps. (See also *IEEE 802.3z, 1G Ethernet, 1000Base-T, 1000Base-X, Fast Ethernet*.)

HDLC (*High-level Data Link Control*)   A generic data link layer protocol, developed by ISO, for layer 2 transmission over communication links. HDLC manages synchronous, code-transparent, serial information transfer over a link connection. (See also *LAPB, LAPD, SDLC*.)

HDSL (*High-Bit-Rate Digital Subscriber Line*, or *High-Speed Digital Subscriber Line*)   An alternative specification to T1 for the physical implementation of DS-1 1.544-Mbps transmission over two pairs of twisted wire. HDSL offers 1.544-Mbps transmission over four wires that do not require the special engineering of T1 as well as supporting half speed over one wire pair. (See also *DSL, SDSL*.)

HDSL2   A newer version of HDSL that supports DS-1 1.544-Mbps transmission over a single pair of wires.

header   The front portion of a packet (PDU, SDU, cell, frame) that contains protocol and control information such as network addresses, sequence numbers, and routing information. (See also *trailer*.)

higher layers (for ATM)   The top layer in the ATM reference model. It refers to user-specific applications and protocols like TCP/IP, FTP, SNMP, and others that operate over ATM.

HIPPI (*High-Performance Parallel Interface*)   A high-speed LAN standard that operates at 800 Mbps, usually used in the interconnection of supercomputers and optical networks (e.g., SONET).

HOL (*head-of-line*)   The head position of a buffer (i.e., located inside a switch). A phenomenon called HOL blocking is associated with the HOL and refers to the fact that frames or cells in a (FIFO) queue must wait for the HOL cell to depart first.

hop (**for frame relay**)   A single trunk line between two switches in a frame relay network. An established PVC consists of a certain number of hops, spanning the distance from the ingress access interface to the egress access interface within the network.

host   The end-point-attached station in a network connection. A host is identified as either a source (original sender) or a destination (final receiver).

HSSI (*High-Speed Serial Interface*)   A high-speed (tens of Mbps) interface between a CSU/DSU and a DTE.

HTML (*HyperText Mark-up Language*)   See *WWW*.

HTTP (*HyperText Transfer Protocol*)   The underlying protocol in the WWW, which provides the necessary tools and capabilities for retrieving information (in the form of text, audio, voice, video, and images) and allows the user to navigate through different documents and sites (by clicking on the various hyperlinks).

hub   A LAN device that interconnects several stations. Also used loosely to mean any central point in a network. (See also *bridge, concentrator, gateway, router, switching*.)

Hz (*hertz*)   Signal or channel frequency unit (1 Hz = 1 cycle per second).

IC (*Integrated Circuit*)   A circuit constructed on a silicon substrate and composed of transistors, resistors, wiring, and other similar components using microscopic components and fabrication techniques. (See also *ASIC*.)

IDSL (*ISDN Digital Subscriber Line*)   A variation of ISDN for digital data access circuits in which the two B-channels are combined into a single 128-Kbps dedicated connection. (See *DSL*.)

IEC (*interexchange carrier*)   Same as IXC.

IEEE (*Institute of Electrical and Electronic Engineers*)   A standards and specification organization active in the areas of computers, communications, electronics, and information processing.

IEEE 802.1p   An IEEE specification that defines an additional 4-octet field in the LAN header (Ethernet, Token Ring, and FDDI) to support up to eight levels of transmission priority. It is intended for applications such as real-time desktop video conferencing and multicast video.

IEEE 802.1Q   An IEEE specification that defines an additional 4-octet field in the LAN header (Ethernet, Token Ring, and FDDI) to support virtual LANs. It holds VLAN membership and security information. (See also *VLAN*.)

IEEE 802.1x   An IEEE specification for operating in a full-duplex mode on a single station Ethernet, Token Ring, or FDDI LAN port.

IEEE 802.3   An IEEE LAN specification for the CSMA/CD protocol operating at 10 Mbps. (See also *Ethernet, 10Base-T*.)

IEEE 802.3u   An IEEE LAN specification for the CSMA/CD protocol operating at 100 Mbps. (See also *Ethernet*, *Fast Ethernet*, *100Base-T*.)

IEEE 802.3z   An IEEE LAN specification for the CSMA/CD protocol operating at 1000 Mbps. (See also *Ethernet*, *Fast Ethernet*, *1G Ethernet*, *1000Base-T*, *1000Base-X*.)

IEEE 802.4   An IEEE LAN specification for the Token Bus Protocol.

IEEE 802.5   An IEEE LAN specification for the Token-Passing Protocol. (See also *Token Ring*.)

IEEE 802.6   An IEEE specification for the DQDB Protocol.

IEEE 802.9   An IEEE LAN specification for a high-performance LAN architecture supporting integrated services (e.g., multimedia) by combining ISDN and LAN features and characteristics.

IEEE 802.12   An IEEE LAN specification for the DQDB Protocol.

IETF (*Internet Engineering Task Force*)   A body responsible for developing specifications required for the interoperable implementation of the Internet. This includes the development and support for TCP, IP, and the suite of Internet applications including FTP, SMTP, Telnet, and SNMP. IETF is also involved in coordinating specifications for new features and capabilities that might operate over the Internet as well as the interfaces with other technologies such as frame relay and ATM. Approved specifications are called RFCs. (See also *Frame Relay Forum*, *ATM Forum*, *ITU-T*, *ANSI*.)

ingress   Movement of frame relay frames from an access device toward the frame relay network. (Contrast with *egress*.)

interface device   Provides the interface between the end device(s) and a frame relay network by encapsulating the user's native protocol in frame relay frames and sending the frames across the frame relay backbone. (See also *encapsulation* and *frame-relay-capable interface device*.)

interLATA   A term that refers to services exchanged between Local Access and Transport Areas (LATAs). (See also *LATA*, *intraLATA*.)

Internet   A worldwide computer communications network that interconnects thousands of smaller-scale networks (e.g., WANs, LANs, MANs) and millions of computers and users. Email (electronic mail) and the WWW are two of the most commonly used Internet services.

internetworking   The ability to provide ubiquitous information transport (e.g., through adaptation) between two or more (normally nonhomogeneous) interconnected networks or systems (e.g., computers). (See also *IWF*, *IWU*.)

interoperability   The ability of ubiquitous operation and communication across products from different vendors and service providers (e.g., computers, networks, switches, protocols.)

interworking   See *interoperability*, *internetworking*.

intraLATA   Services offered within a LATA. (See also *LATA, interLATA*.)

intranet   An integrated, high-speed private network that is internal to a company and that allows the access and distribution of corporate information and promotes collaborative computing among the company's staff. Utilizing the same services and applications as the Internet, including browsers, an Intranet can be thought of as a company's small private internet.

inverse multiplexing   Techniques for configuring two or more circuits so that they appear to operate as a single higher speed circuit. They are primarily used to create capacity in increments that would not normally be available with available discrete circuits, such as between DS-1/T1 (1.544-Mbps) and DS-3 (44.756-Mbps) circuits.

I/O (*Input/Output*)   The input or output (software or hardware) port of a device, protocol, application, or system.

IP (*Internet Protocol*)   A networking protocol for providing a connectionless (datagram) service to the higher transport protocol. It is responsible for discovering and maintaining topology information and for routing packets across homogeneous or heterogeneous networks. Combined with TCP, it is commonly known as the TCP/IP protocol suite.

IPv4 (*Internet Protocol, version 4*)   See *IP*.

IPv6 (*Internet Protocol, version 6*)   An enhanced version of the IP, developed by the IETF, intended to support integrated and multimedia services and a much larger range of IP addresses than IPv4.

IPX   A layer 3 protocol similar to IP that was developed and is supported by Novell.

ISDN (*Integrated Services Digital Network*)   An ITU-T protocol reference model that provides a ubiquitous, end-to-end, interactive digital service for data, audio, and video. ISDN is available as BRI (using local loop technology adapted to carry digital signals at 160 Kbps) and PRI (utilizing DS-1/E1 technology at 1.544/2.048 Mbps). (See also *B-ISDN, DSS1, PSS1*.)

ISO (*International Standards Organization*)   An international, voluntary, standards-making organization, located in Geneva, Switzerland, that is active in establishing and promoting standards in a wide variety of fields, including information technology. ANSI is the U.S. representative on ISO. (See also *Frame Relay Forum, ATM Forum, IETF, ITU-T*.)

isochronous   Any transmission stream in which the timing relationship between the segments of information in the traffic stream must be accurately reproduced at the destination. Thus, the source and destination must operate using the same source clock or the destination must be able to reconstruct the source clock from information received in the traffic stream itself. Examples of isochronous information are voice and video. (See also *non-isochronous*.)

ISP (*Internet Service Provider*)   A company that provides Internet access services to individual users and businesses.

ITU-T (*International Telecommunications Union–Telecommunications Standardization Sector*)   A U.N.-treaty-based standards and specifications body, formerly known as CCITT, whose published recommendations cover a wide spectrum of areas involving definition of terms, basic principles and characteristics, protocol design, description of models, and other specifications. It is part of the International Telecommunications Union (ITU), founded in 1948 to promote telephony and telegraphy issues. (See also *Frame Relay Forum, ATM Forum, IETF, ISO, ANSI*.)

IXC (*interexchange carrier*)   A public switching network carrier that provides (in conjunction with the local exchange carriers—LECs) interLATA and intraLATA access services. With the implementation of the Telecommunications Act of 1996, the distinctions between IXCs and LECs are fading.

IWF (for ATM) (*Interworking Function*)   The set of protocols and procedures to support interoperation (protocol interworking) between a non-ATM end system and an ATM switch. IWF functions entail fragmentation, reassembly, encapsulation, protocol conversion, multiplexing, and demultiplexing of the traffic forwarded from one device to another. (See also *NIWF, SIWF, IWU*.)

IWU (*Interworking Unit*)   A device that supports an IWF. Bridges, routers, switches, and gateways are examples of IWUs.

J2 (*Japanese Signaling Level 2*)   Japanese standard for digital transmission at 6.312 Mbps.

Java   A sophisticated, object-oriented programming language platform introduced by Sun for developing advanced application and management tools for the Web. It enables Web applications to run transparently over the Internet and offers robustness and independence over the underlying operating system.

jitter   Delay variation. In the context of voice, it is the variation between voice samples generating distortion in the delivered voice signal. In the context of ATM, it is the variation in cell interarrival times caused by transmission and queuing delays in circuits and ATM switches along the virtual circuit path.

JPEG (*Joint Photographic Experts Group*)   A standard developed for encoding, transmitting, and decoding still images.

KB (*kilobyte*)   One thousand bytes.

Kbps (also kbps) (*kilobits per second*)   Transmission speed or rate of 1000 bits per second.

kHz (*kilohertz*)   One thousand hertz (Hz).

killer application   The application driver or enabler that dominates (in terms of usage, capabilities, resource utilization, usefulness, design considerations, accessibility, performance) on a technological platform, characterized as a technological innovation or revolution. For instance, the Web is seen by many as the current killer application for the Internet.

km (*kilometer*)   One thousand meters (1 km = 0.621 miles).

LAN (*local area network*)   A network that interconnects PCs, terminals, workstations, servers, printers, and other peripherals over short distances (usually within the same floor or building). Various LAN standards have been developed, with Ethernet as the most widely used. Others include the Token Bus and the Token Ring Protocols. (See also *intranet, VLAN, FDDI, CAN, MAN, WAN.*)

LAN segment   In the context of a frame relay network supporting LAN-to-LAN communications, a LAN linked to another LAN by a bridge. Bridges enable two LANs to function like a single, large LAN by passing data from one LAN segment to another. To communicate with each other, the bridged LAN segments must use the same native protocol. (See also *bridge.*)

LAPB (*Link Access Procedure-Balanced*)   An X.25 data link layer protocol, defined by ITU-T. LAPB is based on HDLC.

LAPD (*Link Access Procedure for the D-channel*)   A data link layer protocol, defined by ITU-T, for use in ISDN. The D-channel carries signaling information for circuit switching. The LAPD protocol is based on HDLC.

LAPF (*Link Access Procedure for Frame Mode*)   A data link layer protocol, defined by ITU-T, for use in frame relay. The (full) LAPF includes flow control and error detection and correction. It is based on HDLC.

LAPF Core   A subset of the LAPF protocol that does not include flow control or error correction. The LAPF Core, rather than the full LAPF, is typically used to implement frame relay networks.

LATA (*Local Access and Transport Area*)   Geographically defined telecommunication areas in the United States, within which a local carrier can provide communications services. A typical LATA contains several area codes. (See also *interLATA, IntraLATA, LEC, IXC.*)

leaky bucket   A flow control algorithm used in ATM where cells are monitored for their compliance with the established connection parameters. Nonconforming cells are either tagged (as violators) or dropped from the network. The analogy is taken from a bucket (memory buffer) with a hole in its bottom that allows the fluid (cells) to flow out at a certain rate.

LEC (*local exchange carrier*)   An intraLATA telecommunications service provider. With the implementation of the Telecommunications Act of 1996, the distinctions between IXCs and LECs are fading.

LIFO (*last-in, first-out*)   A method that determines the order in which packets in a queue are served; the last to join the queue prior to a service completion becomes the first to be served next. (See also *FIFO.*)

link A physical means for transferring traffic between two network nodes (e.g., switches, hosts). A link is characterized by its transmission rate, which is also called link capacity or speed, and is synonymous with the total bandwidth of the underlying physical medium.

LLC (*Logical Link Control*) The upper half of the data link layer in LANs that performs error control, broadcasting, multiplexing, and flow control functions. (See also *MAC*.)

LMI (*Local Management Interface*) An ITU-T–defined interface that provides an end-system user with network management information related to the local access circuit. LMI specifications have been defined for frame relay and for ATM (called ILMI in the ATM specifications).

LSB (*least significant bit*) The lowest-order bit of a binary value. Sometimes the LSB is shown on the left side and sometimes on the right side of diagrams.

M13 (*DS-1/DS-3 multiplexer*) Device that multiplexes 28 DS-1 signals into a single DS-3 signal and vice versa. (Pronounced "em one three," not "em thirteen.")

MAC (*Medium Access Control*) A set of protocols that are the lower sublayer of the data link layer and provide the basis of the IEEE LAN specifications. Generally, MAC determines the way devices can transmit in a broadcast network. (See also *LLC*.)

MAC Address (*Media Access Control Address*, or *Medium Access Control Address*) A 48-bit (6-octet) field in a LAN header that uniquely identifies an end station. There are two such fields, one identifying the source and the other identifying the destination of the LAN frame.

MAN (*metropolitan area network*) A network that provides regional connectivity within a metropolitan area. MANs "fit" between LANs (or CANs) and WANs.

MB (*megabyte*) One million bytes.

Mbone (*Multicast backbone*) A technology for the digital broadcasting and multicasting of audio and video over the Internet.

Mbps (*megabits per second*) Transmission speed or rate of 1 million bits per second.

MCR (*Minimum Cell Rate*) For ATM, an ABR traffic parameter (in cells per second) that defines the minimum transmission rate to which the network will constrain a source in the event of network congestion. (See also *PCR*, *flow control*.)

message A long stream of information bits. It can be thought as a concatenation of several packets or PDUs.

message switching A switching technique based on the exchange of messages between the network nodes. There is no need to establish a connection or dedicated path. Also known as store-and-forward, message switching is not suitable for real-time or interactive traffic. (See also *circuit switching*, *packet switching*.)

MHz (*megahertz*)   One million hertz (Hz).

MIB (*Management Information Base*)   A data structure that defines the objects, their attributes, and their values that are to be managed by the Network Management System (NMS). The contents of an MIB, the values that its objects can have, and the actions taken by the management system based on those values determine the scope and capabilities of the NMS. Both SNMP and CMIP protocols are based on manipulating MIB objects.

microwave   A medium for wireless transmission within the 100- MHz to 100-GHz frequency band, mostly used in satellite, TV, long-distance, and cellular telephony.

MMF (*multimode fiber*)   A type of optical fiber used for optical transmission over distances up to three miles. In a multimode fiber, several propagation paths exist inside the fiber medium, which can cause light dispersion over distance. As a result, both distance and capacity are constrained. However, because of the relatively large diameter of multimode fiber, it is easy to install and more rugged. It is typically utilized in building and campus environments. (See also *SMF*.)

modem (*modulator/demodulator*)   A physical device that converts a digital signal (binary voltage pulses that represent bits) to an analog signal (frequency waveform) and back again. Digital-to-analog conversion is called D/A or modulation, while analog-to-digital conversion is called A/D or demodulation. A modem is typically attached to a computer to allow access to the analog local subscriber loop of the public telephone network.

MPEG (*Motion Picture Experts Group*)   A video technology standard, capable of presenting VCR-quality motion video. It specifies the digital encoding, transmission, and decoding protocol. The most recent version is MPEG2.

M-Plane (*Management plane*)   Part of the ATM reference model; provides the necessary management functions, capabilities, and services for coordination and monitoring across the C-plane and U-plane and down across the various ATM layers. M-plane tasks include OAM, fault management, accounting management, security management, and configuration management. CMIP, SNMP, and Local Management Interface functions are supported under the M-plane.

MPLS (*Multiprotocol Label Switching*)   An IETF working group to develop a standard, public specification for layer 3 switching that would encompass the positive aspects of approaches developed by vendors such as Cisco, IBM, Ascend, and others. It is intended to extend and integrate IP routing protocols (e.g., OSPF) so that switches and routers can interoperate.

mpt-mpt (*multipoint-to-multipoint*)   Refers to the mode of connection or signaling where there are multiple sources (senders) and destinations (receivers).

ms (**also msec**) (*millisecond*)   One-thousandth of a second (1 sec = 1000 ms).

MSB (*most significant bit*)   The highest-order bit of a binary value.

MTU (*Maximum Transfer Unit*)   The maximum allowed (over the physical medium) data unit (e.g., packet) that is supported by the network hardware or software.

multicasting   Selective transmission of a packet from a source to a group of receivers (destinations). (See also *broadcasting*, *unicasting*.)

multimedia   An integrated way of presenting to the user different kinds of information such as text, data, images, video, audio, and graphics. However, in practice multimedia usually includes either voice or video.

multimode fiber   See *MMF*.

multiplexer   A local networking device (mux) used for multiplexing.

multiplexing   A method where multiple (input) streams of information are combined by a multiplexer (mux) into a single (output) stream so they can share a common physical medium. The capacity of the output link has to be at least equal to the aggregate capacity of the input links. (See also *inverse multiplexing, demultiplexing, FDM, STDM, TDM, WDM*.)

mux (*multiplexer*)   See *multiplexer*.

native applications   Classical applications that have been developed for non-frame relay or non-ATM communications platforms (e.g., LANs).

NDIS (*Network Driver Interface Specification*)   A device driver specification for a NIC, originally developed by 3Com and Microsoft, that has become a generic implementation for PCs and LAN devices.

network layer   Layer 3 in the OSIRM; responsible for routing and network management (establishing, monitoring, and terminating connections; traffic and congestion control).

NIC (*Network Interface Card, or Controller*)   The hardware communications circuit board required for the DTE (workstation, PC) to access the network. (Same as *Adapter Card*.)

N-ISDN (*Narrowband Integrated Services Digital Network*)   Predecessor to the B-ISDN; encompasses the original standards for ISDN, namely, BRI and PRI, typically at DS-1/E1 rates (1.544/2.048 Mbps) and slower.

NIST (*National Institute of Standards and Technology*)   A Department of Commerce agency responsible for establishing national standards and implementing policies in various advanced technology areas. Previously known as the National Bureau of Standards (NBS).

NIWF (*Network Interworking Function*)   An IWF that supports the tunneling (encapsulation) of a non-ATM protocol, such as frame relay, into ATM cells for transport across an ATM network. An NIWF is required at both ends of a virtual circuit. (See also *SIWF*.)

NM (*Network Management*)   Defines all the necessary management functions to ensure that a network is operational. The management functional model, as defined in the OSI, includes the following types of management (known, for short, as FCAPS): fault, configuration, accounting, performance, and security. (See also *NMS*.)

NMS (*Network Management System*)   A set of OAM&P functions and services for setting the required hardware and software parameters used in managing a network.

NNI (for frame relay) (*Network-to-Network Interface*)   Specifications for connecting one carrier's frame relay network to another carrier's network

node   Generally, physical equipment (e.g., computer, switch) in a network.

non-isochronous   Any transmission stream in which the timing relationship between the segments of information in the traffic stream is not critical to the value or meaning of the information as it is received at the destination. Thus, the source and destination do not need to operate using the same clock source. Virtually all data applications are examples of non-isochronous information. (See also *isochronous*.)

NSAP (*Network Services Access Point*)   An OSI concept; the service access point (SAP) between the network and the transport layers. It identifies a DTE by a unique address. (See also *E.164*.)

OAM (*Operations and Maintenance*)   A set of network management functions similar to those in OAM&P.

OAM&P (*Operations, Administration, Maintenance, and Provisioning*)   A set of network management functions and services that provide network management tools and control (e.g., resolving network problems, providing for equipment installation, monitoring usage, accounting, configuration, policy implementation, etc.). It is similar to OAM.

OCI (*Optical Carrier Interface*)   See *OC-n*.

OC-n (*Optical Carrier-n*)   ITU-T standards for transmission over optical fiber at *n* times the basic rate of 51.84 Mbps (e.g., OC-3 is 155.52 Mbps, OC-12 is 622.08 Mbps, and OC-48 is 2.488 Gbps). (See also *STS, STM*.)

octet   A group of 8 bits; less ambiguous than *byte* since the term "byte" has been used to identify other groupings of bits (such as 6 or 7). All international documentation uses "octet."

ONI (*Optical Network Interface*)   An interface between an optical fiber network (e.g., backbone) and a nonoptical network (e.g., wireless, wire, satellite).

OSI (*Open Systems Interconnection*)   The OSI reference model (OSIRM) defined by ISO consists of seven layers specifying the protocols and functions required for nodes to communicate using the underlying network infrastructure (physical medium, switches, routers, bridges, multiplexers, intermediate nodes) and enables user-defined applications to access the network. The seven layers are (starting from bottom) physical, data link, network, transport, session, presentation, and application.

OSIRM (*Open Systems Interconnection Reference Model*)   See *OSI*.

OSPF (*Open Shortest Path First*)   A least-cost (in terms of delay, data rate, and dollars) routing protocol developed by ARPA as an improvement to RIP. Called a link-state protocol, an OSPF router transmits routing updates about its local links only when there are changes to the state of the links (up, down, congestion, etc.). (See also *BGP, EGP, RIP.*)

packet   A data transfer unit that is of variable or fixed size and is passed from one network node to the other. Several packets can belong to the same message, but they each have their header and/or trailer and may be routed independently through the network. Often used to describe the unit of information passed from OSI layer 3 to layer 2, but also used more generically. (See also *cell, frame, PDU, SDU.*)

packet switching   A networking method where packets are switched (relayed) from node to node. X.25 is an example. The transmission channel is occupied only for the duration of the transmission of the packet. (See also *circuit switching, message switching.*)

PAD (*packet assembler/disassembler*)   Used in packet switching networks (e.g., X.25), a device attached to a terminal and responsible for grouping and ungrouping octets (and any control information) into packets for network transmission.

parameter   A numerical code or value that controls an aspect of terminal and/or network operation. Parameters control such aspects as page size, data transmission speed, and timing options.

payload   The part of a packet that contains the actual information (control information and/or user data) to be carried. In general, it refers to what remains after stripping off the header and trailer of a PDU (encapsulated packet).

PBX (*Private Branch Exchange*)   A customer-owned circuit switch that creates connections for telephones, faxes, terminals (modems), or other voice-grade communications equipment and provides access to the public telephone system.

PC (*personal computer*)   Any type of desktop or laptop computer.

PCM (*pulse code modulation*)   A technique for converting an analog voice signal to digital format. It requires sampling the analog signal 8000 times per second and converting each sample to an 8-bit value. Hence, PCM requires a 64-Kbps digital channel to carry one voice connection. Used extensively in public voice networks. (See also *ADPCM, DS-0.*)

PCR (*Peak Cell Rate*) For ATM, a traffic parameter (in cells per second) that characterizes the maximum source transmission rate. The fraction 1/PCR represents the minimum intercell interval (the time between two cells) over a given virtual connection (VC). The usage parameter control (UPC) is responsible for policing the PCR of each virtual circuit. Any cell that violates the PCR is discarded.

PCS (*Personal Communication Services*) A type of digital cellular service that provides a user with better-quality, lower-cost, interoperable, and more function-rich cellular communications capabilities.

PD (*Propagation Delay*) The delay encountered by a packet while it is traveling on a link across a network (transit delay).The total, end-to-end propagation delay is the sum of the individual propagation delays (between adjacent nodes); therefore, it depends on the actual geographical distance between the source and the destination.

PDH (*Plesiochronous Digital Hierarchy*) A hierarchy that refers to the DS-0, DS-1, DS-2, and DS-3 (and sometimes E-1, E-2, etc.) signals for digital transmission across multiple networks without a common reference clock.

PDU (*Protocol Data Unit*) A term originated by ISO to describe the information passed between layers (through the protocol interfaces) and containing control (header and/or trailer) and data (payload) information. In ATM, cells are PDUs, while in frame relay, frames are PDUs. (See also *packet, SDU.*)

peer entities Entities (software packages) that belong to corresponding (peer) layers.

PHY (*physical layer*) See *physical layer*.

physical layer Layer 1 (the lowest layer) of the OSI reference model. It supports the transmission of bits over a physical medium.

PIU (*Path Information Unit*) IBM term for the SNA layer 3 PDU.

PM (*physical medium*) The actual transmission interface. Examples include interfaces such as T1, DS-3, E1, E3, E4, OC-n, and UTP.

PON (*Passive Optical Network*) An optical network where several users share a common fiber link, based on TDM and WDM.

POP (*point of presence*) A term inherited from the telephone networks to describe a switch, a multiplexer, or a concentrator that resides between a local access network (e.g., LATA) and a backbone (IXC) network.

POTS (*plain old telephone system*, or *Service*) The conventional telephone system (analog or digital) that employs circuit switching.

PPP (*Point-to-Point Protocol*) An Internet protocol for host dial-up connections. PPP frames can support the transport of various encapsulated protocols.

presentation layer   Layer 6 in the OSIRM; responsible for the presentation format of user application data, such as data encryption, conversion, and compression, that takes place using the appropriate coding (source) and decoding (destination).

PRI (*Primary Rate Interface*)   An ISDN specification that provides 23 64-Kbps B-channels and 1 64-Kbps D-channel (on a DS-1 circuit) or 30 64-Kbps B-channels and 1 64-Kbps D-channel (on an E-1 circuit). (See also *BRI*.)

primitives   Abstract service language for defining various system operations such as function calls and system library calls, along with any parameters, to allow communication across two adjacent layers of any architecture, such as OSIRM or ATM.

private network   A communications network comprising dedicated circuits between customer-owned network devices (multiplexers, switches, routers). (See *public network*, *VPN*.)

protocol   A set of rules that govern (establish, maintain, and manage) end-to-end or node-to-node communication between two peer (at the same level) entities across a network.

PSS1 (*Private Subscriber Signaling 1*)   Specifications for ISDN D-channel signaling between two private ISDN PBXs. (See also *DSS1*, *Q-sig*, *CAS*.)

PSTN (*public switched telephone network*)   A generic name for the worldwide public telephone network. (See also *VPN*, *public network*, *private network*.)

pt-mpt (*point-to-multipoint*)   Refers to the mode of a (unidirectional) connection or signaling where there is one source (sender) and multiple destinations (receivers).

pt-pt (*point-to-point*)   Refers to the mode of a (unidirectional or bidirectional) connection or signaling where there is a single source (sender) and destination (receiver).

PTT (*postal, telegraph, and telephone*)   Government authorities responsible for providing public postal, telegraph, and telephone services. In most countries they also regulate and control communication and networking issues.

public network   A communications network in which the circuits and switches are owned by a company providing public communications services. (See also *private network*, *VPN*.)

PVC (*permanent virtual circuit*)   A virtual connection (VC) established by the network management system between a source and a destination that is kept in place (used in X.25 and FR protocols).

Q.922 Annex A (Q.922A)   The international standard that defines the structure of frame relay frames. All frame relay frames entering a frame relay network must conform to this structure. (See also *LAPB*.)

Q.922A frame   A variable-length unit of data, formatted in frame-relay (Q.922A) format, that is transmitted through a frame relay network as pure data (i.e., it contains no flow control information). (See also *packet*, *frame relay frame*.)

Q.931 An ITU-T recommendation for specifying the UNI signaling protocol in N-ISDN.

Q.933 An ITU-T recommendation for specifying the UNI signaling protocol in frame relay.

Q.2931 An ITU-T recommendation derived from both Q.931 and Q.933 to provide ATM SVC signaling specifications and standards.

QoS (*quality of service*) Refers to the set of parameters that characterize the performance of a given virtual circuit. Often, QoS refers to average performance characteristics, not just worst-case behavior. (See also *service classes*, *QoS classes*, *traffic contract*, *traffic control*.)

QoS classes (for ATM) (*quality of service classes*) The following QoS classes are defined by the ATM Forum to identify performance characteristics of an ATM connection. For each specified QoS class 1 through 4, there is one specified objective value for each performance parameter identified as applicable to that class. With the exception of class 0, these QoS classes relate directly to the ITU-T service classes. (See also *service classes*, *QoS*.)

QoS class 0 (*no equivalent ITU-T service class*) The best effort service with no objective specified for the performance parameters. Also called the *unspecified QoS class* (i.e., UBR).

QoS class 1 (*ITU-T service class A*) The parameters for circuit emulation and constant-bit-rate video. Class 1 should yield performance comparable to current digital private line services (i.e., CBR).

QoS class 2 (*ITU-T service class B*) The parameters for variable-bit-rate audio and video. Class 2 is intended for packetized video and audio in teleconferencing and multimedia applications (i.e., rt-VBR).

QoS class 3 (*ITU-T service class C*) The parameters for connection-oriented data transfer. Class 3 is intended for interoperation of connection-oriented protocols, such as frame relay (i.e., VBR-nrt and ABR).

QoS class 4 (*ITU-T service class D*) The parameters for connectionless (datagram) data transfer. Class 4 is intended for interoperation of connectionless protocols, such as SMDS and IP.

Q-sig (*Q-Signaling, also known as Q.sig*) ITU-T name for PSS1; refers to the Q reference point in the ISDN reference model.

RADSL (*Rate-Adaptive Digital Subscriber Line*) A variation of ADSL that adapts the actual data rates to the condition and capabilities of the local loop circuit. (See *DSL*.)

RBOC (*regional Bell operating company*) A local service telephone company that results from the breakup of AT&T in 1984.

RFC (*Request for Comment*)   A document that contains proposed standards and specifications for review and approval within the IETF. RFCs can be approved or just archived as historical recommendations. The name is somewhat anachronistic since the approved specifications continue to be called RFCs.

RIP (*Routing Information Protocol*)   An older routing protocol, called a distance vector protocol, based on the full exchange of information about the topology of the network between neighboring nodes. That means that a router has to maintain and transmit large routing tables, making it inefficient as the network grows. (See also *EGP, OSPF.*)

RMON (*Remote Monitoring*)   A network probing and performance monitoring method for collecting information about the network's status. RMON is useful for network management and maintenance. (See also *OAM&P.*)

ROBO (*remote office/branch office*)   The branch offices of a larger company. (See also *SOHO.*)

ROLC (*Routing over Large Clouds*)   Protocol specifications developed by the IETF for supporting efficient IP routing over large networks (e.g., ATM, FR, SMDS).

router   A networking device for receiving, forwarding, and delivering packets (or messages) between end systems. A router is more sophisticated than a bridge, and it operates at the network layer, layer 3. Routers exchange topology and reachability information with each other using a routing protocol such as RIP or OSPF. They support end-system layer 3 communications protocols such as IP or IPX. A router that can support more than one end-system protocol is called a multiprotocol router. Routers support a connectionless service in that the end-system packet (e.g., IP, IPX) must contain the full address of the destination, and routing protocols forward the packet based on that address. (See also *hub, bridge, gateway, switching.*)

routing   A (layer 3) network management function responsible for forwarding packets from their source to their destination. Numerous routing protocols exist and are implemented in routers, depending on the various network topologies, requirements, and capabilities needed. BGP, EGP, OSPF, and RIP are the most common examples of routing protocols. Frame relay networks perform routing as part of the connection establishment procedures (for SVCs) and, subsequently, switch cells based on that pre-established route. (See also *router, switching.*)

RSVP (*Reservation Protocol*)   A control protocol developed to support different QoS classes for IP applications (such as video conferencing and multimedia) and to reserve resources in an IP-based network. RSVP's functionality can be thought of as resembling that of a traffic contract in an ATM environment.

RTCP (*Real-time Transport Control Protocol*)   A network management protocol used in RTP that monitors the offered QoS and identifies the participating parties in a multipoint session (e.g., videoconference). Other functions include monitoring packet sequence and delivery and reporting network conditions and reception quality back to the sender.

RTP (*Real-time Transport Protocol*)   An Internet protocol to provide end-to-end transport of real-time, integrated traffic (video, audio) and to support QoS for multimedia applications (such as videoconferencing). (See also *RTCP*.)

SAA (*Service Aspects and Applications*)   Specifications for the APIs, including the services, primitives, and functionality, for any given services such as LANE, frame relay, or SMDS.

SAP (*Service Access Point*)   Software interface between OSIRM layers through which layers can communicate with each other by exchanging PDUs. SAPs are identified as OSI addresses.

SAP (*subnetwork attachment point*)   The unique address maintained by a sub-network for each of the DTEs attached to it.

SAP (**for Novell**) (*Service Advertisement Protocol*)   A broadcast protocol within Novell's LAN protocols by which attached stations advertise their services and availability.

SAR (**for ATM**) (*segmentation and reassembly*)   A method of partitioning (segmenting) frames (variable-length packets) into cells at the source, and reassembling these cells back into information frames at the destination. These tasks occur at the lower sublayer of the AAL, which is therefore called the SAR sublayer. At the source end the SAR segments the data from the information frames into payloads. It then adds any necessary header and/or trailer bits to the data and passes the resultant 48-octet payloads to the ATM layer. Each AAL type has its own SAR format. At the destination, the cell payload is extracted and converted to the appropriate PDU.

SCCP (*Signaling Connection Control Point*)   An SS7 layer that provides network functions such as address (e.g., ISDN or telephone number) translation into an SS7 number.

SCP (*Service Control Point*)   A term used in SS7; typically a computer or a sophisticated switch that accesses large databases in order to provide fast and reliable services. (See also *SSP, STP*.)

SCR (**for ATM**) (*Sustainable Cell Rate*)   An ATM traffic parameter (in cells per second) that characterizes a bursty source and specifies the maximum average rate at which cells can be sent over a given ATM virtual connection (VC). It is enforced by the UPC for VBR (rt and nrt) virtual circuits.

SDH (*Synchronous Digital Hierarchy*)   A hierarchy that determines signal interfaces for very-high-speed digital transmission over optical fiber links. (See also *OC-n, SONET*.)

SDLC (*Synchronous Data Link Control*)   An IBM data link layer protocol, from which most of the other data link layer protocols were derived. SDLC is used at layer 2 in IBM's SNA. (See also *HDLC, LAPB, LAPD, LAPF*.)

SDSL (*Single-pair Digital Subscriber Line*)   A specification for supporting one half of the capacity of DS-1 1.544-Mbps signaling on one wire pair. (See also *DSL, HDSL, HDSL2*.)

SDU (*Service Data Unit*)   The PDU passed down from a higher layer, which becomes the SDU (input) to that lower layer. After any required processing, it is passed down as a (new) PDU to the next lower layer. The SDU identity is maintained between the peer layers at each end of a connection.

service categories (for ATM)   CBR, VBR-rt, VBR-nrt, UBR, and ABR. (See also *QoS classes*.)

service classes   Specified by ITU-T, the four service classes (classes A through D) that define specific performance characteristics of different connections. The ATM Forum has defined five QoS classes (four specified QoS classes 1 through 4 that match the ITU-T classes and one unspecified QoS class). (See also *QoS classes, QoS*.)

session layer   Layer 5 in the OSIRM. It controls (establishes and maintains) the logical connection (session) between two (peer) communication processes.

SG (*Study Group*)   ITU-T-appointed committees to work on developing recommendations and specifications for a new service, system, method, or technology.

signaling   A method for controlling a connection by means of exchanging messages for establishing and clearing a connection (e.g., a telephone call). ISDN's DSS1 and PSS1 (Q-sig), Q.933, and SS7 are examples of signaling protocols.

single-mode fiber   See *SMF*.

SIWF (for ATM) (*Service Interworking Function*)   An IWF that supports the conversion of a non-ATM protocol into ATM cells for transport across an ATM network. With full conversion, an SIWF is required only at the non-ATM end of a virtual circuit. The other end is a fully compliant ATM end system. (See also *NIWF*.)

SLIP (*Serial Link, or Line, Internet Protocol*)   An Internet protocol for host dial-up connection. SLIP frames are encapsulated IP datagrams in which SLIP adds just a few octets of control data. (See also *PPP*.)

SMDS (*Switched Multimegabit Data Service*)   A connectionless, fast packet-switching B-ISDN service, based on 53-octet cells (not the same format as ATM cells). It originally targeted the interconnection of different LANs into a switched public network. It is used also to interconnect WANs and MANs at speeds up to 45 Mbps.

SMF (*Single-Mode Fiber*)   A type of optical fiber for transmission over distances up to 25 miles or more between repeaters. SMF has a single propagation path (inside the fiber) that the emitted light beam follows, and thus there is no interference or distortion. As a result it can carry greater capacity over longer distances than multimode fiber can. However, single-mode fiber is thinner than multimode fiber and requires greater care in installation. It is most typically used in wide area networks. (See also *MMF*.)

SMTP (*Simple Mail Transfer Protocol*)   The protocol specification developed to support electronic mail (email) services.

SNA (*Systems Network Architecture*)   An IBM-proprietary, host-based, 7-layer network architecture, where logical channels are created between end points.

SNAP (*Subnetwork Access Protocol*)   A protocol that allows IP traffic to be delivered or routed through a subnetwork. SNAP frames are encapsulated IP datagrams where a header and a trailer, used by the underlying subnetwork, are attached. Subnetwork Access Protocols are often used in a LAN environment to allow for multiprotocol encapsulation.

SNMP (*Simple Network Management Protocol*)   An IETF-defined standard for exchanging management information between network management systems and network components. It is normally found as an application on top of the User Datagram Protocol (UDP). (See also *MIB, CMIP, NMS*.)

SOHO (*small office/home office*)   A small, independent office. (See also *ROBO*.)

SONET (*Synchronous Optical Network*)   An ANSI-defined standard for high-speed and high-quality digital optical transmission. It has been recognized as the North American standard for SDH.

SONET/SDH   The SONET standard in North America; the SDH standard internationally.

SPVC (*soft permanent virtual connection*)   A PVC-type connection where SVCs are used by the network for connection setup and automatic failure recovery. It is also called Smart PVC.

SS7 (*Signaling System Number 7*)   A common-channel signaling specification developed by CCITT that is widely used in telephone networks. It was also designed to provide the internal control and network intelligence needed in ISDNs. (See also *SCCP*.)

SSP (*Service Switching Point*)   Refers to the SS7 protocol; a connection point for CPE signals to access a public network and provide enhanced user services.

STDM (*statistical time division multiplexing*)   An asynchronous, intelligent TDM method that allocates time slots on demand (dynamically) to users rather than pre-allocating fixed time slots. It offers a more efficient utilization of capacity for bursty data traffic.

STM (*Synchronous Transport Module*)   An ITU-T definition for the signaling and physical standards for SDH. (See also *STS, OC*.)

STM-1 (*Synchronous Transport Module-1*)   An ITU-T–defined SDH framing and transmission standard for digital transmission on optical fiber at the rate of 155.52 Mbps. An STM-1 transmission rate is equal to the SONET STS-3 rate. (See also *STS-1, OC-1*.)

STM-n (*Synchronous Transport Module-n*)   An ITU-T–defined SDH framing and transmission standard for digital transmission in ATM at n times the basic STM-1 rate (n multiplexed STM-1s). An STM-n transmission rate is equal to that of n SONET STS-3s. (See also *STS-n, OC-n*.)

STM-nc (*Synchronous Transport Module-n "Concatenated"*)   An ITU-T-defined SDH framing and transmission standard for digital transmission at STM-n rates as a single concatenated payload rather than as n STM-1s. (See also *STM-n, STS-n, OC-n*.)

STP (*Shielded Twisted Pair*)   Two insulated copper wires twisted together and wrapped by a protective metallic shield. (See also *UTP*.)

STP (for SS7) (*Signal Transfer Point*)   Part of the SS7; performs the translation and switching of the SS7 signaling messages to other SS7 nodes and network elements (See also *SCP, SSP, STP*).

STS-1 (*Synchronous Transport Signal-Level 1*)   A SONET signaling standard for framing and transmission on optical fiber at the rate of 51.84 Mbps. (See also *STM-1, OC-1*.)

STS-n (*Synchronous Transport Signal-Level n*)   A SONET signaling standard for framing and transmission on optical fiber at n times the basic STS-1 signal (n multiplexed STS-1s; e.g., STS-3 is at 155.52 Mbps). (See also *STM-n, OC-n*.)

STS-nc (*Synchronous Transport Signal-Level n "Concatenated"*)   A SONET signaling standard for framing and transmission on optical fiber at STS-n rates as a single concatenated payload rather than as n STS-1s. (See also *STM-nc, OC-n*.)

subnetwork   Also called *subnet*; defined as a set of network nodes (e.g., switches, routers, and other networking devices) connected by communication links. A subnetwork can be characterized as an autonomous network entity. A number of (homogeneous or non-homogeneous) subnetworks can lie between a source and a destination (generally, between hosts); these subnets are interconnected using routers and/or gateways. The Internet is an example of myriads of interconnected subnets.

SVC (*switched virtual connection, or circuit*)   An end-to-end virtual connection established dynamically via signaling procedures. (See also *PVC*.)

Switched Ethernet   A recent Ethernet technology offering much higher performance than shared media, broadcast Ethernet. In Switched Ethernet, shared media hubs are replaced by switches that route Ethernet frames to specific output ports based on the destination MAC address rather than broadcasting the frames on all ports.

switching A method for relaying packets, frames, or messages through a network node that has multiple input and output ports.

T1 A TDM digital channel carrier that operates at the rate of 1.544 Mbps over 2 twisted-pair wires. Often confused with DS-1, it comprises the specifications for framing and transmitting a 1.544-Mbps bit stream consisting of 24 64-Kbps DS-0 channels. DS-1 was originally specified to be transmitted over T1 wiring, but has subsequently been specified on other types of media as well. As a result, the terms "T1" and "DS-1" are often used interchangeably.

T1/E1 The primary rates of T1 (or DS-1 at 1.544 Mbps) in North America and Japan and of E1 (2.048 Mbps) in Europe.

T3 Informally, any TDM digital channel carrier that operates at 44.736 Mbps. It can multiplex 28 T1 signals and it is synonymous with DS-3.

TA (*Terminal Adapter*) A physical device that allows non-ISDN end systems to access a network through ISDN lines and protocols.

Tag Switching An approach proposed by Cisco for integrating ATM switching and IP routing. It is based on a label-swapping forwarding technique: by lookup in a tag table, an incoming tag (carried by the packet) is matched to an outgoing tag (and thus forwarded to the appropriate output). (See also *MPLS*.)

TAXI (*Transparent Asynchronous Transmitter/Receiver Interface*) An interface that provides connectivity over MMF links at a speed of 100 Mbps. The physical-layer specifications for FDDI.

Tbps (*terabits per second*) Transmission speed or rate of 1 trillion bits per second.

T_c (also Tc) (*Committed Rate Measurement Interval*) The time interval during which the user can send only B_c committed amount of data and B_e excess amount of data. According to the standards, the duration of T_c is proportional to the "burstiness" of the traffic. It is computed (from the subscription parameters of CIR and B_c) as $T_c = B_c/\text{CIR}$. T_c is not a periodic time interval. Instead, it is used only to measure incoming data, during which it acts like a sliding window. Incoming data triggers the T_c interval, which continues until it completes its commuted duration. However, vendors often have proprietary implementations of T_c. (See also *CIR, B_c, B_e.*)

TCP (*Transmission Control Protocol*) A standardized transport protocol developed for interconnecting IP-based networks. Operating on top of IP (collectively known as TCP/IP), it is responsible for end-to-end multiplexing, error recovery, reliable delivery, and flow control.

TCP/IP A protocol platform, known also as the Internet protocol suite, that combines both TCP and IP. Widely used applications such as Telnet, FTP, and SMTP interface to TCP/IP.

TDM (*time division multiplexing*) A technique for splitting the total link capacity into several channels to allow different bit streams to be combined (multiplexed). The bandwidth allocation is done by dividing the time axis into fixed-length slots, and a particular channel can then transmit only during prespecified time slots. (See also *FDM, STDM, WDM.*)

TE (*terminal equipment, or end point*) One of the two ends (at the protocol level) of an ISDN connection. It is typically a PBX or a computer. There are two types: TE1 (ISDN compatible) and TE2 (not ISDN compatible).

Telnet An asynchronous, virtual terminal protocol that allows for remote host access.

throughput A performance metric that gives the aggregate maximum bandwidth or capacity (in bps) of a system (such as a switch, link, or network) or the actual bandwidth a user is using for transmission, measured over an observed time interval. *Useful throughput* refers to the "net" throughput achieved by an application (that is, excluding any overhead due to control information included in the packets, retransmissions, etc.).

time slot A fixed period of time, usually equal to the transmission of a (fixed-length) packet (i.e., packet length × transmission rate).

TM (*traffic management*) The set of actions and operations performed by the network (administration) to guarantee the operability of the network. TM is exercised in the form of traffic and flow control. (See also *OAM.*)

Token Bus A medium-access control technique, also known as IEEE 802.4, which allows multiple access to a communication bus. Bus stations are configured in a logical ring. A token (special control frame) is passed around, and a station may start transmitting a data frame after it seizes the token (it can hold the token for a limited time only—in order to ensure fairness). After transmitting a data frame, the station must pass the token on to the next logical station in the ring. Since frames are broadcast, a station that receives a frame not addressed to it discards it. (See also *Ethernet, Token Ring, FDDI.*)

Token Ring A medium-access control technique, also known as IEEE 802.5, based on a token circulating around a physical ring network configuration. A station wishing to transmit waits until it receives the token and then starts transmitting a data frame. Every station on the ring listens to the medium and copies the frame into its local buffer if the frame is addressed to it. After transmitting a data frame, the station must forward the token to the next station on the ring. (See also *Ethernet, Token Bus, FDDI.*)

traffic contract (for ATM) An agreement between the user and the network management agent regarding the traffic class (service type) and QoS (as requested by the user and/or provided by the network) and the user's required compliance (conformance) with the agreed traffic descriptors (e.g., SCR, PCR, MCR, etc.). The traffic contract is negotiated and put into force prior to establishing the connection. Various forms of traffic control can be exercised by the network management in case the user violates its traffic contract (i.e., the user exceeds the predetermined traffic descriptors).

traffic control A mechanism for avoiding congestion or other traffic flow problems in a network, by performing a set of actions for managing the traffic. Traffic control is implemented as a means for testing the conformance of the actual traffic to the traffic descriptors. (See also *traffic shaping*.)

traffic descriptors (for ATM) A set of parameters that characterize the source traffic. These include MCR, PCR, and SCR.

traffic parameters See *traffic descriptors*.

traffic shaping A method for smoothing the bursty traffic rate that might arrive on an access virtual circuit so as to present a more uniform traffic rate to the network. Also a method for assigning priorities to different classes of traffic. (See also *traffic control, UPC*.)

trailer The ending part of a frame (PDU) that contains protocol and control information such as the CRC. (See also *header*.)

transport layer Layer 4 in the OSIRM. It handles end-to-end (source-destination) reliable communication (error detection and correction, sequencing, flow control) across a network.

trunk In the context of frame relay, a communications line connecting two frame relay switches to each other.

tunneling Known also as *encapsulation*, the transparent transport (e.g., through a frame relay network) of user traffic based on another protocol (e.g., SNA, Token Ring), thus providing internetworking capabilities.

UBR (*Unspecified Bit Rate*) A best-effort ATM service category . No QoS parameters are specified and no quality commitment is provided by the network management. The only traffic parameter specified is PCR, and all submitted traffic has the CLP bit in the ATM header set to 1 (eligible for discard in the event of congestion). (See also *QoS class 0, CBR, VBR, ABR*.)

UDP (*User Datagram Protocol*) A connectionless transport protocol that operates on top of IP. In UDP there is no guarantee of packet sequence, delivery, or acknowledgment capability, which makes UDP unreliable (nonguaranteed). However, it is simple and adequate for many query-response-type applications (e.g., SNMP). (See also *TCP*.)

UNI (*User-Network Interface*) The interface, defined as a set of protocols and traffic characteristics, between the CPE (user) and a frame relay or ATM network (switch). The frame relay specifications support only one frame relay UNI. The ATM Forum specifications support two standards: one between a user and a public ATM network, called the public UNI, and one between a user and a private ATM network, called the private UNI, or PNNI.

unicasting The case where a packet generated by a source is sent to a single destination. (See also *multicasting, broadcasting.*)

UNIX A sophisticated, high-performance, multitasking operating system that typically runs on workstations.

UPC (for ATM) (*Usage Parameter Control*) The traffic control entity that monitors and enforces a virtual circuit's conformance with the source's traffic contract and parameters. UPC, commonly known as traffic policing, is performed at the UNI. It is needed to regulate any (unintentional or malicious) noncomplying source traffic (i.e., traffic that violates parameters, such as PCR, as specified in the traffic contract). (See also *flow control, traffic control.*)

U-Plane (*User-plane*) The upper part of the B-ISDN model (ATM reference model); responsible for handling user services (such as transport of text, video, and audio), application-specific protocols (such as frame relay, SMDS, FTP, and TCP/IP), and various APIs. (See also *C-Plane, M-Plane.*)

utilization A performance metric that gives the fraction of time a system (e.g., a switch) is busy (processing, transmitting), usually observed over a long period of time (i.e., when the system has become stable).

UTP (*Unshielded Twisted Pair*) A twisted-pair (copper) wire without any protective metallic sheathing. There are two common categories: a lower grade CAT-3 and a higher grade CAT-5. (See also *STP.*)

VBR (*Variable Bit Rate*) One of the ATM service categories that supports the transport of bursty traffic as opposed to continuous bit rate (CBR) traffic. VBR traffic is characterized by an average (SCR) and peak (PCR) cell rate. Depending on the timing requirements of the application between the source and the destination, there are two VBR types: real-time VBR (VBR-rt) and non-real-time VBR (VBR-nrt). (See also *CBR, UBR, ABR.*)

VBR-nrt (*Non-Real-Time Variable Bit Rate*) One of the two VBR service categories for transmitting traffic where timing information is not critical. VBR-nrt is suited for bursty, delay-tolerant data traffic. Also known as nrt-VBR. (See also *VBR-rt, VBR, CBR, UBR, ABR.*)

VBR-rt (*Real-Time Variable Bit Rate*) One of the two VBR service categories for transmitting traffic that is time sensitive. It is suitable for carrying bursty, or low-bit-rate, delay-sensitive traffic such as packetized (compressed) video and audio. (See also *VBR-nrt, VBR, CBR, UBR, ABR.*)

VC (*virtual circuit, virtual connection, or virtual channel*) A connection that is set up across the network between a source and a destination where a fixed route is chosen for the entire session and bandwidth is dynamically allocated to the user. (See also *connection-oriented, connectionless network, PVC, SVC*.)

VCI (*Virtual Channel Identifier*)   A 16-bit value in the ATM cell header that provides a unique identifier for the virtual channel (VC) within a virtual path (VP) on a given physical circuit that carries that particular cell. VCIs 0 through 15 are reserved for ITU-T assignment. VCIs 16 through 31 are reserved for ATM Forum assignment. (See also *SVC, PVC*.)

VDSL (*Very High-Bit-Rate Digital Subscriber Line*)   An emerging specification to provide connectivity and broadband services to residential customers. VDSL supports data rates of 13 to 50 Mbps downstream (to the customer) and up to 1.6 Mbps upstream (to the network). (See *DSL*.)

videoconferencing   Real-time audio- and video-based communication between two or more parties (users) at transmission rates ranging from 1.5 Mbps up to 45 Mbps. B-ISDN services are designed to fully support video-conferencing.

virtual channel   See *VC*.

virtual circuit   See *VC*.

virtual connection   See *VC*.

VLAN (*virtual LAN*)   A networking environment where users and devices that may belong to independent LANs are interconnected and communicated in such a way that they appear to be on the same (traditional) LAN workgroup. VLAN is the IEEE 802.1Q standard.

VLSI (*Very Large Scale Integration*)   An integrated circuit technology that makes it possible to fabricate hundreds of million of transistors into a single chip.

VPI (*Virtual Path Identifier*)   A value in the cell header that identifies the virtual path (VP) to which the cell belongs. The field is 8 bits in cells traversing a UNI circuit and 12 bits in cells traversing network circuits. (See also *VCI, VC*.)

VPI/VCI (*Virtual Path Identifier/Virtual Channel Identifier*)   The combination of the VPI and the VCI, used to identify a specific segment of an end-to-end virtual circuit (VC) between two ATM devices, and to switch cells in an ATM network.

VPN (*virtual private network*)   A network in which resources (such as bandwidth and buffer space) are provided, on demand, to the users (usually by the public carriers) in such a way that the users view a certain partition of that network as a private network. The advantage of the VPNs over private networks is that VPNs allow a dynamic use of public network resources while retaining much of the controls, operational characteristics, and security of a private network at much lower costs (personnel, equipment, service costs). VPN services are available from PSTN carriers for voice services and from ISPs for intranet support.

VT (*virtual tributary*)   Specifications that define SONET/SDH subrate connections. Specifications have been defined to support DS-1, DS-2, DS-3, E-1, and E-3 connections, for example.

WAN (*wide area network*)   A network that typically spans nationwide distances and usually utilizes public telephone circuits. (See also *LAN, CAN, MAN*.)

WDM (*wavelength division multiplexing*)   A technique for transmitting several wavelengths of light simultaneously on a single optical transmission medium. Each wavelength carries traffic at a specified bit rate, such as STS-3 or STM-1. A popular approach for WDM is to concatenate several 2.5-Gbps (STS-48, STM-16) traffic streams onto a single optical fiber. (See also *DWDM, FDM, TDM*.)

Web   See *WWW*.

WFQ (*weighted fair queuing*)   A fair queuing (FQ) discipline where each queue (e.g., in a router or switch) is assigned a weight in order to ensure guaranteed service by efficiently allocating the transmission bandwidth.

WWW (*World Wide Web*)   An interactive, multimedia, Internet-based application that has become extremely popular and useful because of its highly integrated (mostly visual) presentation and distribution of information; its ease and speed of accessing commercial, personal, or Internet services; and its advanced Internet search facilities (search engines). A user can navigate and browse through the various documents and (Internet) sites simply by clicking (using a pointer device) on the associated (hyper-) links. HTTP is the protocol that forms the basis of the WWW. Audio, video, and text information is presented on the Web under a special language called HTML (which creates the actual hyperlinks).

X.25   One of the first CCITT standardized public (data) packet-switching network layer protocols. Originally designed to operate over unreliable communications links, it supports both virtual circuit (VC) and datagram services.

X.121   The ITU-T network address standard for X.25-based networks.

xDSL   The general name for a variety of digital subscriber line (DSL) technologies. (See also *ADSL, HDSL, VDSL, IDSL, RADSL*.)

References

[ACT95]   "Voice over Frame Relay—A White Paper," *ACT Networks*, 1995.

[ANSI-T1.607-91]   *DSS1—Signaling Specification for Frame Relay Bearer Service*, American National Standards Institute, 1991.

[Black96]   Black, Uyless. *Frame Relay Networks: Specifications and Implementations, 2nd Ed.*, New York: McGraw-Hill, 1996.

[Brown98]   Brown, Dave, and David Willis. "Videoconferencing on Frame Relay Networks," *Network Computing*, Sept. 15, 1998.

[DC97Dec]   "Data Comm 1998 Market Forecast," *Data Communications*, December 1997.

[DNA-99]   Taylor, Steven. *1999 Frame Relay Market Webtorial—Initial Results*, Distributed Networking Associates, May 1999.

[FRF1.1-96]   *FRF.1.1 User-to-Network Implementation Agreement (UNI)*, Frame Relay Forum, 1996.

[FRF2.1-95]   *FRF.2.1 Frame Relay Network-to-Network Interface Implementation Agreement*, Frame Relay Forum, 1995.

[FRF3.1-95]   *FRF.3.1 Multiprotocol Encapsulation Implementation Agreement*, Frame Relay Forum, June 1995.

[FRF.4-94]   *FRF.4 Frame Relay User-to-Network SVC Implementation Agreement*, Frame Relay Forum, 1994.

[FRF.5-94]   *FRF.5 Frame Relay/ATM PVC Network Interworking Implementation Agreement*, Frame Relay Forum, December 1994.

[FRF.6-94]   *FRF.6, Frame Relay Service Customer Network Management Implementation Agreement (MIB)*, Frame Relay Forum, 1994.

[FRF7-94]   *FRF.7 Frame Relay PVC Multicost Service and Protocol Description*, Frame Relay Forum, 1994.

[FRF.8-95]   *FRF.8 Frame Relay/ATM PVC Service Interworking Implementation Agreement*, Frame Relay Forum, April 1995.

[FRF9-96]   *FRF.9 Data Comparison Over Frame Relay Implementation Agreement*, Frame Relay Forum, 1996.

[FRF.10-96]   *FRF.10 Frame Relay Network to Network SVC Implementation Agreement,* Frame Relay Forum, 1996.

[FRF.11-97]   *FRF.11 Voice over Frame Relay Implementation Agreement*, Frame Relay Forum, May 1997.

[FRF.12-97]   *FRF.12 Frame Relay Fragmentation Implementation Agreement*, Frame Relay Forum, December 1997.

[FRF13-98]   *FRF.13 Service Level Definitions Implementation Agreement*, Frame Relay Forum, 1998.

[FRF.14-98]   *FRF.14 Physical Layer Interface Implementation Agreement*, Frame Relay Forum, December 1998.

[FRF15-99]   *FRF.15 End-to-End Multilink Frame Relay Implementation Agreement*, Frame Relay Forum, 1999.

[FRF16-99]   *FRF.16 Multilink Frame Relay UNI/NNI Implementation Agreement*, Frame Relay Forum, 1999.

[FRF96]   Frame Relay Forum, *A Discussion of Voice over Frame Relay*, Oct. 1996.

[FRFN2Q97]   Kocen, Ross. "VoFR IA Paves the Way for Equipment and Service Interoperability," *Frame Relay Forum News*, 2nd Q 1997.

[FRFN4Q98]   Kite, Paul. "Fax over Frame," *Frame Relay Forum News*, 4th Q 1998.

[Heckart94]   Heckart, Christine A. *The Guide to Frame Relay Networking*, Flatiron Publishing, 1994.

[ITU-Q.922-93]   ITU Recommendation Q.922. *ISDN Data Link Layer Specification for Frame Mode Bearer Services*, ITU, Geneva, 1993.

[ITU-Q.931-92]   ITU Recommendation Q.931. *ISDN User-Network Interface—Layer 3 Specification for Basic Call Control*, ITU, Geneva, 1992.

[ITU-Q.933-92]   ITU Recommendation Q.933. *DSS1 Signalling Specification for Frame Mode Basic Call Control*, ITU-T, Geneva, 1992.

[ITU-Q.933-95]   Revised ITU Recommendation Q.933. *ISDN Signaling Specifications for Frame Mode Switched and Permanent Virtual Connections Control and Status Monitoring*, ITU, Geneva, 1995.

[MCI97]   *MCI Hyperstream Frame Relay Federal Tariff*, Federal Communications Commission, April 24, 1997.

[NC98JUN15]   Willis, David. "Lifting the Fog with Frame Relay Management Products," *Network Computing*, June 15, 1998.

[Newman96]   Newman, David, Brent Melson, and Siva S. Kumar. "Voice over Frame Relay: Imperfect Pitch," *Data Communications*, Sept. 21, 1996.

[Newton98]   Newton, Harry. Newton's Telecom Dictionary, 13th Ed. Telecom Books and Flatiron Publishing, 1998.

[NW97APR21]   Greene, Tim. "New Tool Lets Users Peer into Frame Relay Networks," *Network World*, April 21, 1997.

[Passmore97]   Passmore, David. "Who Needs SVCs?" *Business Communications Review*, June 1997.

[RFC1315]   Brown, C., F. Baker, and C. Carvalho (eds.), RFC 1315. "Management Information Base for Frame Relay DTEs," Wellfleet Communications, ACC, April 1992.

[RFC1604]   Brown, T. (ed.). RFC 1604, "Definitions of Managed Objects for Frame Relay Service," Bell Communications Research, March 1994.

[Sif99]   Sif, Mehdi. "Challenging the IP-VPN Drivers," *Frame Relay Forum News*, 2nd Q, 1999.

[Smith93]   Smith, Philip. *Frame Relay Principles and Applications*, Reading, Mass.: Addison-Wesley, 1993.

[Stallings95]   Stallings, William. *ISDN and Broadband ISDN with Frame Relay and ATM, 3rd Ed.*, Englewood Cliffs, NJ: Prentice Hall, 1995.

[Tanenbaum96]   Tanenbaum, Andrew. *Computer Networks, 3rd Ed.*, Englewood Cliffs, NJ: Prentice Hall, 1996.

[Taylor97]   Taylor, Steven. "SVCs: The End of the Beginning," *Data Communications*, Nov. 21, 1997.

[TR9577-92]   "Information Technology—Telecommunications and Information Exchange between Systems—Protocol Identification in the Network Layer," ISO/IEC TR 9577, 1992.

[VerticalSG98]   Cochran, Mary. "Frame Relay: Where Do We Go from Here?" Keynote Address at Frame Relay Forum 1998 Annual Meeting, Vertical Systems Group, May 1998.

[VerticalSG99]   Dunn, Erin. "Frame Relay and ATM: Competitive or Complementary," Industry Update Session at SuperComm, Vertical Systems Group, June 1999.

[Wexler99]   Wexler, Joanie. "Frame Relay and IP VPNs: Compete or Coexist?" *Business Communications Review*, July 1999.

Index

Addison-Wesley Computer and Engineering Publishing Group

How to Interact with Us

1. Visit our Web site

http://www.awl.com/cseng

When you think you've read enough, there's always more content for you at Addison-Wesley's web site. Our web site contains a directory of complete product information including:

- Chapters
- Exclusive author interviews
- Links to authors' pages
- Tables of contents
- Source code

You can also discover what tradeshows and conferences Addison-Wesley will be attending, read what others are saying about our titles, and find out where and when you can meet our authors and have them sign your book.

2. Subscribe to Our Email Mailing Lists

Subscribe to our electronic mailing lists and be the first to know when new books are publishing. Here's how it works: Sign up for our electronic mailing at **http://www.awl.com/cseng/mailinglists.html**. Just select the subject areas that interest you and you will receive notification via email when we publish a book in that area.

3. Contact Us via Email

cepubprof@awl.com
Ask general questions about our books.
Sign up for our electronic mailing lists.
Submit corrections for our web site.

bexpress@awl.com
Request an Addison-Wesley catalog.
Get answers to questions regarding your order or our products.

innovations@awl.com
Request a current Innovations Newsletter.

webmaster@awl.com
Send comments about our web site.

cepubeditors@awl.com
Submit a book proposal.
Send errata for an Addison-Wesley book.

cepubpublicity@awl.com
Request a review copy for a member of the media interested in reviewing new Addison-Wesley titles.

We encourage you to patronize the many fine retailers who stock Addison-Wesley titles. Visit our online directory to find stores near you or visit our online store: **http://store.awl.com/** or call **800-824-7799**.

Addison Wesley Longman
Computer and Engineering Publishing Group
One Jacob Way, Reading, Massachusetts 01867 USA
TEL 781-944-3700 • FAX 781-942-3076